Notes on Doctrinal and Spiritual Subjects
Volume 1

NOTES

ON

Doctrinal and Spiritual Subjects,

BY

FREDERICK WILLIAM FABER, D. D.

PRIEST OF THE ORATORY OF ST. PHILIP NERI.

"Defunctus adhuc loquitur."—*Heb. xi. 4.*

VOL. I.

MYSTERIES AND FESTIVALS.

FOURTH THOUSAND.

JOHN MURPHY COMPANY,
PUBLISHERS.

BALTIMORE, MD.:
200 W. LOMBARD STREET.

NEW YORK:
70 FIFTH AVENUE.

NOTES

ON

DOCTRINAL AND SPIRITUAL SUBJECTS.

VOL. I

U   ⅅ

U   ℛ

TO

ANNE, DUCHESS OF ARGYLL,

𝔗𝔥𝔢𝔰𝔢 𝔙𝔬𝔩𝔲𝔪𝔢𝔰

ARE RESPECTFULLY DEDICATED

IN REMEMBRANCE OF HER FRIENDSHIP FOR

THE AUTHOR

AND WITH A GRATEFUL SENSE OF HER MANY KINDNESSES

TO THE

CONGREGATION OF THE ORATORY.

U 𝔇

PREFACE.

DURING the two years which have elapsed since Father Faber's death, the question has been frequently asked, whether any manuscripts had been left by him for publication. Although no completed works were found among his papers, it has been thought advisable that a selection should be made from them, and published in continuation of the works which have already appeared. The extensive circulation to which his writings have attained in England, and still more upon the continent, seemed to warrant the hope that the publication of such of his manuscripts as would admit of it would be welcome to those who have found in his former works a source of spiritual profit.

The contents of these volumes have consequently been selected from a large mass of miscellaneous papers. It is not, however, without some diffidence that the results of the selection are now published, as they consist entirely of notes, which in their present form were not meant to be made public. They have been left for the most part in the unfinished state in which they were found . as it has been thought better to let them appear incomplete than to give them another form by alterations which might expose the Author's meaning to misinterpretation. They will be judged, not by themselves alone in their fragmentary character, but in connection with the many complete and finished volumes which were published in the Author's lifetime.

The notes are of two kinds,—those which were made by the Author in preparation for his sermons or lectures, and those which contain materials for works intended for publication. With regard to the latter, it was his custom to cast in several forms, each advancing a step nearer to completion, the works which he proposed to publish, and to keep them by him, sometimes for years, before he sent them to the press. The notes of the treatises on the Holy Ghost and Calvary, which are included in the present volume, were prepared six years before his death, but, with the exception of a few pages of Calvary (p. 223), no further progress was made. If they do not present the attractions of a finished work, they give at least the outlines of it, and the form in which he meant to treat it.

The arrangement of subjects which was adopted by the author in his volume of Hymns has been followed as nearly as was practicable. Of the seven Parts which make up the whole Collection, three are published in this volume: the first, treating of God, His Attributes, and the Three Persons of the Most Holy Trinity; the second, of the Sacred Humanity of Jesus, including the Mysteries of the Passion; and the third, of our Blessed Lady and the Saints. The second volume will contain the fourth and fifth parts, relating to the Church, the Sacraments, Controversy, and the Spiritual Life, together with the sixth, which is of a miscellaneous character, concluding with the seventh, which treats of the Four Last Things and Purgatory.

A column has been added to the table of contents, for the purpose of giving, when it could be ascertained, the date of each sermon. With a few exceptions they were all preached in the Church of the Oratory, at King William Street, Strand, from 1849 to 1853, and at Brompton after that date.

It only remains to say a few words concerning the object of the present work. It is intended to serve as a collection, wherein may be found considerations in a short form upon the chief Mysteries of the Faith and the Spiritual Life, and from which religious communities and those engaged in missionary labor may draw materials for meditation and instruction. To many it will be interesting as an illustration of the methods of thought and work which were habitual with Father Faber: and it is believed that those who heard his sermons with pleasure and profit, will be glad to have some record of them, however imperfect; while those whose privilege it was to live within the circle of his love will rejoice that his words should not be lost, but should continue the work of increasing upon earth the love and honor of Almighty God, our Blessed Lady, and the Saints, which he strove so successfully to promote.

JOHN E. BOWDEN.

THE ORATORY, LONDON,
  Feast of the Purification,
Eighteenth Anniversary of the English Oratory,
      1866.

U.   ℞

CONTENTS.

Part I.

GOD AND THE MOST HOLY TRINITY.

SECTION I.

THE DIVINE ATTRIBUTES.

SECTION II.

THE HOLY GHOST.

Part II.

THE SACRED HUMANITY OF JESUS.

SECTION I.

OUR BLESSED LORD.

U

SECTION II.

THE PASSION.

U.

Part III.

OUR BLESSED LADY AND THE SAINTS.

SECTION I.

OUR BLESSED LADY.

U.   ℞

SECTION II.

THE SAINTS.

U.   ℞

Part First.

GOD AND THE MOST HOLY TRINITY.

SECTION I.

THE DIVINE ATTRIBUTES.

I.

THE THREE EPOCHS OF THE HOLY TRINITY.

I KNOW not whether deep awe or deep tenderness is more excited in us, when we think of the overwhelming mystery of the Holy Trinity. If thought remains thought, then deep awe; but if thought quickly lights up into prayer, then most exquisite tenderness, and a certain trembling familiarity, which is the most piercing joy in life.

We feel—

1. As children born abroad, and told great things of our home, and beginning to travel thither when grown up.
2. As flying with an angel, yet feeling the farther off from earth, the nearer home.

Let us see what we have to do with the Holy Trinity: we feel as if we should lie on our faces, and speak low, when we speak of this adorable, transcending Life of the Uncreated and the Eternal.

I. First Epoch.—The Eternity before Creation.

1. It is God's immensity which makes Him so intimate to our littleness.
2. The loneliness of God.
3. The Companionship of the Divine Persons.

3

U. ℞

4. We lying clearly in the knowledge of God from eternity.

5. We also, our own secret selves, quickening the thrills of His love, before heaven and earth, matter or spirit, light or angel, space or time existed.

So it was our old home.

II. Second Epoch.—Our own lifetime.

1. Daily life of the Most Holy Trinity—Generation and Procession.

2. No shadow of mutability has passed over the Divine Majesty because of Creation.

3. Yet the Sacred Humanity of Jesus is in the midst —Mary's throne—Angels and souls.

4. Momentarily the Will of the Three Divine Persons concerns itself for us.

5. Our place there is fixed—preparations made—intense interest taken in it.

So it is our present home, from which we are absent but for a while.

III. Third Epoch.—Our immortality.

1. The life of the Most Holy Trinity still going on in blissful changeless peace.

2. Yet we actually beholding it, and drinking our own immortal life out of the vision.

3. Delight of being exclusively engrossed with God: and God *as it were* exclusively with us.

4. Whether there be new creations or none, we are still in glorious rest with Him.

So it is our future, our only, our unspeakably happy home.

My brethren! all this is but a fragment of our Catechism; but if these things be so, oh happy predestinated

U.

souls; what have we to do with sin, with self, with worldliness?

———

II.

THE SPIRIT OF ADORATION.

Fear remains in *sæculum sæculi*, therefore in Heaven: *tremunt potestates:* so on earth the substance of religion, the successful avoiding of sin, perseverance and perfection, all consist in the genuine spirit of adoration.

I. The Mystery of the Most Holy Trinity: the worship in heaven.

1. The angels, hiding their faces with their wings, &c.
2. Our Blessed Lady: her profound humiliation.
3. The Sacred Humanity of Jesus, filled with the spirit of adoration.
4. No familiarity in heaven with the unveiled ever new majesty of God.
5. There must be awe, as the mystery is not comprehended, even by Mary.
6. No intrinsic impossibility of sinning—all depends on the Vision, not on us.
7. Awfulness of the coruscations of the Eternal—what words can tell?
8. Height of celestial joy in this very awe: the Vision will not harm us: it is our life.

II. The spirit of adoration—what must it be to us unclean on earth?

1. Examples of it.—(1) Old Testament. (2) Jesus. (3) Mary. (4) Apostles. (5) Dying Saints.
2. Want of it the reason of so little perseverance in the devout life.

U.   ℞

3. Faults against it.
    (1) Criticism of God's ways.
    (2) Light speeches, such as we might make about
        Saints.
    (3) Even in prayer—1. want of preparation, 2.
        posture, 3. petulance.
4. Ways of practising it.
    (1) Respect for the Name of God; special com-
        mandment about it.
    (2) Fear of His judgments: humble views of—1.
        Death, 2. Judgment, 3. Purgatory, 4. Sin, 5.
        Security of salvation.
    (3) Doing things slowly.
5. Evils which the neglect of it brings, or rather
    blessings which the practice brings.
    (1) It leads to little talk, and so closes a huge
        river of sins.
    (2) To self-contempt, and so makes the prime law
        of charity easy.
    (3) It moderates and sobers joy which otherwise
        would make us childish and giddy.
    (4) The more we realize the dignity and immensity
        of God, the more we desire Him.
    (5) It gives us greater confidence in Him, as
        reverence always does; we trust what we
        revere.

The awfulness of making free with God: the Eternal
Father, the sacredness of His Majesty. His very goodness causes us to tremble; the infinite blessing of His
not passing us over and ignoring us! Sometimes in
the stillness of the night, in the hush of prayer, it
might so seem as if we might come to die and He forget us. Oh the blessing of being encompassed, girded

U.   Ⓟ

up, wound round and pressed to Him with His everlasting presence, universal knowledge, and illimitable
power! O God, our God! how admirable is Thy Name!

III.

DEVOTION TO THE OMNIPOTENCE OF GOD.

I. Characteristics of the Attribute.
    1. The result of all the rest of God's Perfections.
    2. And also the means by which they all work and
       magnify themselves.
    3. Its grandeur shown by its very *limits*—(1) It
       cannot do wrong. (2) It cannot give way. (3)
       It cannot require assistance.
    4. Its peculiar connection with Mercy; see xi. and
       xii. chaps. of Wisdom. Its connection with de-
       votion to the Eternal Father, and to the choir
       of Thrones.
    5. Grandeur of its (1) silence, (2) facility, (3) tran-
       quillity, (4) unobtrusiveness, (5) forbearing ten-
       derness.
II. Spirit the devotion will breed.
    1. Immense increase of faith.
    2. Huge courage.
    3. Indomitable cheerfulness.
    4. Familiarities with God; looking at Omnipotence
       as our ally.
    5. Rest of soul, through submission; Creation lean-
       ing on Omnipotence, and Omnipotence embrac-
       ing, fondling it as it leans.
III. Miscellaneous.
    1. It is very necessary for the time in which we live.

U

2. It makes our way of working more quiet, and also more consistent, less vacillating.
3. It breeds in us a greater habitual idea of the sovereignty of our most dear God.
4. It makes us more gentle with others, and more humble in exercising influence.
5. It impregnates our soul with the savor of eternity.

IV. Attitudes of the Devotion.

1. Adoring the beauty of the Attribute.
2. Submitting to it as a master.
3. Co-operating with it as a fellow-worker.
4. Looking at it as a fast friend, who will always be interfering for us, when needed.
5. Regarding it as lending its magnificent self to us to use in our own way.

How it fills us with a glorious overwhelming faith in the final victory of right.

IV.

THE DELIGHT OF THE INCOMPREHENSI-BILITY OF GOD.

I. Delight of it to Himself.

1. Like the Generation of the Son, it is a kind of jubilant consciousness of all His perfections.
2. It is the outspreading of His peace.
3. It is the vastness of His liberty, which is the most mysterious of all things in God.
4. It gratifies His secrecy ; S. Austin calls Him *Ens secretissimum.*
5. Sole prerogative—of being able to comprehend Himself!

U.

6. Yet not a loneliness. The Three Persons comprehend the Divine Nature and Essence.

7. Joy in the Sacred Humanity as a visible proof of
the Divine Incomprehensibility : incommunicable even to It. His omnipotence cannot make
Him comprehensible.

8. The secret regions of God probably most full of
jubilee to Himself, as incommunicable because
too high to communicate—yet this is, of course,
a human way of speaking.

9. Each attribute has eminences inconceivable;
besides that, there are unsuspected incommunicable perfections.

10. The wonder of His simplicity amidst all this,
intense jubilee to Him because of His unity.

II. Delight to us.

1. To our love, that He will always be above our
comprehension, and *all* comprehension.

2. It ardently quickens our desires to know and to
explore Him.

3. It helps us to measure eternity — we can hardly
believe in the inexhaustible.

4. It helps us to realize the unsearchable riches of
His mercy, which His Incomprehensibility con-
fers upon Him.

5. It wins and weans us from all created beauty.

6. It gives us such intense intellectual peace: silence
of objections, freedom from temptations.

7. Joy of faith: the unknown things of God leave
something like faith in heaven even.

8. Room for vastness of worship and love: our best
idea of God is His Incomprehensibility.

9. Delight that we can wonderfully comprehend so

much—and desire to love more that we may
comprehend more. Delight of saints in hidden
ways of God and Incomprehensibility of judgments. (S. Paul, Romans xi.) Our Lord also
" hid from wise and prudent."

10. But we can love Him as incomprehensible, though
not *know* His Incomprehensibility.

III. What is Incomprehensibility ?

1. God is incomprehensible by the very force of being
God.

2. Lights of nature, grace, and glory.

3. The blessed see some things they cannot comprehend; and some they do not see at all; yet God
is seen *totus sed non totaliter.*

4. The least things in God are incomprehensible.

5. S. Teresa's peculiar devotion to it.*

IV. The shadow of His Incomprehensibility is our own
reward, "eye has not seen, nor ear heard," &c.

V.

THE PREPARATIONS OF THE DIVINE WORKS.†

I. In reality, how fearful a thing it is to think that to
be Christians we must be like God! He so high,
and we so low! He with such perfections, we with
such miseries! Let us see how God works, *e. g.*,
in the Birth of Christ. So unlike what we should
have expected is real majesty.

---

* Le cose difficili da intendersi mi cagionano divozione, e quanto
piu sono incapibili, tanto maggior divozione provo verso di esse.—
Sentenziario, p. 58, sent. 937.   † Christmas Eve.

1. He waits with patience.
   (1) The world was left in sin for four thousand years.
   (2) Yet how He must have yearned to redeem it: how different our precipitate zeal.
   (3) He will have Mary His creature to anticipate the time: how much *we* have to do with God's works.
2. He works with modesty, and a sort of Divine Bashfulness: and this for all He is God.
   (1) He seeks silence and obscurity: *e. g.*, the Immaculate Conception, and the Annunciation.
   (2) Few words, and no praise: so all the circumstances of the Nativity.
   (3) He puts things out and leaves men to thwart them, as if He were regardless of success.
3. He works with a spirit of Divine Love.
   (1) He ignores the world, and takes it neither into His counsels nor His calculations.
   (2) All for love; His own glory, the merits of Jesus, the favors of Mary, all mean our salvation.
   (3) There is a sort of poetry about all the circumstances of His works, because of their excessive sweetness and heavenly pathos: not only to win our hearts, but because He is God, as if He could not help being beautiful and sweet and touching.
II. So we also should work.
   1. In our daily duties and occupations.
   2. In all the affairs of our spiritual life.
   3. Yet instead, eagerness, self-trust, and human respect are our three principles of human life;

its body is self-trust, its soul is human respect, its spirit eagerness.

Look at Mary and Joseph all to-day.—1. Journeying on. 2. Bethlehem. 3. The cave, how quiet, modest, retiring, and uneager: yet the world had not seen Jesus yet. It was without Him. Think of the world without Jesus—in all its relations. But so it is with Mary; still by nature, she is more still by grace; still by grace, she is more still now that she bears the Fountain of Grace and the Lord of Glory. It is just like the Annunciation: the magnificence of Mary is her tranquillity.

VI.

THE MERCY OF GOD.

The thought of God the sunshine of the world—study of His character and attributes—His personality.

I. What mercy is, especially in God.

  1. Mercy in a human sense involves our suffering ourselves, or our liability to suffer, the same or like or some sufferings.

  2. Mystery of it in God, Who—(1) can suffer nothing, (2) is infinitely just, (3) omnipotent, and (4) omniscient.

  3. Divine gifts to men—(1) from justice, (2) from liberality, (3) from goodness.

  4. Distinction between goodness and mercy in God.

II. Works and Manifestations of Divine Mercy.

  1. Attributes of God, as seen by the blessed, or by Saints in ecstacy, beautiful, satisfying the immortal spirit.

U.   ℞

2. Out of mercy came the mysterious work of creation—creatures out of nothing, mercy separating
them from the mass of possible things.

3. Manner of creation—He made angels and men in
a supernatural state of grace.

4. Gift of immortality, hindering them from falling
back into the abyss of nothingness, which theo-
logians call a perpetual *redemption*.

5. Mercy to mankind, going beyond mercy to angels
—(1) Fall. (2) Incarnation. (3) Iteration of
Sacrament of Penance.

6. Mercy to sinners—

(1) Meekness—does not let His anger break out,
is not disgusted.

(2) Patience—waits for sinners, dissembles, tires
out our passions by longsuffering.

(3) Benignity—always ready to receive; no number of sins, or kind, repel Him, yet think
what sin is.

(4) Clemency—*citra condignum* in hell.

7. Mercy to the good, whom St. Paul calls vessels of
mercy.

(1) Anyhow greater than to sinners.

(2) Ways—1. Adoption. 2. Protection against
evil spirits. 3. Affability. 4. Punishments
in this life. 5. Magnificence of gifts, consolations, and augmentations of grace.

(3) Unspeakableness of heaven and beatific vision
at last.

III. Special adoration of God's Mercy.

1. Picture of mercy—(1) In hell. (2) In heaven.
(3) The whole *being* of Purgatory. (4) Spread
like the waters of an ocean over earth. (5)

U.

Gloriousness of it in God Himself, in the depths of the Unspeakable Godhead.

2. Mary a vessel gleaming full of mercy, without judgment, that men might fall in love with its beauty and adore it—in her it is apart, not as in the Sacred Heart of Jesus; her consequent devotion to this attribute.

3. So take the hint from this, and daily get her to worship the mercy of God and bless it for us.

Spirits gazing on the Divine attribute of mercy— unreckoned centuries of eternity go by—still it seems ever new, ever wonderful, ever fresh, as the dilated spirit drinks in the view. Will the time ever come, when we, imprisoned here amid the weariness of life, the captives of our own offensive littleness, the victims of pain, age, and want, shall be ourselves a beauty, a bright spot, a notable magnificence, thus, in the full blaze of the golden heavens, worshipping with the strong thrills of an immortal ecstasy the mercy of the Holy and Everlasting God, the Simple and Undivided Trinity?

VII.

GOD WHO IS RICH IN MERCY.*

We want many things of God: we shall never cease to want many things of Him; when we possess Him in the incredible happiness of our grand eternity, though we shall possess Him, we shall still want Him. If He were to speak to me now, and I had to say

* Feast of the Precious Blood, 1860.

U.   ℞

the one thing, only one, which I most wanted of Him, could I hesitate in my answer for one moment? Father! I want *mercy*. If I think of the past I want mercy; of the present, mercy; of the future, mercy; of eternity, mercy. St. Paul, prisoner at Rome, writes to the Ephesians, and calls God—God who is *rich in mercy*: this name of God is exceedingly sweet; it sings in my ear like an angel's song: beautiful things came out of that marvellous mind of St. Paul's: none ever more beautiful than this—God who is rich in mercy.

I. What is it for God to be rich.—To be rich is to have superfluity, more than we want. God *more* than He wants! What a thought!

1. The immensity of His treasures.

2. The variety of them.

3. Their delightfulness to creatures. Can God possibly create two things more insatiable than the spirit of an angel and the soul of a man?

4. His liberality.

5. But in mercy, St. Paul hints, eminently, unspeakably, unimaginably rich.

II. The inside of the treasury of God.

1. Creation—what a vastness it is, what an outpouring it was!

2. Grace, its beauty and abundance.

3. Mary with her sorrows, joys, glories, and dear offices.

4. Jesus, with His immensities of Bethlehem, Nazareth, and Calvary.

5. The unsearchable magnificence of His own ever blessed Self.

III. Mercy sweetening life.

1. Are we in trouble about our past life? Hark,

U.   ꝛ)

how sweet that apostolic voice! Listen, it is an angel singing, Rich in mercy!

2. Trouble about present vileness? The very wild flowers from the earth breathe forth the words, the silence tingles into a sound, and articulates, Rich in mercy. It is like one of those beams of God which sometimes fall athwart the darkness of our prayer.

3. Trouble about those we love, whom we have long prayed for, and who seem past prayer? Rich in mercy! Blessed be St. Paul for that lucky word, or rather, Blessed be the Holy Ghost for that tender inspiration!

4. Trouble about our dead, whose faults come pertinaciously to mind? Rich in mercy!

5. A death to die, and a judgment to go through? These are panics such as to be almost unbelievable—yet they are infallible: Rich in mercy. Yes! in a torture of believing love, we cry, it is the utterance of our human faith, Rich in mercy!

IV. We often talk of a thing we know till it strikes us that we do not know it. Familiarity has a way of making things strange to us. What is mercy? What an unanswerable question! but let us try to answer it.

1. It is all the wants of the creature satisfied in one.

2. It is all his difficulties answered and turned into revelations.

3. It is all the sweetnesses of God put into one.

4. It is the beautifulness of God to us: (1) Power become gentle. (2) Wisdom dissolved into kindness. (3) Magnificence made tender. (4) Justice

grown indulgent. (5) Love's delight in us, fidelity to us, inability to do without us.

5. Oh no! mercy is far more than all this; look up into God, wait awhile till your eyes get accustomed to the blaze, look up to His highest heights, gaze into His deepest depths—there now, you see mercy. Oh, how unutterably beautiful! and you may read the new name God gave to mercy—and when He gave it the songs of the angels thundered round the throne as they had never done before—Thou shalt call His name Jesus; for He shall save His people from their sins.

All this is incredible: it is incredible; but faith manages to believe many incredible things. If all this be true, what becomes of the justice and sanctity of God? I do not know, I cannot think, I must not question. Sin is encouraged? I hope not; but if men take scandal with the justice of God, no wonder they take scandal with the mercy of God: for it is more excessive, more unexpected, more out of place, more unaccountable. God must see to it. God must provide. I grant it is a difficulty, a miracle, a secret, a mystery; but to faith one phrase, which St. Peter invented, and which I will put alongside of that word of St. Paul's on which I have been commenting, one phrase unlocks the whole, answers the whole, illuminates the whole,—the whole Church is sounding it to-day as through a silver trumpet:—The Precious Blood!

VIII.

THE MERCIES OF GOD.

Each one's life is a miracle of mercies: like the lives of the Old Testament Saints and patriarchs.

I. The multitude of God's mercies.

  1. God is not distracted by the numbers of His creatures.

  2. The continual outpouring of His mercies upon them.

  3. What a mercy from God must be like; think then of their multitude.

II. The variety of God's mercies, like vernal and autumnal woods.

  1. Different to different persons.

  2. No two of the same person's mercies are the same.

  3. Varieties, slow and sudden, unasked and long prayed for, silent and loud, direct and indirect, secret and public.

III. The way in which He does them.

  1. As if laying Himself under an obligation instead of conferring one.

  2. For the purpose of gaining our love.

  3. In such a way as to make us feel more free with Him instead of less free.

IV. The way they are mingled with sorrows.

  1. They come before sorrows to make us better able to bear them.

  2. The sorrow is always less raw than it seemed as if it inevitably must be.

  3. They follow like the rain when the lightning has come: then be on the watch for His mercies;

as the flower which the hot sun has caused to droop, when the rain comes, lifts up its colored eye to heaven, and breathes sweet odors on the air.

V. Their perseverance.

    1. They do not cease because of our ingratitude and sin.

    2. They do not wear out like human kindnesses.

    3. They multiply as we grow older.

VI. Their sweetness.

    1. Special sweetness in the circumstances and adaptations of each.

    2. Timely sweetness—always in season—only God's kindness is always seasonable—human kindness is often harsh for want of this.

    3. Extra sweetness, more than needed or promised, or than is natural; every mercy of God is a very supernatural thing.

VII. Conclusion.

    1. What a picture of God it gives us! He so loves thanks.

    2. Also what a picture of ourselves, yet what a joy to have such a God as ours.

    3. Yet all this is only a shadow of the mercies of heaven.

Yet earth's mercies end in heaven's mercies. How many secret mercies of each one of you is but the beginning of a gladness and a glory that shall be eternal. Oh let us go home and think of our good God, and weep secret tears of joy over the beauty and the pleasantness, over the patience and the plenty, over the freedom and the kindliness, of our Father's exceeding goodness.

IX.

THE DIVINE FORBEARANCE.

The immensity of the Majesty of God, and so the dreadfulness of offending Him, and the unspeakable wonder of His being so patient and still under it all. London at this hour.

I. God's forbearance generally.

   1. With individuals, nations, and the world.

   2. His silence.

   3. His continuance of blessings, and so seeming approval.

   4. His forbearance lasting even through a quiet dëathbed.

   5. Then the awakening.

II. His forbearance with our own selves; which none but we can know, for none else know the depth of our own badness.

   1. The graces heaped upon us.

   2. Our relapses and fresh rebellions.

   3. Continual hourly new forgivenesses.

   4. Negligence in His service.

   5. Poorness and ungenerosity of it.

III. Our present state.

   1. We on earth—many less guilty in hell.

   2. God's present love of us.

   3. The reason of this—because He sees us in Christ.

   4. Our resolutions for holiness.

   5. Present practice—for the rest of Lent—Devotion to the Passion.

Shut out the world from our hearts, even while working for the world with our hands—catch His

U.　　　　　　　　　　　　　　　　　　Ⓟ

voice—hear the dropping of His Precious Blood—His
low sighs, not so much of suffering as of love—by
Easter we may kiss His wounded feet.

X.

GOD'S PATIENCE WITH US.

I. His slowness to anger.
  1. Number of our offences.
  2. Increase of graces.
  3. Delay of punishment.
  4. Gentleness of punishment.
  5. Even when punishing He often is not angry.

II. His disinterested sweetness in His disappointments
    with us.
  1. As if His glory was nothing to Him.
  2. What He cannot get in one way He tries to get
     in another.
  3. If He fails He will not give it up.
  4. He acts as if *He* had made a mistake in asking
     too much.
  5. He does not make things decisive, as if He said,
     Well, now try this Cross, my child.

III. His incredible allowances, and the interpretations
    of His wisdom.
  1. His knowledge of us as our Creator, fountain of
     millions of mercies, which would seem foolish
     to the sharp-eyed blindness of the world.
  2. He sees no fault when we often see much.
  3. What He sees in secret all goes to extenuate our
     faults.
  4. He sees how much are stupidities well meant.

U.

5. He sets such a value upon *efforts.* No mother is so blind as the all-seeing-God.

IV. His marvellous indulgence.

    1. Evil ways less heavy in His scales than in those of man.

    2. While good weighs far more heavily.

V. His own astonishing placability.

And all this because He is the Father of our Lord Jesus Christ.

XI.

"KNOWEST THOU NOT THAT THE BENIG- NITY OF GOD LEADETH THEE TO PENANCE?"

Is there any one present who does not wish to change his life? However good, he must be in a sad delusion. At this present moment where should we be, if we had our due? In eternal punishment, for sin, and through the absence of grace to which we have had no title. If we could always think this thought, how changed our lives would be!

I. The benignity of God is what has saved us—and it is the characteristic of His benignity always to be leading us to penance.

    1. At last it overcomes our hardness, by its very patience and forbearance.

    2. Were there less benignity, penance ever being accepted would be simply incredible.

    3. It makes the penance not only possible, but even sweet, by supernatural aids.

4. Think of the punishment of resisting such a benignity, and the reward of obeying it.

5. It is because it is benignity that it presses penance, because it knows we cannot be saved without it.

So then penance is necessary to salvation—look at it as we will.

II. Practice.

1. Have we ever done worthy penance for our sins?

2. Anything *like* worthy penance?

3. *Any* penance at *all?*

4. Are we going to do any?

5. What steps are we going to take?

III. That I leave to yourselves: only I would urge upon you the three grand helps, and not helps only, but facilities also, of penance.

1. Continual remembrance of *our* sins.

2. Continual remembrance of *His* Passion.

3. Continual remembrance of an undoubting faith in hell. The devil's worst and most fatal preparation for the coming of Antichrist is the weakening of men's belief in eternal punishment. Were they the last words I might ever say to you, nothing should I wish to say to you with more emphasis than this, that next to the thought of the Precious Blood, there is no thought in all your faith more precious or more needful for you than the thought of Eternal Punishment.*

---

* Fourth Sunday in Lent, 1863. This was the last occasion but one on which Father Faber preached.

U.   ℞

XII.

"THE BRUISED REED HE SHALL NOT BREAK, AND SMOKING FLAX HE SHALL NOT QUENCH."

Many things in life are questionable: but this at least is unquestionable: here we are all agreed.

I. If there be one thing more certain than another it is that we must not go into the eternal fires of hell: this is beyond controversy.

    1. No difficulties in religion are to be thought of in comparison of this necessity.

    2. No sacrifices are too great to be made to ensure this.

    3. No length of efforts is too long to be sustained in order to escape this appalling doom.

Hence we must take religion as we find it: we must accept God on His own terms.

II. The many beautiful descriptions of God and of our Saviour in the Bible; none seems to me so beautiful as that one in Isaias xlii.: The bruised reed He shall not break, and smoking flax He shall not quench.

    1. Observe that the Father says of our Lord's Sacred Heart, My soul delighteth in Him: I have given My spirit upon Him; then afterwards, The bruised reed He shall not break, and smoking flax He shall not quench.

    2. Then our Lord in St. Matthew xii., *hurt* at their wanting to stop His doing good on the Sabbath, tells those that He heals not to make Him known —and the Evangelist quotes Isaias, and says our Lord did this to fulfil that prophecy.

3. The beauty of the Three Years' Ministry comes from this: the woman at the well; the woman taken in adultery; the great clear shining love of the great apostles, even that prince of divine lovers, that model of heavenly enthusiasts, St. Peter, once it was only smoking flax; that conflagration of love, which has set the Church on fire for centuries, the Heart of Magdalen, once it was only smoking flax; that furnace in which millions of hearts are for ever being molten, the heart of Paul, once it was flax that smoked so little and so feebly that it needed the Eye of God to see that it smoked at all.

III. The ways in which this is true of God.

1. The immense value He sets on the slightest smouldering of piety and love in our souls; how He nurses beginnings; how He coaxes fears and entices relapses; we read of no feast days among the angels, but those to celebrate the return of sinners to their Father and their God.

2. In falls—the huge allowances He makes; Jesus even gave scandal by it; slow to anger, swift to pardon; long in leaving, instantaneous in coming back; nay, *effort* is *always* victory in His sense, even when it is defeat.

3. He sees good where we do not see it; it is greater to Him than it even *looks* to us, and He makes more of it; St. Teresa even says that often what seems faults to us are not faults at all to Him.— Comfort of this. Surely without offending against humility we may trust we have some bruised purposes, ah, sadly bruised, of good, some smoking flax, to the eyes of Jesus visible, of divine love!

Now, look at ourselves, at the kindest amongst us, how different we are: we go about life doing just the reverse, breaking the bruised, quenchiug the smoking; our very love is ungainly and unloving, and our charity such a poor miserable shadow of what it is in God; we are so clumsy, so awkward, so harsh, so dry, so stiff, so pedantic, so unaccommodating, so humiliatingly untender and ungraceful.

And what a miracle the opposite is in God! how the vastness of His immensity can leave us so at ease and at large! the terrific extremity of His power can be so smooth, so soft, so light—the frightening exactions of His spotless holiness, so kindly, so forbearing, so easily contented, so sweetly unimperious. Oh what an incredible God! what must heaven be simply as the place where God's goodness has its own unhindered and eternal way! See how beautiful this is—the extreme indulgence of an earthly mother has to come out of the very foolishness of her love! the far more extreme indulgence of our Heavenly Father would be impossible to anything but the boundless wisdom of a God. Ah Lord! with such a God as Thee it will not be hard to save our souls.

XIII.

GOD OUR FATHER.

I. The beauty and consolation of this idea.

    1. It destroys the sense of loneliness in the world;

    2. Gives a new and consoling view to afflictions and chastisements;

U

3. Makes the sense of weakness more endurable;

4. Enables us to *trust* God for problems we cannot solve.

5. Sense of relationship with all our fellowmen.

II. How it enters into all spiritual actions.

  1. In sin.

  2. In sacraments.

  3. In aiming at perfection.

  4. In temptations.

  5. In suffering.

III. How God is our Father, and proves Himself so.

  1. In the ordinary events and course of life.

  2. In protection from evils which we shall only know at the day of doom.

  3. In answers to prayer.

  4. In doing good to those we love.

  5. In forbearance, and the continuance of grace.

IV. *How* He is our Father.

  1. Not nominally, but really.

  2. This comes out of creation.

    (1) Marvellous sensible love.

    (2) Identity of interests.

    (3) Reflection of Self.

  3. The Father of our Lord Jesus Christ.

  4. He has made Himself still more our Father by covenant; and He effects what He promises.

  5. Additional ties of grace and glory.

Happy sunshine of this thought—(1) more trust in Him; (2) more freedom with Him; (3) more generosity towards Him.

———

U.

XIV.

THE JOY OF BEING THE PROPERTY OF GOD.

There is one wish ruling over all mankind, and it is a wish which is never in any single instance gratified; each man wishes to be his own master. It is a boy's beatific vision, and it remains the grown-up man's ruling passion to the last. But the fact is, life is a service; the only question is, whom we will serve?

I. What it is to become the property of our own selves.
  1. Habits of sin which imperiously rule us even to pain and to death.
  2. Misery of many wants, which gnaw us if we do not satisfy them.
  3. Continual mortification of not getting our own way.
  4. The few ruling passions—so as often to upset reason.
  5. There is not a vestige of liberty left to us.

II. The property of the world.
  1. Success is a perpetual struggle—what absence of repose.
  2. Unbearable tyranny of human respect.
  3. False promises of worldly pleasures.
  4. Total want of sympathy, and kindliness in the world.
  5. Way in which all about us, reputation, privacy, time, passes from under our own jurisdiction.

Moreover those two services make us in effect the property of Satan.

U.

III. The property of God. "I belong to God—what is all else to me!" Blessing of this indifference to us; most unhappiness is from want of indifference.

1. We belong to Him by all titles; but He will have us give ourselves to Him of ourselves.

2. In His service every hardship has its own reward, every sorrow its special consolation.

3. In sorrow the sweetness,

    (1) As coming from our Father.

    (2) As deeply compassionated by Him.

    (3) As eternally rewarded.

4. In joy,

    (1) That it is pleasing to God.

    (2) Of a heavenly character, and

    (3) Leaves the soul at rest.

5. In work,

    (1) It is for God.

    (2) No fretfulness about success.

    (3) Full of spirit and courage.

6. In weariness,

    (1) Sweet sense of fatigue for God.

    (2) How He rests us with beautiful soft thoughts and visitations.

    (3) He is no taskmaster.

7. In death,

    (1) Full of solemnity but not of terror.

    (2) A beginning, not an end.

    (3) Tremulous joy of increasing nearness to God.

And then He takes His property back again, dearest of Masters, and we go to Him, and then and not before, and there and not elsewhere, we are at rest; for His bosom is the weary man's own house—his very own delightful home!

XV.

GOD'S LOVE OF SINGLE SOULS.

A soul of mediocrity: its unexciting commonplaceness to us.

I. God's view of it.

1. Intense interest simply because it is a soul.
2. Eternal choice of it, and mysterious preference of it to other possible souls.
3. Desire to have its eternal companionship, as if an augmentation of His glory.
4. A certain peculiar glory destined for it.
5. It represents some definite peculiar beauty and excellence in God Himself.

II. His behavior to it.

1. Every single perfection exercised for it, and livelily interested in it.
2. The yearning character of His immense love for it.
3. The way in which He interests all other creatures in it.
4. His separate devotion to that one soul.
5. The devices and condescensions with which He makes love to it.

III. The Three Persons.

1. The Eternal Father
    (1) Is stirred in all the abysses of His Paternity;
    (2) Would give His Son a second time for its salvation;
    (3) Receives it, as a returning prodigal, again and again.
2. The Eternal Son.

U.　　　　　　　　　　　　　　　　　　ꟼ

    (1) The immensity of His wisdom makes Him
        love it all the more.

    (2) Ready to be crucified a second time for that
        one soul alone.

    (3) Continual communication of Himself to it in
        grace and sacraments.

  3. The Eternal Spirit.

    (1) His immense Will bent on that one soul.

    (2) His faithful, pathetic pleadings with it, as
        if almost there might be some unhappiness
        in God.

    (3) How tenderly His omnipotence handles that
        single soul.

So it is as if the Holy Trinity could not bear to part
with the creature who had been an eternal idea in His
mind, an eternal love in His affections.

And all this is for my one soul—my soul just as it is
now—my soul just as I know it to be! Surely, I must
either lose my faith, or die of love.

XVI.

THE STRANGENESS OF GOD'S LOVE
FOR US.

Many persons go about the world without in the
least seeming to see anything strange or preternatural
in life; nay, none of us realize how much is involved
in common things and everyday expressions. God's
love of us—we take it for granted—let us look into it.

I. How do we know God loves us?

1. It is not our own loveliness.

U.   D

2. Nor the state of the world, with sickness, death,
&c.

3. We find a difficulty in religion, from the facility
of sin, chance of hell, &c.

4. Yet there is something in our nature which refuses
to let us believe in the possibility of the Creator
not loving His creatures.

II. Why does He love us?

1. Not for our merit's sake.

2. Not for any dignity or intrinsic worth we have.

3. Because of His own adorable perfection of infinite love.

III. What kind of a love does He love us with?

1. The very absence of all worth on our part shows
that His love is a wonderful thing, quite different
from human love.

2. His love of us as our Creator.

3. His love of us as our Redeemer.

4. All the imaginable kinds of human love together
approach not to this.

IV. What a support to us this consideration is!

1. He will accept our least services.

2. It is not easy to weary and exhaust His love.

3. Past blessings and graces are a sort of guarantee
for future ones.

4. There must be a loving meaning in all adversity
and suffering.

5. How wonderful must be that state in which these
two wonders, the two loves of Creator and Redeemer, are satisfied and fulfilled in the creature's
glory.

Importance to ourselves and acceptableness to God
in our having a most vivid faith and a bold trust in

God's love of us: it is quite a sign of predestination
—to feel as if we could *not* be lost, for all we are the
miserable perverse sinners that we are. No! God is
for us—who shall be against us?

XVII.

"BE NOT DECEIVED—GOD IS NOT MOCKED."

How the Bible is always *startling* us! We children
of men are deeply fallen, but are we come to this—
that we dare to mock God? It seems incredible. We
children of men are indeed far gone in folly: but are
we come to such downright madness as this, that we
mock God? Yet an apostle thinks it needful to warn
us against it. There are few things in the Holy
Scriptures stranger than this.

I. To mock God.

    1. The scene in Herod's courtyard: what if His
       Divinity had burst forth!

    2. God in His Majesty, amidst the burning angels,
       and the vast fires of heaven.

    3. God with the inexorable pressure of His just
       hand in hell.

    4. But even in hell no one dares to mock.

    5. To mock God! unspeakable, unimaginable wild-
       ness! I never heard even of madness that did
       it. Yet an apostle thinks it a sin we are not
       unlikely to fall into.

II. Who mocks God? I fear there is no one of us

who has not at some time mocked Him. What if
we are mocking Him now? as in Herod's court.
What it is to *promise to God.*

1. Those who promise to him and do not perform
   —perhaps hardly mean to perform when they
   promise.
2. Those who perform carelessly and indifferently.
3. Those who do not take even the trouble to promise, like not answering a man when he speaks
   to you.
4. Those who delay, trusting to future repentance.
5. Those who do some things for God, and leave
   other things undone, as if they were His judges
   and superiors.

III. Playing a part with God is a mockery of Him.

1. Shirking examination of conscience and self, for
   fear of discovering things to change.
2. Indefinitely adjourning correspondence to grace.
3. Bargaining with God for reserves.
4. Praying for what we seriously do not wish.
   Thy will be done, &c.
5. Trying to outwit Him—to have both worlds—
   to make him equal to others, not sovereign, &c.

Oh, it makes one desperate to see how men go on
with God. Do you not see that He is not in the
least the God your conduct makes Him out to be?
Do you not perceive that everything is mockery of
God which is not the fear of Him, the day-long, the
life-long fear of His most holy and everwhelming
Majesty? You—you who have not the courage to
throw God off altogether, but are serving Him with
half a heart—you who pray at times, who come to
church, who give an occasional alms, but to whom

fashion, pleasure, frivolity, expensiveness, amusement, are far more sensibly sweet than God—do you imagine God does not see through you? Do you imagine you will succeed? Do you suppose you will surprise God, and slip into a heaven by a stratagem? Fools! Fools! Do you not see the enormity of the impertinence, which even your very religion is to His unspeakable truthfulness, to His inexorable sanctity? Oh incredible audacity of human nature, audacious in its levity, audacious in its insincerity! How a cruel, a very cruel, but strictly just eternity will swallow up souls by millions, because they would neither face this honest truth, nor live upon it—that everything is mockery of God except a downright genuine conversion of the heart!

XVIII.

GOD SO LITTLE LOVED.

I. Some things are so serious that we say we cannot allow them to go on any longer; and then it is amazing what the power of our wills can do. Now here is a very serious matter—God being so little loved. Can we look on this with indifference?

1. The honor of God being so little loved.
2. His immense majesty.
3. His own incomparable goodness to us.
4. What must happen to those who do not love Him?
5. What danger those are in who love Him so little.

U.   ℞

6. All the miseries of this life are because of God not being loved.

7. Hell is also filling hourly.

8. And all the while the love of God seems really growing less and less.

II. Do you mean to say that we are indifferent to all this? No.

1. Are we doing anything to hinder it?

2. Does it give us any real sorrow or uneasiness?

3. Was life then meant for other things to be attended to, and this to be neglected?

4. Is religion a private luxury—a simple sofa of sweet soft thoughts for conscience to lie down upon and take its ease?

5. Love is work—God must have work from us—real thorough work.

6. We can at least begin with ourselves and increase our own love of Him;

7. And we must begin at once, to-day, this morning;

8. And we must begin manfully and in earnest. We want conversion—nothing short of it—look at the past; it will never do.

III. But we cannot stop at self. Is our piety to go to sleep while the world is perishing?

1. Are all these souls to perish and we not to lift an arm?

2. But what can we do? Oh! rather what can we not do?

3. Prayer is pretty well omnipotent, and we can all do that.

4. But have we ever set ourselves to pray down the sins of London?

5. But I must have something more than prayer

U.   ⓓ

—God's cause is in fearful case—I must have great things.

6. Can you not send a child to school, or bring a sinner to the sacraments?

7. Or give more abundant alms to good works?

8. Driven to a holy despair by the awful scenes of dead and dying souls around you, what sacrifices are you making for Him who sacrificed Himself upon the cross for you?

Look the crucifix in the face, and answer these questions, not to me, but to Him.

XIX.

MORE FOR GOD.*

My brethren, I wish you would be more for God than you are!

We have been among the mountains lately, the dark mountains of the Passion, and the illuminated heights of the Resurrection: now let us look at ourselves, at our own height, our place before God, our union with Him, our practice of virtues, our correspondence to grace.

  I. Easter questions.

1. Will this do? Is it safe, just as it is? Is it satisfactory?

2. Is it capable of being improved?

3. If so, of what sort of improvement?

4. Have we actually set about this work?

* Low Sunday, 1861.

5. If not, why not? For what reason have we de-
   layed? Have we decided not to improve?

II. More for God

  1. Do you not *need* to be so?
    (1) Is God satisfied?
    (2) Could you die as you are?
    (3) Do you look forward to never being more
        than you are? If you do, you will not even
        be saved.

  2. Do you not *wish* to be so?
    (1) The marvellous contentment of it.
    (2) The safety of it.
    (3) The immense recompense.

  3. Yet is it not easy?
    (1) More for God—if it were but a little more.
    (2) More for God—if it were but gradually
        more.
    (3) And even were it hard, would it not be
        worth while.

III. All for God.

  1. This surely is the sweet and glorious thing.*
  2. The wonder that we can be anything else. It is
     the common sense of life.
  3. This alone makes life bright, and death delight-
     ful, and eternity so replenished with glory.
  4. Yet, alas! how little we are for God—how in-
     significant His place in our lives.
  5. Then I will be contented to ask you to be more
     for God, somewhat more than now. Nay, I
     will ask you only this. By His Cross and
     Passion, and by His glorious Resurrection, to
     resolve now to be more for God than you are.

* Eccles. xliii. 32.

U,   ℞

At least deliberate about it—at least seriously entertain the idea.

For your own sake, for God's sake, I cannot bear that you should be so little for God as you are. I do not ask you to be all for God, only to be more for God, more for God than you are. I ask no more than this, because I think I should get no more. Is it want of faith in you or want of love for you? Oh, not want of love for you, but it is want of faith in you. Ought I to be ashamed of this want of faith, or ought you to be ashamed? Anyhow, of one thing I am ashamed: I am ashamed to look a thousand Christians in the face at Easter, and yet not dare to ask them to be all for God. But I dare not, and therefore I do not. But will you try to be *a little more* for Him than you are?

XX.

WILL YOU COME TO GOD NOW?

I. Years have passed, and each year God called you. He urged you, He begged, He prayed, He entreated, He made great promises. But you would not. The world, youth, riches, honors, above all things, pleasures, were tempting. God was put off. Will you come to God *now?* If we would not then, why should we now?

1. Because we have lived longer, and we cannot help learning more and more that the salvation of the soul is our grand and only work. Will you come to God now?

2. Because, if it was always dangerous to delay, it

always grows more dangerous. Will you come
to God now?

3. Because we *have* enjoyed our share of the world,
and it is at least God's *turn* now. Will you
come to God now?

4. Because, when we see others who serve God, and
think it all over, we suspect we magnified both
the difficulties and the dulness of being religious.
Will you come to God now?

5. Because the world, we must confess, has disappointed us. Will you come to God now?

6. Nay more, it has been an exceedingly heavy yoke
upon us. Will you come to God now?

7. Because death is advancing very rapidly. Will
you come to God now?

8. Because we cannot face the eternal tortures, and
repentance grows harder by delay. Will you
come to God now?

9. Because there is an irresistible sweetness in God's
very invitation. Will you come to God now?

II. Practical Reflections.

1. God is waiting to forgive, eager to forgive.

2. His salvation is abundant, complete, and full of
delightful pleasantness.

3. Our past sins will be all obliterated.

4. We shall get ample supplies of grace for the
future.

5. Peace, rest, brightness—will gather round our
remaining years: and all these things will be
the greater, the younger we are when we give
ourselves to God.

Can there be a heaven upon earth, a joy that is
more than a match for any sorrow? Oh yes! it is

U.   Ⓐ

the joy of those who have trusted God's goodness, the blessedness of those who have found peace and pardon in Jesus Christ.

XXI.

A TASTE FOR GOD.

We are apt to exaggerate the change which death makes in ourselves, because it makes so tremendous a change in our position. We must not confound these two things: as the tree falls, so shall it lie.

I. What will cause our joy in heaven?

   1. It is a life of prayer, praise, vision, and contemplation.

   2. To an evil spirit or impenitent soul it would be the sheerest monotonous misery.

   3. God, and only God, is the direct bliss of heaven.

   4. He is also the joyousness of the indirect joys in heaven.

   5. So the best we can take to heaven is a taste for God and the things of God: our real *tastes* are not the best prophecies of our predestination.

II. What are our tastes now?

   1. Distinguish between our tastes and our frailties; as a miser may be led into expense by love of pleasure.

   2. Are prayer, sermons, services, distinctly pleasures to us?

   3. Have we a taste for God, and the things of God?

   4. How is our taste for God, alongside of our taste for the world?

U.

5. Scripture moreover assures that the two are incompatible.

III. A taste for God is a magnificent grace; it is such a security to us; such a thing to rest upon; such a proof to us that we are drawn into a supernatural world.   In what it consists.

1. Sweetness in the thought of God.

2. The thought of God quietly making itself the center, and righting itself after struggles.   We have disturbances, but gravitate back to God when they are past.

3. Resting in God, even when there is no sensible sweetness.

4. Contentment, coming of this rest.

5. Something inward which is beyond words.

6. It does not in itself secure holiness, but it goes far towards doing so.

7. It is a gift of God, yet I incline to think it can be acquired.

IV. How it is to be cultivated and dealt with.

1. It must be taken care of, and defended against dangers.

2. And even augmented by our own efforts.

3. We must not presume on it, as if of itself it would kill worldliness like some antidote.

4. We must not be afraid of its manifest encroachments towards sovereignty.

5. Its growth is in a life of prayer.

6. Its health is in sweet patient lovingness to all around us.

7. To ourselves it is our life, the budding of our eternity: not a sight or hearing, or an odor, or even a taste, though we call it so: it is a

U.   ℞

touch of God, yet not a touch outside us, but a
touch on our souls within us, and so causing a
taste; a touch in the dark, which often makes
us lie still and thrill with love.

XXII.

OUR HOME IN GOD.

In the Bosom of the Most High God, amid the
astounding marvels of the Most Holy Trinity, amid
the boundless silences and the uncreated fires of the
illimitable majesty of God—there is our home—there
is to be our life—there are our interests, our tastes,
and our occupations for all eternity! What an incredible faith, incredible even from the very exceeding-
ness of its simplicity. What grave, broad thoughts it
suggests to us, and yet such homely, plain practical
truths! The grandeur of the Mystery of the Most
Holy Trinity makes us children all at once.

I. Description of our Home.

  1. Multitudinous Majesty of God, outlying beyond
     all spaces, full of countless ever-flashing life.

  2. The ravishing loveliness and eternal surprises of
     His Attributes.

  3. The adorable grandeur and sweetness of the
     Three Persons.

  4. The immensity of the revelations of the Vision;
     and yet,

  5. The jubilee of the incomprehensibility of God.

II. The life we lead in that Home.

  1. Beauty beyond all imaginable beauty.

2. Interestingness, fascination, and absorption.
3. Joy that would break the hearts of all .the men who ever have been created is not as one drop to our joy in the Bosom of God.
4. Magnificence of the love with which we can love there.
5. But overwhelming ecstacy of the love with which we are loved.

III. The life we are now living is at once nothing, and yet all in all to that life.

Practical Conclusions.

1. Are our present tastes and interests fitting us for it?
2. Are our present occupations congenial to it, and practising for it?
3. How immensely we must be changed even to bear, let alone enjoy, that other life!
4. How obviously our spiritual life must be our one care here!
5. What is it we want? what is it we must cultivate? *A desire for God!*

My brethren! is it well with our souls? How shall we know? Each passing year does the sense of exile grow upon us, the feeling that earth is not our home? Do we become less interested in worldly things, and more weary of them, yet with an active, practical, charitable weariness? Does a kind of Christian discontent spread more and more over our souls, and yet grow more peaceful, as we grow more discontented? All this is well; but it must pass into something higher, something deeper, something sweeter —into a hunger and a thirst for God!

Part First.

GOD AND THE MOST HOLY TRINITY.

SECTION II.

THE HOLY GHOST.

45

U

I.

THE HOLY GHOST. *

CHAPTER I.

THE PROCESSION OF THE HOLY GHOST.

WE are going to dare to mount up into the eternal life of God, to see what we may be able to see regarding the Holy Ghost, the Third Person of the Undivided Trinity. We must leave far behind us all the ideas and images of earth. Our inquiry must itself be an act of worship, and its end be more holiness and fresh love. We must be content sometimes with words, which seem to have but little meaning, the little meaning being not in the thing signifying, but in their way of signifying it, with momentary glimpses of bright things, which are almost immediately withdrawn again—with reverent guesses—with truths half seen—with pictures, which though seen, rather puzzle us than represent anything intelligible. Are we willing to hazard such an enterprise? Let us see.

    I. The effects upon the soul of investigating any portion of the mystery of the Holy Trinity.

    1. The unworldliness which the inquiry gives.

* The five following chapters are the sketch of a proposed Treatise.

(1) Because the images and ideas are all unearthly.

(2) Because we know the intense and transcen-
dental truth of it all.

(3) Because it helps towards either self-oblivion
or self-contempt.

2. There is a reality in everything about God—so
that we cannot come in contact with Him without something happening to us: a child amid
tools and machines, metals and precious stones,
of which he does not know the names or uses,
or to whom the names are only hard words, yet
has grown in mind by what he has seen : how
much more then with the things of God !

3. From this reality it comes to pass that some substantial effect is wrought by this in our souls.

(1) Our faith is enriched, and also invigorated by
the exercise.

(2) A celestial standard of beauty, as yet beyond
the grasp of our own thoughts, is infused into
our souls.

(3) The powers of the soul probably gain new
capabilities by contact with God.

4. We unconsciously gain, and hereafter find out, a
better understanding of the mysteries around us,
e.g. creation, the permission of evil, the variety
of graces in men, the exclusiveness of truth,
God's seemingly arbitrary ways with His creatures, and other problems, of which each individual mind has one or more peculiar to itself,
haunting and distressing it by its distorted
shapes and exaggerated shadows.

5. The knowledge we obtain by such inquiries

gradually dawns into a *clearer* and *quieter* view of God.

6. Love outgrows knowledge, and comes from the inquiry, even when there are so few appreciable results; this is partly because of—

(1) The reality of God.

(2) The standard of beauty infused into us.

(3) Our own personal concern with the mystery in question.

7. It is always to be remembered that it is our own eternal home which we are looking at.

II. The object of our present inquiry is the Holy Ghost: Who is He?

1. True and Eternal God.

2. One only, however, of the Three Divine Persons.

3. The last of the Three in order, but All co-equal.

4. Of Whom many marvellous distinctive things have been revealed.

5. Who manifests a peculiar love of ourselves, proper to Himself, and shown in His own way.

6. Who has been mixed up secretly with all our lives since childhood.

7. Who is actually dwelling in us at this moment in a peculiar manner, over and above the omnipresence of God—quite different from the dwelling of the Blessed Sacrament within us, yet only to be paralleled by that.

III. The life of God.

1. It is the same this hour that it ever was: as it never had any beginning, so it has had no past history—but it is one simple act never begun, never finished, never in process from a beginning,

never on its progress towards an end, never
left incomplete.

2. All acts in God are necessary; else God would
not be perfect, there would be something in
Him which need not have been there, which
He could do without, and this it would be
blasphemy to say. Inside Himself, God has no
liberty: to the grandeur of His simplicity liberty
would be a feebleness and an imperfection.

3. Unity of Essence:—this unity is so unspeakable
that the word is below the meaning; all closest
unities are but far-off shadows of it: it consists—

  (1) In singularity.
  (2) In-indivisibility.
  (3) In simplicity.
  (4) In identity.
  (5) In plenitude.

4. Trinity of Persons.

  (1) The Unbegotten Father.

  (2) By His knowledge of Himself and all things
begetting the Word.

  (3) And these Two, as one principle, by Their
love of each other and of all things, breathing
forth the Holy Spirit.

  (4) And the Holy Spirit returning upon the
Two, and being their junction, expression,
joy, term, and love.

  (5) All co-equal, co-eternal, consubstantial: one
substance as described above.

  (6) No sort of inequality; only priority of order
and emanation.

  (7) Yet with the most extraordinary distinct-
nesses as Persons.

5. This is the completion of the life of God,—which causes it to result—

(1) In the most stationary immutability.

(2) In the most vital activity.

(3) In the most indefinable simplicity of act.

(4) In the most profound peaceful separateness, yet universality.

(5) All combining in the most unimaginable abysmal beatitude.

IV. The Procession of the Holy Ghost.

1. His procession is not from the Divine Essence viewed as apart from the Two Persons, but from the Two Persons as subsisting.

2. He proceeds from the Two Persons, as one principle.

3. He proceeds by the way of the will, as the Son by the way of the understanding: hence the Procession is not a generation.

4. To use a human word, the method is by respiration:—and therefore is—

(1) From the interior.

(2) From the ardor of love.

(3) Perpetually, by the, so to call it, identical reciprocity of the love of the Father and the Son.

(4) Refreshing as it were the inward heat,—the necessity in God of this refreshment, if we may dare so to speak.

5. From the triple love of the Father and the Son.

(1) Appreciation.

(2) Benevolence.

(3) Complacency.

6. The love of us and of all creatures, entered into

the love by which He proceeded, not *necessarily*, but as a matter of fact, *per accidens et concomitanter.*

7. This Procession is eternal, and is eternally going on every moment, as part of God's life, like the breathing of a living man.

8. Yet He who thus proceeds is in all respects co-equal, co-eternal and consubstantial with Those from whom He proceeds.

V. Certain eminences of the Holy Ghost.

1. What He does for the Person of the Father.

(1) Gives Him an exercise for His unbegotten fecundity.

(2) Gives Him an expression for His love of the Son.

(3) Is as it were the terminal ocean to Him as fountain of deity.

2. What He does for the Person of the Son.

(1) Gives Him an exercise for the fecundity the Father communicated to Him.

(2) Gives Him an expression for His love of the Father.

(3) Illustrates the distinctness of His Person from that of the Father.

(4) Is the occasion to Him of the grandeur of being, with the Father, the principle of a Divine Person.

3. What He does equally for Both of Them.

(1) Unspeakably sanctifies Them by the exercise of love.*

(2) Returns to Them Both as an impulse;

(3) And is reflected by Them;

* Bail, Théologie Affective, 2me. Traité, Med. xii.

U

(4) And draws an eternally beautiful life out of Them.

(5) By a procession which is to Them, as well as to Him, an infinite beatitude.

4. He is the bond or chain or kiss of the Father and the Son.

    (1) For they have no plurality as the principle of Him, but one simple sovereign unity.

    (2) They have but one relation to the Holy Spirit, not Each of Them a separate relation ;

    (3) And he has but one relation to them.

    (4) The Father could not be this bond ; for the Son and the Holy Ghost have different relations to Him.

    (5) Nor the Son for the same reason ; because the Father and the Holy Ghost have different relations to Him.

    (6) Unutterable strength of this uncreated Bond, who is a Person.

    (7) The life of God is completed in it—not *held together* by it; for that would imply composition, which is impossible.

5. He is the term of the interior productions and necessary acts in God.

    (1) The last Person produced, as if God would mix with creatures unless He has a term, a term to His infinite life !

    (2) The only Person not Himself producing, but returning backwards rather.

    (3) His knowledge of Himself essential and speculative, not productive.

    (4) The same is true also of His will.

U

(5) Note then that the fulness of God and the repose of God is not in knowledge but in love: the Holy Ghost is the uncreated sabbath of the life of God!

VI. He is the jubilee of the Father and the Son.

1. Because He is their term—and so completeness—and so beatitude.

2. Because He is *Genitoris Genitique suavitas*, as St. Austin calls Him.

3. Because love is akin to joy.

4. Because the seat of jubilation is in the will, and He proceeds by the will.

5. His procession is itself the endless, everlasting, divinely musical, stately-gleaming, unimaginable jubilation of the Holy Trinity, within itself, and also in all creations lying in its external omnipresence.

VII. He is the fulness of the Father and the Son.

1. His not producing is not rightly infecundity—no infirmity; nay, it is His very personal eminence, and characteristic perfection; for all characteristics of the Divine Persons are perfection.

2. He is fulness, which is akin to joy.

3. He is fecund with the high fecundity of falling back upon the Father and the Son, and, as it were, completing them, and bounding the boundless Trinity.

4. He is the crown of fecundity, because He is the jubilation of fecundity.

5. He is fecund, because He has drunk in, and possesses in Himself all the power of the Godhead to produce by will; He holds all possible

uncreated love, and is the Ocean of the Father's
unbegotten Fountain.

Such is the Holy Ghost, all beautiful, all holy, in
His unimaginable Procession, and who is condescending
at this moment to be wrapping us all round with His
eternal love, longing to lead us willing captives to the
shores of His jubilant eternal Sea!

CHAPTER II.

THE HOLY GHOST AND CREATURES.

THERE was a time, or rather there was a timeless eternity, when God was all in all; no space, no matter,
no created spirit, no life out of God: no place where
life could be, no conditions under which life was possible: creation then lay a complete ideal in the mind
of God, in the clear soft light of His decrees; a procession, but not an eternal one, a procession which
was one day to be. The date came when time should
be born, a certain indiscernible point in unsuccessive
eternity, and then creation lay outside of God, though
in His lap.

I. Creation might have been eternal.

 1. The possibility of this throws considerable light
  on the life of God.

 2. We must beware of thinking that the Divine
  life had to be completed before Creation could
  take place; the Generation of the Son, and the
  Procession of the Holy Ghost, are always going
  on, posterior to Creation as well as prior to it.

3. The eternity of Creation is possible.

   (1) On God's side, because His power is eternal, and He could at any moment have created.

   (2) On the side of creatures themselves.

      1. Because creatures never *began* to be possible: they were possible from eternity.

      2. Though not capable of being eternal by essence, creatures may be eternal by participation.

   (3) On the side of the act of creation itself, because—

      1. The action of God is instantaneous.

      2. Such an action on His part, as Creation, would not be the less free, because it was eternal.

      3. Creation, rightly considered, is not a transition from non-being to being, but the production of a whole thing from no presupposed subject.

      4. Yet even if it were but such a transition, non-being need only precede the creature in nature and not in fact.

4. All this applies more easily to permanent things. Billuart* thinks it more probably would not apply to successive things; still even this is not certain; for our ideas are so welded now to things as they are, we can hardly put ourselves in a position to judge of such a question.

5. God doubtless could have made a non-successive creation.

6. St. Thomas says that without revelation the

    * De Opere Sex Dierum. Dissert. 1, art. vi.

temporal nature of creation is credible, but not demonstrable.

7. As a matter of fact, creation is temporal, and that it is so is *de fide.*

II. Creation lying outside of God.

   1. The immeasurable quantity of strange inanimate matter.

     (1) Of various composition;

     (2) Of magnificent and subtle properties;

     (3) Of extreme beauty and variety of form;

     (4) Reducible to very considerable simplicity, perhaps to one element—and to one force;*

     (5) Whose inner life seems unattainable;

     (6) And is a life of continual protean change.

     (7) Indestructible, and now everlasting.

     (8) It is as it is, for some deep reason unknown to us.

     (9) Doubtless bearing on itself the most intimate transcript of His perfections, Who made it.

   2. Life is an especially godlike gift.

     (1) To be organic is an approach to life, and is a state doubtless full of divine wonders beyond our sciences.

     (2) Life requires peculiar and subtle conditions, and varying adaptations.

     (3) It is also inimitable by any marvels of man.

     (4) Countless varieties of life from angels down to zoophytes: and all have feelings, character and consciousness of their own.

     (5) It is a secret into whose ultimate recesses it seems as if we could never penetrate.

 *See Smee's Monogenesis of Physical Forces, and per contra Faraday's conservation of Forces.

U.   ℝ

(6) Yet life is always a happiness: the greatest of treasures which *most* creatures have, if not all; indeed it is the greatest, for a martyr is only one who has the courage to change a lower life for a higher.

(7) It is most plainly an outpouring of God's goodness, even in his beatitude.

3. Double life, material and spiritual.

   (1) Material life.
     1. Ever changing.
     2. The greater portion of it simply mortal.
     3. Yet capable of supernatural operations, in man at least, which immortalize it.
     4. Strange unions of matter and spirit, as in sacraments, and certain mental conditions.
     5. Glorified life of matter, without any violence done to nature.

   (2) Spiritual life.
     1. Immortal, but not intrinsically so.
     2. Its extreme simplicity is an approach towards God.
     3. Its changes—their peculiarity, as in angels when they fell.
     4. Horror of spiritual wickedness, because it is seeming to come into such immediate antagonism to God.
     5. Immense capabilities of glory which a spirit has.

   (3) All this creation shaped out of the Divine mind.
     1. God was never an uncreating God.
     2. No change passed over Him, when he realized His idea.

3. Hence no incompleteness or overlooked minuteness is possible in creation.

4. It was the work of all God's combined perfections.

5. The product therefore quite as much of His love as of His wisdom : perhaps more so, inasmuch as His uncreated Love was the Person next to creatures :

6. And, as we shall see, creation was at least let loose through His love ;

7. And when fallen, brought back neither by Wisdom alone, nor by Love alone, but by both together; and in the case of the individual soul by Love as inclusive of Wisdom.

4. The Divine Concurrence keeping Creation out of nothingness.

(1) There is nothing in creation to which God has given an independent existence.

(2) God is, as it were, the life underlying, sustaining, and rendering possible our life.

(3) If He were to withdraw His concurrence for one moment, it would all fall back with hideous relapse into nothingness.

(4) The Divine Presence is more intimate to us than even the principle of life.

(5) It is threefold—

1. By Essence, His substance embracing and penetrating all the extremities of the world.

2. By presence, eyes, knowledge, light, no darkness.

3. By Power, the activity and vigor of all

activities and vigors, the fountain of
forces.

(6) Conservation is the same act as Creation, and
indivisible from it.

(7) No effort, no successive attentions, on God's
part, necessary to this calm concurrence.

5. His own glory is the end of all creation, and of
all possible creations.

(1) God's essential glory is untouched by creation—which leaves no mark on it.

(2) He is necessitated by His perfections to seek
His own glory in all things: self-love is
divine holiness.

(3) We are left free to fulfil this glory—

1. Either by making our happiness identical
with it,

2. Or by magnifying His perfections through
the ill-success of our opposition to them.

(4) But we are necessitated to fulfil it in one of
these two ways.

(5) Hence there is no neutrality possible for
creatures, with regard to God.

6. Yet creation is wholly unmingled with God.

(1) Impossibility of any such mixture

1. On the side of God, because of His completeness, perfection, and unity of substance.

2. On the side of creation, because of its
composition, derivation, and essential dependence.

(2) Concurrence, even with evil actions, is a
wonderful display of the agency of God's
purity.

U.   ℞

(3) Yet extreme awfulness of sin, of which the Divine Concurrence gives such a stupendous view.

III. Creation lying outside, yet in the embrace of God.

1. What is meant by nature.

(1) That which is due to the shape and capacity of a thing as God designed it.

(2) That which is not out of the reach of its acquisition.

(3) That which is congenial to it, and can blend with it, without the infusion of any supernatural principle, *i.e.* with the common concurrence of God.

2. Natural unions with God.

(1) The union of origin, conservation, and last end, with the Divine Essence.

(2) The union of dependence, filial humility, and accountableness, which seems to draw us to the Father.

(3) The union of the light of reason with the light of the Word, which joins us to the Son.

(4) The union of will and love of God, simply as the Author of nature, which joins us to the Holy Ghost.

3. The order of grace.

(1) Sanctifying grace a participation of the Divine nature—a quality of the soul or habit.

(2) Actual grace an impulse of the Divine Will: varieties and powers of it.

(3) Nature cannot merit the first grace, nor can the last grace be merited: so that the world of grace floats separately, as it were, from the world of nature.

U

4. Creation was in a state of grace, to angels and
   men, who alone were capable of grace.
   (1) Unnecessary love of this.
   (2) It was so both to angels and men.
   (3) So that reasonable nature was never tried by
       its sole self: both trials were of creatures in
       a state of grace.
   (4) This shows the closeness of the Creator's
       embrace of creation.
   (5) And that we, by sin, did no less than struggle
       out of His arms.

5. Unions of grace.
   (1) A higher knowledge of God.
   (2) Virtues, not only more heroic in degree, but
       different in kind.
   (3) The union of merit, through a supernatural
       principle.
   (4) The substantial indwelling of God far beyond
       concurrence.
   (5) The Father more our Father because we have
       a supernatural real worship.
   (6) Greater union with the Son is the fountain of
       grace.
   (7) Our wills capable of closer union with the
       Holy Ghost.
   (8) The ultimate union of seeking and enjoying
       God for ever.

6. The Incarnation of the Second Person.
   (1) The Creator still more closely embracing His
       creation.
   (2) Yet it was in the original idea of creation:
       nay, the fontal idea of it all.
   (3) The propriety of the Second Person being

incarnate, because of the connection between the Word and creatures.

(4) The Incarnation was efficient by anticipation, both for angels and men.

(5) Yet that previous efficacy, at least so far as men are concerned, is not to be compared with the change it has now actually wrought on the earth; witness the unopening of Limbus.

7. Unions because of the Incarnation.

(1) Sacramental Unions.

(2) The unions of grace are now more lofty and more entire.

(3) Mystical unions and likeness to Jesus.

(4) Unions since the Incarnation differ—

    1. In kind. (1.) New Mission. (2.) Sacraments. (3.) Other uses of matter.

    2. In degree: constantly approaching, and at last emanating in transformation.

    3. In method. (1.) Sacred Humanity. (2.) Imitation of Jesus. (3.) Christian Vocations.

(5) Union is the special work of the Incarnation, itself the greatest of all created unions.

8. The indwelling of the Third Person.

(1) Its substantial reality

(2) By sanctifying grace.

(3) By His gifts. Vasquez says, *non ratione augmenti habitus gratiæ, sed ratione aliorum donorum.*

(4) By His impulses, pleadings and inspirations.

(5) By His plenary presence in the Church, which is our enclosure.

U

9. Unions through Him.

    (1) The processes of justification and sanctification the same before Christ as after, so far as they are interior.

    (2) Yet in some sense the Holy Ghost was not given until redemption was actually accomplished He follows the Word in the order of our salvation, as in the order of the Trinity.

    (3) All unions with Jesus are completed in Him, and by Him.

    (4) His own extraordinary intimacy with the saints.

    (5) Even within our souls His posture is the same as it is in the divine life, a peculiar unitive relation to the Father and the Son.

10. The order of glory.

    (1) Glory in reality is not an order distinct from grace, only a time and place and fixed ultimate condition of it.

    (2) Free will threading its way through the superincumbent weight of spiritual helps and appliances.

    (3) In the actual order of Providence nature has no end, no natural end ; we cannot see what reasonable nature is to end in ; it has to rise out of itself into a supernatural end.

    (4) Thus glory becomes the normal state of nature at the last.

    (5) The creature is meant to look the Creator in the face—this is its glory.

11. It is then we have the person of the Eternal Father.

U.   Ⓡ

(1) Words of the Apostle St. Philip: Lord! show us the Father, and it is enough.

(2) We must become likenesses of Christ, and we shall be so after the resurrection, and only then shall we be satisfied, and our satisfaction will be in being with the Father.

(3) The Father is to be all in all, when the mediatorial kingdom of Christ comes to an end.

12. We shall indeed possess the whole Trinity.

(1) The Three Divine Persons will belong to us as an enjoyed possession.

(2) We shall dwell with Them for evermore, intuitively beholding Them as They are.

(3) Creation rose out of the Incarnation, and by the Incarnation the wandering creation is brought home to the Creator.

IV. The Threshold of the Uncreated.

1. The freedom of all divine acts outside God— importance of this truth, that Creation was free.

2. The oneness of action in all that the Three Divine Persons work outwardly.

3. The doctrine of Mission, Visible and Invisible.

(1) Temporal, yet representing the processions in the Holy Trinity: the world of grace mirroring the Holy Trinity, momentarily and perpetually, as does the world of matter, though less intelligibly.*

(2) Mission threefold in the individual soul.

1. First Justification.

---

*See "Creator and Creature," p. 170. "Blessed Sacrament," p. 277, &c.

2. Each augmentation of grace.

3. Eternal beatitude.

(3) It is to produce an end, and its end is that a Divine Person should begin to exist in us in a new manner, as in a temple, and that the soul thereby may possess or enjoy God in a new manner—so that Mission touches on heaven, touches on the Beatific Vision.

(4) Imperfect Missions.

1. Reason's knowledge and love of God, which is not a fresh possession and enjoyment of Him.

2. Actual graces, which are rather a knocking at the door than an indwelling.

3. Infallibility of the Pope is rather a moving of the intellect.

(5) The Father is not sent, and the Son is sent only by the Father.

(6) The Son and the Spirit are not sent separately.

(7) But mission is attributed to each separately by appropriation.

(8) The unsent Father is always present in invisible Missions.

(9) The reality of Mission—the Persons substantially present.

(10) Horror of heresy as impeding Mission: it is like an imprisoning of God's mercy within Himself, and restricting His liberty in His own Creation.

4. All creation is stamped with the likeness of the Uncreated, probably far beyond our powers of perception,

5. And this is a Trinitarian likeness.

U,

6. Yet perhaps each Person has some relation of His own to creatures, though inexpressible, just as relations constitute the Persons in God.

7. If we begin with the Father, we travel down to the Holy Ghost, and rest in Him as the Threshold of the Created.

8. If we start with matter and zoophytes, and travel up to the Holy Ghost, we rest in him as the Threshold of the Uncreated.*

9. How we get the right view of Him with regard to creatures: there is nothing *between* the created and the Uncreated; the Uncreated Spirit confines on creation, creation confines on Him.

10. Thus the shadow of. the Uncreated on the created doubles back like the shadows in a mountain lake: the first choir of angels, the Seraphim, representing the near Term of the Godhead, the Holy Ghost; the second choir, the Cherubim, the Word and Wisdom of the Father, which is the Son; and the Thrones in their kingly peace and stability, the Person of the Father. This explains why devotion to the Eternal Father and devotion to the choir of Thrones co-exist by a kind of instinct in so many saints and others, who were probably not conscious of the reason. Yet the personal angels, who stood alone, follow the personal order in the Blessed Trinity: Michael the angel of the Father, Gabriel of the Son, Raphael, with his characteristic mixture of pathos and joy, of the Holy Spirit.

*Holy Ghost nearest to creatures—Henricus de Balbis in Thomas of Jesus. De Orat. Div. lib. iv. cap. ix. p. 388–90, 8vo. ed.

U,   ℞

V. The Holy Ghost the end of creatures.

1. Creatures come down to the brink of His sweet-watered sea and pass in.

2. The powers and affections of the Sacred Heart of Jesus to return into Him.

3. The immaculate heart of Mary, with the holiness of Joseph, the Baptist, the Apostles, and the hierarchy of the Incarnation, pass into Him.

4. The love of the Seraphim, the science of the Cherubim, the peace of the Thrones, the empire of the Dominations, the energy of the Virtues, the force of the Powers, the dignity of the Principalities, the defence of the Archangels, the charity of the Angels, all pass into Him.

5. So do all hearts of men that are grace-touched and virtue-loving.

6. To flow down into Him is the beautifulness of life.

7. Yet we are not lost in Him, but find there the eternal distinctness of eternal life.

VI. The History of the Holy Ghost.

1. Eternally proceeding from the Father and the Son, which He is doing while we are speaking.

2. Joining in the predestination of Jesus and Mary.

3. Brooding over Creation.

4. Immense nameless communications of grace to the Angels, through the Seraphim His own choir: some think all the three first choirs receive light *immediately*, not mediately.

5. Intense love of the Sacred Humanity of Jesus.

6. Inspiring patriarchs with desires and prayers to hasten His coming.

7. The poet of the prophecies describing the life and passion of Jesus beforehand.

8. In the heart of David dictating the psalms.

9. Sanctifying Mary, David's daughter, and His own spouse.

10. Preparing, creating, or fashioning the Body of Jesus, by overshadowing Mary.

11. His share in the Magnificat.

12. Sanctifying St. Joseph. *

13. Given immeasurably to Jesus.

14. Descending at the Baptism of Jesus

15. Driving Him into the wilderness, and then commissioning Him to preach.

16. His love of the apostles.

17. His passing with the breath of Christ into them, which was an adumbration of His eternal Procession by spiration.

18. Meeting Jesus in the Ascension Cloud.

19. Descent on Mary and the Apostles at Pentecost.†

20. Dwelling in and building up the Infant Church, *almost* visible, so manifest was His agency.‡

21. Punishing Ananias and Sapphira, visible sample

---

* The Holy Ghost was Himself the conjugal love of Joseph and Mary, and so the Bond of the Earthly Trinity as of the Heavenly. Raffaello Maria Vita di S. Giuseppe, p. 48, v. Bethlehem, p. 433.

† Giry says it was revealed that the Holy Ghost rested on Mary in one flame, and *thence* separated off into tongues. Vies des Saints, vol. i, p. 145.

‡ For the Holy Ghost after Pentecost compared with the Holy Ghost before, see Thomas of Jesus, De Orat Div. lib. iv. cap viii.

Visible descents were frequent in the primitive church, because the sins of Christians had not interposed obstacles between them and the effusions of the Holy Spirit. Mistica Ciudad, Lib. vii. cap. xiii. No. 226.

of many like invincible providences, or at least indiscernible interferences, so suitable to our Lord's words about the sin against Him.

22. Welcoming Mary His Spouse at her Assumption, and joining in her Coronation.

23. Inspiring the epistles.

24. Giving St. John the Apocalypse.

25. Acting in the Church now as executor of Jesus, tutor of the Saints, and teacher of Mary His Spouse. *

Such is a sketch of God's huge creation, and the action of the Holy Ghost in it, and His position with reference to it. It is equally peculiar with His place in the Divine Life of the Holy Trinity.

CHAPTER III.

THE HOLY GHOST AND JESUS.

As creation sprang out of the Incarnation, and the Incarnation embraces and is the reason of creation, the relation between the Holy Ghost and creation leads necessarily to his relation with Jesus: it is in Their mutual relation to creation that we must now bring them together.

I. The History of Creation.

1. The Predestination of Jesus.

(1) Eternal in the Divine Mind.

* For the story of the Holy Ghost, electing the Archbishops of Ravenna, beautifully told, see Tufo, Hist. de Teatini, cap. 88, p. 355.

For office of Holy Ghost in Purgatory, v. Finetti sopra il Purgatorio, cap. 28.

    (2) It was for the same reason as we may suppose creation at all, viz., love: only it was the cause of the rest of creation, the nucleus round which creation gathered.

    (3) It was the first externation of the goodness of God.

2. The Date of Creation.

    (1) It took place at a fixed and foreordained time.

    (2) A moment which had a vast reasonableness, unrevealed, and beyond our powers of discovery.

    (3) We may be sure it had to do with the predestination of Jesus.

3. The Angels.

    (1) The eldest-born of God's creatures.

    (2) Of a different nature from that which was predestined for the Word.

    (3) All their graces were from Him, and because of Him Incarnate, though not in the shape of redemption.

4. The Creation of matter.

    (1) Original matter out of nothing: one atom could fill the universe.*

    (2) Gradual cosmogony was perhaps meant as a visible Bible to the angels, full of types and prophecies of Jesus, and loud hymns of material forces which their intelligence could translate.

    (3) Perhaps the angels took part in the cosmogony; certainly in the custody and administration of the finished world.

        * Smee's Monogenesis.

5. The Trial of the Angels.

    (1) I am inclined to place this after the creation of matter, at least of primary matter; else their trial would be less significant, regarding the material nature of Jesus.

    (2) The presentation of Jesus to their intellects and wills, the Word clad in an inferior nature, to be so worshipped.

    (3) Ample grace was given, yet one-third fell, and fell irrevocably.

6. The epochs of the material world.

    (1) Science would lead us to infer that they have been of enormous duration.

    The glory of God in the evolutions of matter, inorganic, organic, and animated — in the lawfulness of uniformity, or the restrained and balanced fury of catastrophes.

    (3) Glory to Him from the activity and contemplation of the angels; for though the idea of the predestinated Jesus was not yet fulfilled, their interest in the material world centred round Him as their Incarnate King; it brought them into an affectionate relation with matter.

7. Preparation for Jesus.

    (1) Sin changes His manner of coming.

    (2) All history of patriarchs and Jews a preparation for Him.

    (3) Pagan history, with its outworn and outwearing mythologies and philosophies, partially a preparation, but also a working out of the proposition of His necessity, from the rampant growth of all corruption, and the tyranny of decadence in all its shapes.

8. He comes.

   (1) Mary's Immaculate Conception, and fifteen
years.

   (2) The Thirty-three Years, with all their mysteries, living on still as it were in the hearts
of men.

   (3) The Passion-death the only terms of redemption with the Father.

9. The Church.

   (1) This is the living and real continuation of the
Incarnation.

   (2) The earthly dwelling of Jesus in the Blessed
Sacrament till the day of doom.

   (3) The Church is as it were a part of heaven in
exile upon earth.

10. The place of the Holy Ghost in the Church.

   (1) To carry on the work of Jesus:—in pope,
theology, sacraments, priesthoods—the Holy
Oils are *breathed* into in order to consecrate
them.

   (2) To fill it with the precise spirit of Jesus, and
to fill it abundantly: this spirit of Jesus is
the practical exorcism of the world and its
spirit from the Church.

   (3) It is a sort of Palestine to Him, the sphere of
His activity, His dispensation. so to speak.

II. The devotion of Jesus to the Holy Ghost.

1. He begins teaching Nicodemus about Him, and
in connection with the special Christian gift of
regeneration.

2. He establishes His apostolate by the imparting of
the Holy Ghost.

3. He declares sin against Him to be unlike sin

against Himself, and some sin unpardonable, as
if by the terror of this to defend His affectionate
familiarities from profane liberties.

4. He knew the beautifulness of His own visible
presence, yet said it was expedient He should
go away, in order that the Holy Ghost should
come; so Jesus seems in a certain sense to abandon the field to Him.

5. He left His own work incomplete, for the Holy
Ghost to finish; He did little more than make
a beginning, so far as His ministry went.

6. He made the office of the Holy Ghost one of love
to Himself—to bring to mind all that He (Jesus)
had said.

7. He let Himself be immensely sanctified by Him.

8. He possessed Him without measure.

III. The devotion of the Holy Ghost to Jesus.

1. His Conception, which is especially appropriated
to the Holy Ghost.*

2. This devotion disclosed at our Lord's baptism and
transfiguration.

3. His munificence to the Mother of Jesus.

4. No one can profess our Lord's divinity but by the
Holy Spirit.†

5. He defends His Person, Natures, Sacramental
Presence, and Mother from heresies in all ages.

6. He steps in in confirmation to strengthen the
wavering loyalty of Christ's soldiers.

7. In ordination He, as it were, multiplies the sphere
of Jesus, as Jesus by the Incarnation had already
enlarged the sphere of the Holy Ghost.

8. His way of leading the apostles into all truth

* Billuart, v. 340.   † 1 Cor. xii. 3.

U.   ℞

was by bringing to their minds all the words of Jesus.

9. The saints, who are the handiwork of the Holy Ghost, are but multiplied likenesses of Jesus.

IV. The Holy Ghost and Mary.

1. Mary is inextricably bound up with Jesus, from His predestination downwards.

2. She stood in separate relations to each of the Three Divine Persons.

3. Her relation to the Holy Ghost was that of Spouse: what does that imply?

   (1) That as He was the term of God, the Incarnation took place through His overshadowing Mary.

   (2) That He fashioned the Sacred Humanity of Jesus.

   (3) That He did this with her consent.

4. He overshadowed her at the incarnation as it were to shield her, and keep her alive in that mystery, just as she was miraculously kept alive beneath the Cross.

5. Her different sanctifications were great indescribable operations of His.

6. His descent on her at Pentecost, as if more with her now that she was childless.

7. As Spouse, she rightfully occupied His position in the earthly Trinity.

V. The Holy Ghost and the Incarnation.

1. His connection with the Sacred Humanity, both Soul and Body: Jesus, being full of the Holy Ghost, returned from the Jordan, and was led (driven out, Mark i. 12) by the Spirit into the desert. Luke iv. 1.

U.

2. It seemed as if the Incarnation, as it were, let Him loose, and gave Him space.

3. This would be a personal reason for His having so much to do with the preliminaries and preparations of it.

4. Pentecost was His advent, as it were, with His *new* Mary; and the apostles were almost as much His as they were our Lord's.*

5. He has the same end as Jesus, the exaltation of the Father: for He is the Spirit of adoption, by whom we cry Abba, Father; just as the Father sent Him in the *Name* of Jesus. John xiv. 26.

VI. The Holy Trinity.

1. All these things were done in the utmost unity by the Holy Ghost and by Jesus.

2. The Sacred Humanity belonging, and infinitely dear, to all the Three Persons.

3. The Holy Trinity absolutely One in its action in all these things;

4. Yet variously representing its distinctness of Persons.

5. Nevertheless those representations are but appropriations.

6. In Mission now One comes forward, now Another: One manifests Himself in the effect, visible or invisible, where all are really present.

7. Yet by far the greatest amount of Mission is appropriated to the Holy Ghost.

* The operations in the "fond de l'âme" in high mystical states are a miraculous union of the Holy Ghost parallel to what the Second Person does in the Blessed Sacrament.—Barbançon, Secrets Sentiers, chap. 13, p. 325.

U.   ℞

8. The Father is not sent, but present, and operating concomitantly with the others.

9. Impossibility of our clearly understanding this: but so it is in all discourses of the life and action of God, whose unimaginable simplicity falsifies every word we say.

VII. On what we may reverently conceive the devotion of Jesus to the Holy Ghost was based.

1. On His love, as a Divine Person Himself, for the person of the Holy Ghost.

2. On the worship which in His Human Nature He paid to the Holy Ghost.

3. On gratitude, as it were, for His Sacred Humanity being specially fashioned by the Holy Ghost.

4. On His immense love of holiness, and delight in the operations of grace

5. On His love of Him as the Spouse of His Mother. ·

6. On His choice of Him as His successor in the Church.

7. On the peculiar sympathy between His Human Nature and the Divine Nature of the Holy Ghost.

(1) Because of the Love of His Human Nature for the Holy Ghost in consequence of its exceeding Holiness, which was the work of that Divine Person, and an unparalleled communication of the Divine Nature by sanctifying grace to a created Nature, similar to that in some measure which His own Divine Person communicated to His assumed Nature.

    (2) Because of the substantial indwelling of the
        Holy Ghost in His Human Nature by
.   Mission, the most magnificent of all His
        Missions : so that He dwelt in Jesus eternally
        by the beautiful mystery of Circuminsession,
        and temporarily by Mission.

Love of the Holy Ghost is therefore a prominent
feature of the spirit of Jesus. Unless we also have
a very special love for Him, we are not yet thoroughly
penetrated with the spirit of Jesus.

CHAPTER IV.

THE HOLY GHOST AND THE SOUL.

THE multitudes of souls which there are in the world
—their variety and varying circumstances : there is
not one with whom the Holy Ghost has not had most
numerous, complicated, and persevering relations, if
they have come to man's estate.

  I. His names are illustrations of His work in the
      individual soul.

    1. Spirit.

      (1) This represents the method of His uncreated
          origin.

      (2) It also expresses His office in the soul.

      (3) He is in the soul the initiative, representative,
          and ally of all immaterial interests.

      (4) The hiddenness of His work is in fact an
          excellence of its spirituality.

      (5) His method of operations is peculiarly subtle,
          delicate, and spiritual.

2. Love.

   (1) He is Himself an uncreated Love;

   (2) And also the fountain of all holy created love.

   (3) He is wedded indissolubly to a state of grace, which is a state of love.

   (4) He never comes to us without augmenting our love, and our love is never augmenting without His coming to us substantially.

   (5) He breeds in us especially a love of Jesus.

3. Paraclete.

   (1) This is expressive of the tenderness of His office towards us: St. Athanasius notes that the word does not occur in the Old Testament.

   (2) Comforter, inwardly comforting us—especially—

     1. In the uncertainty of our salvation: the wonder that this is bearable: He makes it so.

     2. In temptation: we occasionally see how powerless we are of ourselves.

     3. In exile from God, continued for so many years of mortal life.

   (3) Advocate,* which is comforting us outwardly, by getting us aid: mystery of a Divine Person being called an Advocate.

   (4) Both these offices flow from His love.

   (5) The last is the same office as that of the Sacred Humanity and the Five Wounds in heaven: only the wounds are silent, the Spirit has unutterable plaints.

4. Gift.

   (1) All good gifts are from Him;

       * Corn. a Lapide in Rom. viii. 26.

(2) Yet all from the Father.

(3) Because He is Himself the gift of the Father and the Son.

· (4) He also gives Himself.

(5) And with Himself gives Them.

II. His most ordinary operations in the soul are those of grace.

  1. Sanctifying grace is the foundation of everything; and it is His Mission.

  2. His indwelling in the soul substantially by grace.

  3. By each augmentation of grace He dwells there in a different manner from what He ever did before.

  4. Then there are the inward pleadings and struggles of actual grace.

  5. So that one while He looks like natural conscience, another while like Guardian Angel.

  6. His share in the sacraments: ordination—consecration—*illapsus*.

  7. What we call the interior life is the life we lead with Him in our souls.

III. His gifts, which are still higher operations.

  1. He has some very special gifts, seven in number, with which he works in souls: they are marvellous tools, undreamed possibilities of grandeur of soul, unsurpassed forms of beauty, working miracles with our natures without doing violence to them; by them we touch, and taste, and relish, what we know by faith.

  2. They are infused habits, enabling us to graceful promptitude in the service of God, on which His actual impulses play as on sweet-voiced keys of music. the divine germs of all real

U   ℗

human heroicity, foundation of all high principles, mine of all supernatural instincts, freeing
us from the slavery of creatures, and giving us
liberty. Isaias arranges them in their mutual
connections and attractions.* They also have
occult connections with the fruits of the Holy
Ghost, and our Lord's Beatitudes.

3. Wisdom—to see the causes and fitnesses, and
   taste the savor, of divine things : the fruit and
   beatitude—
   (1) Fruit :—Faith.
   (2) Beatitude. Blessed are the peacemakers : for
   they shall be called the children of God.

4. Understanding—to penetrate more intimately into
   the truths of faith : how much is supernatural
   in the operations of a Christian intellect !
   (1) Fruit :—Faith.
   (2) Beatitude. Blessed are the clean of heart :
   for they shall see God.

5. Science—to judge correctly of human things, according to God's view and the principles of grace.
   (1) Fruit :—Faith.
   (2) Beatitude. Blessed are they that mourn :
   for they shall be comforted.

6. Counsel—to direct the actions of faith : grace
   for details, is my own view of it.
   (1) Fruit
      A. Some say none, because its own operation
      is its fruit.
      B. On my view, goodness.
   (2) Beatitude. Blessed are the merciful : for
   they shall obtain mercy.

*Lallement (English Edition), pp. 142, 143.

7. Piety—softness to God and to others; giving
right instincts.
  (1) Fruit:—Benignity and joy.
  (2) Beatitude. Blessed are the meek: for they
  shall possess the land.
8. Fortitude—to suffer, to dare, and to persevere in
daring; also to protect us against ourselves.
  (1) Fruits:—Longanimity and patience.
  (2) Beatitude. Blessed are they that hunger and
  thirst for justice: for they shall have their
  fill.
9. Fear—to repress our pride and forwardness, and
to give us the gift of adoration: in the edifice
of the spiritual life, this is the foundation.
  (1) Fruits:—Modesty, temperance, and chastity.
  (2) Beatitude. Blessed are the poor in spirit:
  for theirs is the kingdom of heaven.
10. These gifts, grand thought! can grow, and do
grow with our fervor and charity: yet there
is sometimes, as in tepid priests and mere up-
to-the-mark religious, a mere physical growth
of them, without any corresponding actual
growth, or any proportionate eliciting of them
in acts of perfection.*
11. They are very delicate—and are almost instantly
tied up by the thinnest ligatures of venial sin.
12. Also they insist on being our masters: we must
abandon ourselves to them, and give them their
fling.
IV. The fruits of the Holy Ghost, such as are specially
named so in Scripture, are the results of the
maturity of grace.

* Lallemant (English edition), p. 148.

U.

1. They are certain holy actions performed.
   (1) With agility.
   (2) With promptitude.
   (3) With sweetness.
2. There is a maturity about them, which is a fourth quality, distinguishing them even more than the other three from common virtuous actions.
3. They very peculiarly fill the soul with God: this also probably results from their maturity.
4. They represent the Holy Ghost Himself and His divine life.
5. Fruits :—Charity—because He is the love of the Father and the Son.
6. Joy—because He is the jubilee of the Father and the Son.
7. Peace—because He is the bond of the Father and the Son.

N.B.—These three fruits are the fountains of all the rest: the remaining nine of the twelve are more or less concerned with these three, and more or less subordinate to them.

8. Patience—moderate excess of sadness, and secures joy.
9. Meekness—allays anger, which disturbs charity, joy, and peace.
10. Goodness — an energetic inclination to benefit others, which is joyous charity.
11. Benignity — the doing of this cordially and genially : geniality is an emanation of the Holy Ghost.
12. Longanimity—against weariness and fatigue, which hold charity, joy, and peace under pressure and in dulness.

U

13. Faith—a facility in believing, without repugnance or dulness.

14. Modesty — gracefulness of body, manners, and speech, so as to be the outward beauty of charity, joy, and peace.

15. Temperance — refraining bodily appetites and inordinations by mortification, so as to protect the rights of our spiritual nature, and make *room* for charity, joy and peace.

16. Chastity—the virtue of purity: a kind of return to innocence, or preservation of it—so as to make the soul a fair temple of charity, joy and peace.

V. His ways, familiarities, and excesses.

   1. Gratuitous gifts, not necessarily sanctifying the receiver, but part of the Holy Ghost's love of the Church.*

     (1) Word of wisdom — knowledge of eternal things, so as to talk of them persuasively.

     (2) Word of science — intuitive gift of counsel about moral and human things.

     (3) Faith—eloquence and clearness to teach and make plain the hard mysteries of the faith.

     (4) Healing—to cure diseases and heal wounds.

     (5) Virtues — miracles unconnected with the human body.

     (6) Prophecy—seeing or making public things future or things absent.

     (7) Discernment of spirits — seeing into hearts and judging of operations in souls.

     (8) Tongues—to speak them or to hear them.

     (9) Interpretation of tongues — to explain diffi-

* Tempesti, i. 379.

culties in Scripture, or hard words in theology, or the tongues which others speak.

(10) All these were in Christ habitually; and of
our Lady, Novatus says,* *Dico satis credible
esse Beatæ Virgini a primo suæ conceptionis
momento omnes gratias gratis datas per
modum habitus a Deo fuisse collatas. Suaderi
potest ex nonnullis Scripturæ locis, et rationi-
bus:* but it was not so with any of the saints;
they possessed them only transiently.

2. His inspirations.

(1) Their frequency, like a man talking softly to
us all the day long, even in crowds.

(2) Their delicacy, like muffled notes of music,
or thin leafy whispers of a breeze, or an
unseen lark up in white air—so short,
enigmatic, fragmentary.

(3) Habit of listening for them—this shapes our
whole life afresh, and gives it a supernatural
posture and attitude.

(4) They multiply by listening, like a bird in
a wood who is answered by another, or as
sounds come in quiet places when we listen;
so we are ever hearing celestial music, broken
now and then by higher surges of wind,
when the world and life are stormy.

(5) All perfection consists in docility to them:
the faults of the saints came from want of
this; it is the subject matter of their faults,
as disobedience to the commandments is the
subject matter of positive sins.

3. His caresses.

* Cap. xix. qu. xiv.

U.   ℞

(1) Sweetnesses—in prayer, suffering, and spiritual occupations: a shred of His jubilee.

(2) Surprises—tears, smiles, holy fear, sudden familiarity with God, momentary contacts and senses of His presence.

(3) Sudden leaps in the road to perfection, out of the common laws of slow acquisition, as when all the species of evil thoughts were suddenly destroyed in the mind of St. Ignatius at Manresa.

(4) Special attractions in the spiritual life, and the whole doctrine of vocation; vocation is His caress; to go against it is to refuse His kiss.

(5) Special and peculiar graces, one or more of which distinguish nearly every man, such as keeping recollected, and the like.

(6) Locutions, out loud or in the heart, common to all the saints.

(7) Violent conversions, unlike the gentleness of unresisted grace: sometimes also He is violent with the saints, and on the whole masterfulness, like the strong wind at Pentecost, is a characteristic of Him.

(8) Curious states of some holy souls, as if free will were almost gone: St. Gertrude could only say what our Lord wished her to say —others could only pray as He wished— others could not hear when worldly things were talked of; but in all these and similar states the spirit of Jesus is the predominant thing which the Holy Ghost produces.

(9) Unions with some one attribute of God—or

one mystery of Jesus—or Mary—or the Blessed Sacrament.

(10) Familiarities with simple souls, the Dove nestling in human wills for ever, with a predilection like that of Jesus: instances from Siniscalchi; St. Gregory, St. Philip, &c.

Look at a building full of strange machinery—so is the soul with all this machinery of the Holy Ghost.

CHAPTER V.

DEVOTION TO THE HOLY GHOST.

WE have seen now Who the Holy Ghost is, and what He has done, and what He does in our own souls; we now come to the practical question of the devotion we ought to have for Him.

I. What devotion to One of the Divine Persons means.

1. Each Person is equal altogether to the other Two: simple adoration is due to Him, as to the One God.

2. Indeed one Person cannot be worshipped without All being so: so that even when directed to One it falls upon All.

3. Such devotion as we pay to Mary, angels, and saints, is impossible; although, as with those inferior devotions, our devotion to Divine Persons rests both on the imitable and the admirable: God is almost more imitable than the Saints, because of His inimitable simplicity.

4. We have a knowledge of the different Persons, and the peculiarities of Their relative sub-

sistence, putting out of view Their absolute Essence.

5. On this knowledge certain feelings rise, which are distinctive.

6. Devotion to One of the Divine Persons is therefore the simple worship of God, into which these distinctive feelings enter; and these feelings direct the acts of the mind and heart peculiarly to One of the Persons, as if specifying, or giving a species to, the worship.

7. Thus it is devotion in the highest sense of devotion : it is adoration of the Divine Essence, not so much limited to One Person by being directed to Him, but with the feelings excited by the characteristics of One Person rather than the other Two *added* to it, which makes it a very special act of worship of the other Two, as the Three Divine Persons are Their own mutual love, and joy, and self-sufficiency.

II. By what means we arrive at devotion to the Holy Ghost.

1. It is founded, first of all, on our knowledge of His peculiar place in the Divine Life.

2. Next on His action in and upon creation, as shown in its history.

3. Next on His connection with Jesus.

4. Next on His work and method in the individual soul.

5. We must make an idea of Him as we do of Jesus. Our devotion to our Blessed Lord is based upon our idea of Him; we should have had a devotion to Him if we had only known that He was our Incarnate Redeemer : but,

having the four Gospels, our idea of Him is more characteristic, intimate, and detailed, and our idea of Him is drawn from them. So must we from Scripture, theology, lives of saints, and our own experience, make an idea of the Holy Ghost.

6. We must ascertain—
   (1) What He is like.
   (2) What He has done.
   (3) What He does.
   (4) How He does it.
   (5) Our own concern with Him, His work, and His Method.

We must then correct our idea by the analogy of faith.

7. This inquiry, and this correction, have been the occupations of the preceding lectures; so we may now build up our devotion, simply recapitulating what we have said. It is important to remember that any *probable* opinion is sufficient to form a principle and foundation for a devotion.*

III. The likenesses of the Holy Ghost.
  1. He has three kinds of likenesses.
   (1) Likeness to the Father, from whom He has received the Father's own likeness.
   (2) Likeness to Jesus—
     1. From whom He has received the likeness of the Son's Divine Nature.
     2. To whose Human Nature He has Himself given the likeness of His Divine Nature.
   (3) Likeness to Mary and the Saints, which is wholly from Himself, and a reflection of Himself.

* Lallemant (English edition), p. 180.

2. His actual likenesses.
  (1) To the Father.
    1. In His habit of pleading with men, as if
       He were their equal, as with Cain, Job,
       Jonas, and the Jews.
    2. In His non-incarnation.
    3. In His repairing His ruined projects, like
       a spider its web, as the Fall, vocation of
       the Jews, Jewish kingdom, &c., and so
       with each soul.
    4. In His jealousy; in this he is less like the
       Son than like the Father.
    5. In His sensitiveness; being so easily
       grieved.
  (2) To Jesus.
    1. In His gentleness.
    2. In His patience, and His power of waiting;
       though here, as we shall see hereafter,
       there is a difference; but in the forbear-
       ance the likeness is complete.
    3. In His minuteness of love.
    4. In His prodigality—He is spendthrift of
       His inspirations, as the Son was of His
       Precious Blood. Oh the waste of inspira-
       tions! yet each one of Them, rightly consi-
       dered, is more wonderful than the grandest
       book ever written, or the finest work of
       art ever designed, let alone executed.
    5. In unity of spirit with Jesus.
  (3) To Mary.
    1. She has borrowed all from Him, and so
       reflects Him.
    2. In her love of Jesus.

3. In her share in the Incarnation.

4. In her union of the deepest pathos with the highest joy ever found in a creature.

5. In her intercessory office.

6. In the way she teaches Jesus, leads to Him, magnifies Him, glorifies Him, hides herself behind Him, so that He may be the more seen.

7. As in long years people grow like each other by living together, so with Mary and her Spouse the Holy Ghost, in her successive sanctifications: she had become so much more like Jesus upon Calvary, that the Holy Ghost founded on that another indescribable sanctification at Pentecost.

(4) To Angels.

1. In invisibility of offices.

2. In fidelity of unwearied ministrations.

3. In joyousness, yet pitifulness for men; as St. Raphael, His own angel, so sets forth with all his joy a romance of sympathy with the sorrows of human life.

4. In the exhibition which they are of countless variety of His graces.

5. In their end, which is to glorify Jesus their King.

(5) To the Saints.

They are His portrait of Himself: they are saints, because He is the Holy Spirit; His gifts in them, His fruits in them—this is their sanctity. They are His Bible, just as the Old Testament reveals the Father, and the New Testament the Son, so the saints of the Church reveal the Holy Ghost.

3. The likeness of His created symbols.

(1) Wind.

   1. Represents His invisibility, with visible effects.

   2. His *seeming* waywardness, as He lists: *i. e.,* no law discernible, but some law deep laid in His uncreated love, working up from beneath the depths of His predestination.

   3. His vehemence, as at Pentecost the rushing wind; so the Church in some ages of the world has been visibly shaken by this wind.

(2) Dove.

   1. The quiet pacific method of His common action.

   2. His brooding character, as at creation over chaos.

   3. His plaintive pathos, like that shy hidden voice of the deep woodland life, that woos and complains, and puts a soul into the summer woods, overruling, yet not by loudness, all other songs of birds.

(3) Fire.

   1. His being the love of the Father and the Son.

   2. His intensity: consuming, refining, transmuting all things, especially all created attachments.

   3. His masterfulness: He will reign alone.

U

(4) Bright Cloud, as at Transfiguration and Ascension.

   1. Light, yet a light that hides—a privacy of glorious light is Thine—breeds love of concealment in others: all sanctity is shy.

   2. Jesus hides in Him, and is borne about on Him as on a car.

   3. Silent *procession* of clouds, varying shapes, melting off and reappearing, hanging about heights, fantastic mutations in blue sky, making light beautiful: all these phenomena are images of Him.

(5) Shadow, as with Mary.

   1. A shadow from creation's garish light.

   2. A shadow which fertilizes, and preserves the dampness, like a wood on the edge of the sandy wilderness.

   3. A shadow which cools nature's heats, and inspires a joyous awe as of God's neighborhood.

IV. His peculiarities as exhibited in His action in creation, and the way in which they each and all correspond to what is distinctive about Him in the Divine Life.

  1. Something so very human about Him, rather than angelic: at least as He reveals Himself to men.

   (1) As if, like the Eternal Word, He was more drawn to our nature.

   (2) The Scriptures specially attribute creature-like feelings to Him.

   (3) Griefs—plaints—Abba, Father—intercession —likeness of dove. This answers to His

U

being next to creatures as the Term of the Godhead.

2. His likeness, in His action in creation, to the Father and the Son, as above drawn out. This answers to His Procession from them Both, as one principle.

3. His tenderness and love, which we have already seen. This answers to His proceeding from the Father and the Son by the way of the will, and not by the way of the understanding.

4. Joy—put forward especially in Scripture as among His most prominent fruits and constant effects. This answers to His being the Jubilee of the Father and the Son.

> The disciples were filled with joy and with the Holy Ghost. Acts xiii. 52.
>
> The kingdom of God is not meat and drink: but justice, and peace, and joy in the Holy Ghost. Rom. xiv. 17.
>
> The fruit of the Spirit is charity, joy, peace, &c. Gal. v. 22.
>
> Receiving the word in much tribulation, with joy of the Holy Ghost. 1 Thess. i. 6.

5. Thus, His created symbols answer to His uncreated relative subsistence.

V. The spirit of devotion to Him; it is as to Jesus in the Passion, not Jesus Risen.

1. A spirit of tearful tenderness and pathos.

2. A spirit of familiarity,—from His intimacy, and the colloquial nature of His inspirations.

3. A spirit of docility—for He is master.

4. A spirit of detachment, because He is the end of creatures: to us God begins with Him.

5. A spirit of holy fear, because, 1. Of what Jesus says of Him. 2. Of what we ourselves know of Him.

6. A spirit of simplicity, as simple souls are His own obvious attraction and devotion.

7. A spirit of truthfulness and reality: *e.g.* Ananias and Sapphira.

8. A spirit of hatred of heresy, as it is a sin especially against Him.

9. A spirit of Humility: He exhibits something in God's tenderness so like what would be humility in creatures: there is nothing in the Divine Nature on which God could base humility— so He bases a sweet semblance of it upon our necessities, and sorrows, and even our transgressions.

VI. The effects of devotion to Him upon the soul.

1. It brings us, as it were, into the life of God.

2. It makes us gradually at home in the mystery of the Holy Trinity, which is our eternal home.

3. It breeds in us the real spirit of Jesus.

4. It makes us interior, yet outlooking, just in the right proportions.

5. It increases His gifts and multiplies His fruits in us.

6. Its most direct effects are to give us facility in believing, and promptitude in serving God.

7. A spirit of the most irrepressible joy, and exclusive rejoicing in unworldly things.

VII. Examples of it.

1. The apostles, in councils, epistles, &c.

2. St. Gregory the Great with the dove at his ear.

3. Blessed Crispin of Viterbo.

4. St. Philip's miraculous heart.
5. It ought to be the spirit of the Oratory.
   (1) Because of its Founder.
   (2) Its occupations—preaching, confession, prayer:
       endless reliance on the Holy Ghost.
   (3) Spirit of joy and brightness: sunniness—it
       accounts for St. Philip's.
   (4) The institute has charity instead of vow.
   (5) Revelation to the Ven. Serafina di Dio. *

VIII. How this devotion concerns us, seen by a con-
      trast between hearts with the Holy Ghost, and
      hearts without Him. †

1. To have, or not to have Him, makes all the difference of the beauty and reality of this life ;
2. And all the destiny of the life to come.
3. It means whether we belong to Jesus or not.
4. Amid Angels the difference is that between
   Michael and Satan.
5. Among men, between Peter and Judas.
6. On the quantity of Him, or intimacy with Him,
   or docility to Him, lies based all the huge difference between saints and common believers.
7. To be without Him is to have been by our own
   fault created for nothing, or worse than nothing,
   to have missed the end of our creation, to be a
   part of everlasting darkness, of everlasting
   unlovingness.

IX. Contrasts between the Holy Ghost and Jesus.

---

* V. note at the end of the chapter, p. 99.

† The devotion of the Curé of Ars to the Holy Ghost, Spirit of
the Curé of Ars, p. 47. See also lives of Grignon de Montfort,
Liebermann, and Desplaces, founder of the Seminaire du St.
Esprit. St. Gertrude's visions concerning the Holy Ghost are
given in her life, lib. iv. cap. 40.

1. We are speaking of peculiarities, not oppositions, in order to clear our view and base our devotion.
2. He is with us now, like a Second Jesus, only without Body, Eyes and Voice.
3. All life the world over, all Christian life is now like the thirty-three years in Palestine, teaching, healing, being beautiful, as the son was then: or rather it is the three years' Ministry prolonged to the Doom—not the Infancy or Passion: this is remarkable, as devotion to Him is in spirit so similar to devotion to the Passion: Jesus Himself continues the Infancy and Passion by means of the Mass and the Blessed Sacrament, while the Holy Ghost continues the Ministry, but continues it in the spirit of Jesus, with peculiarities.
4. His presence such as to make it expedient Christ should go.
5. Seeming contrasts, or say rather, individual features of the Holy Ghost by the side of Jesus.
   (1) He speaks more, is less taciturn.
   (2) More pathetic: it is we ourselves who mostly put pathos into the actions of Jesus when we preach: in the narrative of the Gospels there is a peculiar, almost unpathetic, brightness and simplicity.
   (3) He takes the initiative more.
   (4) He is more touchy and sensitive, if we may venture on such words.
   (5) He seems, with all his devotion to sinners, to have a greater devotion to saints: whereas this was less brought out in our Lord.
   (6) He seems to make more haste: St Ambrose's *nescit tarda molimina Spiritus Sancti gratia.*

(7) He punishes more, as if His justice were more purely divine.

There is ever before me a dim vision of the beauty of the Third Person of the Most Holy Trinity, the eternally proceeding Love of the Father and the Son. I have tried to image Him, as the dove or tongues of fire; then as the sound of the mountain-wind high up, while the woods and lakes lay unruffled in the vales; then as a wondrous shoreless uncreated Sea of Love. But I was discontented. Then I tried to picture His Divine Person, not like the Ancient of Days in Daniel, as the Father, nor like the Lamb slain, as the Incarnate Son, but as a distinct person veiled in light, and the white resplendency of shadow-casting clouds. But it was not enough. Then I pictured Him as if He were the viewless air, which I breathed, which was my life, as if the air were He, going into me and coming out, and He a Divine Person, sweetly envious of the Son, sweetly coveting the Sacred Humanity which He Himself had fashioned, and coming into the world on beautifullest mission, seeking to be as near incarnate as He could be without an actual incarnation; and it was so near that he seemed almost human, though unincarnate. And this was the clearest view I ever could see of that Divine Person.

May He forgive what I have written of Him, and accept it, and bear with me a little longer, till I have drawn my last breath in Him, and breathed it forth again as my first breath of another life, a fresh son newly born at the Feet of the Eternal Father!

St. Mary's, Sydenham,
The Annunciation, 1857.

U.

APPENDIX.

In 1699, on the evening preceding the Nativity of the Blessed Virgin, the special feast of the Oratory at Naples, the servant of God had a revelation which she gave in writing to her director: it is as follows:—

"I should wish to write, not with a pen, but with the tongue of a Seraph, not with ink, but with my own blood, that this letter might be a flame of fire, to consume the whole Congregation, or I should wish to send the very interior of my heart to explain and make you understand what I heard on the eve of the Nativity from the Blessed Virgin herself, and from our and your Holy Father St. Philip regarding his Congregation.

"I saw the Saint with the great Mother of God in a flame of fire, and surrounded with light; I prayed earnestly to him for his Congregation and for each individual of it in particular; and with a sweet countenance, he said to me many beautiful things, of which I will tell you some briefly.

"The saint showed me what his sons ought to be and also the dignity of the Congregation, made as it were after the likeness of God and of the Three Divine Persons, especially of the Person of the Holy Ghost: and he told me, that those who belong to the Congregation ought not to be called by any other name than sons of the Holy Ghost, and that the Congregation ought to be called the Temple of the Holy Ghost; he said, it was not my spirit that founded it, but the Holy Spirit, and as such they ought to work and to be all love for God and their neighbor; I desire nothing of them, but that they burn with that fire, of which they are the sons; and he made me perceive clearly that this is suitable to this Congregation: and I saw the care he has for it, and the many caresses that he bestowed on some of the Fathers and the encouragements he gave them.

U.   ℞

"I also saw that the Blessed Virgin is the Patroness and Protectress of the Congregation, and this consoled me much. Oh why have I not words to express the nobility of the Congregation and its state and high condition, because its members have no other obligation than to love God, who is the summit and perfection of everything; they are children chosen for great heights of spirituality. Oh how noble did it appear to me! and how great did the last imperfection seem in them, on account of the dignity of their condition and the delights of their state, which I saw to be like a meadow, rejoicing in the sweet breezes of the Holy Ghost, who excites His sons to work nobly and of their own free will.

"I knew in general, that in proportion to the nobility of this state, a greater and more immaculate correspondence to it is required: and I saw how frightful is the least stain and dust of imperfection in him who professes it The Saint told me that with great affection he recommended them all to God. All this was in general. May the Lord be ever praised and blessed! I knew then in the mind of the Holy Father what he wished to say to me and what he meant by showing me so many beautiful things. For without speaking he had explained to me the perfection we must have, in order to be children of light.

"It would be monstrous, if fire were to produce snow, light darkness, and crystal mud. I do not know how to explain myself better, but I understand the meaning that the Saint wished to convey. It would be wonderful if a sweet tree produced gall; how much greater a prodigy would it be, if in any sons of St. Philip, who are called sons of the Holy Ghost, any defect were to exist! I saw the sanctity that the state requires and that which he who professes it can easily attain to and ought to possess. I saw the saint caress many of the Fathers and encourage many others I write briefly, for I had a night and a day of such delights as our Lord only knows."

II.

PENTECOST.

I. What can they want who have Jesus? *e.g.* Disciples in Judea.

  1. Fascination of personal influence: His was beyond compare.

  2. Marvellous beauty, variety, novelty, and yet familiarity of His kindness and gentleness.

  3. The secret, nameless, supernatural spell which breathed out from Him.

  4. The sheathing of His Godhead in His human tenderness.

  5. Yet the ever new delight of the knowledge of His Godhead.

II. Yet our Lord Himself said they *did* want something: their want was the Holy Ghost.

  1. A Divine Person who is specially love, and so especially to be worshipped by love.

  2. Overshadowing Mary — John said Jesus would baptize with the Holy Ghost—last day of feast (John vii. 37–39).

  3. What Jesus said Himself—It is expedient that I go away—and that blasphemy against the Holy Ghost is not to be forgiven.

  4. His coming *made* apostles: it was Mary's *second* Pentecost.

  5. So our Lord taught as if the one grand thing He had to teach was devotion to the Holy Ghost. He came to kindle that fire, and He yearned to have it kindled.

U.

III. We too are with Jesus—not in spirit only, but in
　　　literal presence; yet we too need the Holy
　　　Ghost; we need—

1. More love of Jesus Himself.

2. More putting in mind of what He said.

3. A more yearning spirit of prayer.

4. More power against self and worldliness.

5. More, oh, a thousand times more love of each
　　　other. This is the grand want of the world just
　　　now—the want that cries aloud and clamors to
　　　be satisfied, lest the glory of God and the spirit
　　　of Jesus should altogether cease from off the
　　　earth. Here, then, is the way in which devotion
　　　to the Holy Ghost is so acceptable to our Blessed
　　　Lady. She sees the earth perishing, not so much
　　　because men do not love God, as because they
　　　do not love one another. The heathen said of
　　　primitive Christians, not, see how these men love
　　　God—but, see how they love one another.

I seem always to see our dear and blessed God bend-
ing over us, yearning to fill our hearts with, oh such
graces and such a much more exceeding love—and He
cannot, because we will not, make our hearts large with
love of each other!

.

U.　　　　　·　　　　　　　　　　　　　　D

III.

GOD A GOD OF FIRE.*

I. I am come to send fire on the earth, and what will
I but that it be kindled?—St. Luke xii. 49. How
strange this sounds from Jesus, meek and humble
of heart!

  1. Compare the spirit of it with the night of the
  Incarnation and the night of Bethlehem.

  2. Or the quiet fires in the hearts of Mary and Joseph
  in the holy House of Nazareth.

  3. Or with the abysses of the abjection of the
  Passion.

  4. Or with the secret apparitions of the beautiful
  Forty Days after the Resurrection.

  5. Or with the passive, patient stillness of the Blessed
  Sacrament.

II. Yet the scene at Pentecost.

  1. They wait, Mary in the midst, and the chosen few,
  for Him Who is to be so much to them that it
  was well that Jesus should go away.

  2. They wait for Him, Who is eminently the Spirit
  of Jesus, and will bring to mind all He said.

  3. For Him with Whom Jesus in His Human Nature
  has now been ten days in heaven! Oh the marvellous occupations of those ten days!

  4. He comes to them in the vehement majesty of a
  mighty wind, and scatters Himself in showers
  of fire like cloven tongues.

* Whitsunday, 1858.

U.

5. So that Mary and the apostles seemed to the multitudes to be drunk with new wine.

III. God *always* a God of fire.

1. He calls Himself so: The Lord thy God is a consuming fire. Deut. iv. 24.

2. He appeared as such to Isaias; as a whirlwind
and enfolding fire to Ezekiel. St. John says
(Apoc. i. 14), His eyes were as a flame of fire.

3. Burning Bush: in the inner folds of the desert,
and ravines of Horeb, to Moses.

4. (Daniel vii. 9, 10.) His throne like flames; the
wheels of it like burning fire, and a swift stream
of fire issued forth from before Him: vision
seen in the first year of Baltassar, King of
Babylon.

5. In these sweet fires we are to dwell eternally.
Isaias (xxxiii. 14) asks, which of you can dwell
with devouring fire? which of you shall dwell
with everlasting burnings? and the answer is,
he that walketh in justices.

IV. So our religion is a religion of fire.

1. It was the one will of Jesus to kindle this fire on
earth.

2. The Holy Ghost is never otherwise in the heart
than as fire.

3. The fires of the Eternal Father are to be our
everlasting home.

4. What manner of fire should we have then?
Fiery love, fiery faith, fire consuming self, fire
burning the world out of our hearts, fire likely
to make men think us drunk or mad.

5. What is the case in reality? Do we burn?
Are we vehement? Do our hearts throb and

beat tumultuously with love of God? Do we understand that lifelong broken heart of our great father St. Philip, burst with the ball of fire, which was the Holy Ghost?—Oh if our religion be a moral indifference, a calm bargaining with God, a prudential speculation, a discreet fear of hell, a frigid propriety, a servile keeping of the letter of God's law—it may be a religion—but is it the religion written in the Bible? Is it the fire which it was our dearest Lord's one will to kindle?

Oh that that Divine Person would come down upon us with His fire to-day, would break our hearts with the magnificent excesses of the love of God, would burn us with the pain of the great pleasure of His fire! Sweet, gentle, plaintive, vehement, fiery, enthusiast Spirit!—Oh that he would so light His flames in our hearts that from this hour our whole life should be nothing but an unbroken Pentecost!

. IV.

DOCILITY TO THE HOLY GHOST.

In speaking of the Holy Ghost we can either rise up into the ineffable splendors of the Most Holy Trinity, or go down into the most secret and noiseless centre of our own souls: this last to-day.

I. Our union with the Holy Ghost.

1. He Himself actually dwells in us.

2. We are more under His care than the disciples

U.   ⓓ

were under that of Jesus in the Thirty-three Years.

3. He dwells in us in a new way with every augmentation of sanctifying grace.

4. No words can describe the intimate familiarity in which we live with this Third Person of the Most Holy Trinity.

5. His ceaseless action upon our souls, through His love of Jesus and of ourselves.

6. His gifts, and His fruits as well as His graces.

7. His inspirations, multitudinous and incessant.

II. Inspirations.

1. We are with Him as Adam was with God in Eden.

2. To all good persons He is speaking continually.

3. Perfection may be defined as consisting simply of docility to His inspirations.

4. He speaks low, and His operations are very delicate.

5. He loves and expects to be consulted.

6. And furthermore, even when not consulted, a habit of listening to Him is an essential part of the spiritual life; without it, prayer can never be supernatural, or more than a pious habit; not a real familiarity, or union of the soul with God.

7. This life of perpetual secret colloquy with the Third Person of the Most Holy Trinity is what is meant by an interior life.

III. Consequences of not listening to inspirations.

1. Our own spiritual life, and God's designs upon us are nothing but mist, confusion and unmeaning generalities.

U.

2. So we come in outward things to work on impulse, or from natural activity, without consulting, or listening for the Holy Ghost.

3. Hence neither our works nor ourselves have the secret of success, or the root of perseverance.

Oh the sweetness of an interior life—its firmness, its repose, its clear atmosphere,—how beautiful it is, ever at the feet of that Third Person of the Most Holy Trinity learning the secrets of heaven, in whispers of a sweet music, which no ear but ours can hear !

U   ℝ

Part Second.

THE SACRED HUMANITY OF JESUS.

SECTION I.
OUR BLESSED LORD.

ADVENT MEDITATIONS.

I.

THE LIFE OF JESUS IN THE BOSOM OF THE ETERNAL FATHER.

I. His Eternal Generation.
   1. Infinitely noble.
   2. Infinitely pure.
   3. Eternal.
   4. Unspeakable and incomprehensible.
II. His residence in the Bosom of the Father.
   1. His sojourn there.
   2. His going forth.
   3. His sojourn among men.
III. His Divinity.
   1. His union with the Father.
   2. His equality.
   3. His independence.
IV. The mutual love of the Father and the Son.
   1. Their conversation.
   2. Their love.
   3. The fruit of their love, the Holy Ghost.
V. The eternal plan of the Incarnation.
   1. The fall foreknown.

U.　　　　　　　　　　　　　　℟

2. The exclusion of the angels from the remedy of
the Incarnation.

3. The choice of the Word of His Sacred Humanity.

VI. His eternal choice of sufferings.

1. Of the sufferings of His whole life.

2. Of His Death.

3. Of the Cross in particular.

VII. The Predestination of His Mother.

1. His choice of her.

2. That choice the source of her greatness.

3. That choice the source of her graces.

4. That choice the source of her crosses.

THE LIFE OF JESUS IN THE WOMB OF MARY.

VIII. He begins a new life in her womb.

1. Infinitely precious.

2. Infinitely pure.

3. All for us and at our disposal.

IX. His beatitude from the first moment.

1. It was from the first moment.

2. He was the first of all the blessed.

3. He obtains beatitude for us.

X. His clear view of God from the first moment.

1. The first Man who enjoyed it.

2. The only one in this life.

3. More clearly than all men and angels.

XI. His first act of love.

1. The most perfect act which has been or can be.

2. Extended to all the works of God.

3. And ardently to all men.

XII. Ineffable joy from the first moment.

1. His soul's joy in His Divinity.

U

2. His joy in infusing graces into Mary.

3. His joy in destining graces for each one of us in particular.

XIII. His adoration of the Father from the first moment.

1. Humble submission as to the creator of His Sacred Humanity.

2. Profound reverence from His view of the perfections of the Father.

3. Worship from a sense of the nothingness of His soul.

XIV. His praise of God from the first moment.

1. By the affections of His Sacred Heart.

2. By His works.

3. By exciting His Mother's Heart to join with Him.

XV. He thanks God from the first moment.

1. His Soul for the Hypostatic Union.

2. For all benefits received at that moment.

3. For all blessings to all creatures, past or to come.

XVI. His union of Viator and Comprehensor.

1. The state of Viator a violence to the Son of God.

2. A voluntary violence.

3. Love unites these incompatible states.

XVII. Oblation of Himself to the Eternal Father.

1. Offers the graces that instant received.

2. Offers Himself without reserve.

3. And for everything.

4. And with purity of oblation.

XVIII. His compassion for our miseries at that moment.

1. General pity.

2. For sin, our greatest misery.

3. For our sins in particular.

XIX. Takes our sins upon Him from that moment.

   1. Takes the burden with love.

   2. Embraces sufferings needful.

   3. Takes the Cross from His Father's Hands.

XX. Works for the glory of God and our salvation from that moment.

   1. Begins His work that instant.

   2. With fervor.

   3. Continues it with constancy.

XXI. Begins to merit from that moment.

   1. His perfect freedom.

   2. Infinite merits.

   3. Each action infinitely meritorious.

XXII. The desires with which He inspired Mary.

   1. To give Him to men.

   2. To see Him with her eyes.

   3. To serve Him as her Son and her God.

II.

CHRISTMAS DAY.

Love must be to us instead of mind, and heart, and spirit, in order that we may understand and feel, and worship the mystery of the cry of the Infant God breaking the silence of the winter's midnight at Bethlehem. And what was it first of all that the angels sang? Glory to God in the highest. This is the temper in which we must keep our feast.

I. God's glory the first thought.

   1. To look out for it was the habit of their blessed spirits.

U.   ℬ

  2. So also must it be ours.

  3. We lose half the joy of feasts by thinking only of ourselves.

II. But God's glory is the same as man's happiness.

  1. How touching and how beautiful is this thought!

  2. How intensely it ought to make us love God, Who is so mixed up with His creatures.

  3. What a lesson it teaches of trustful submission to His Will.

III. And God's glory in the highest is in His humiliations in the lowest.

  1. This is the grand character of Jesus, and of all His mysteries.

  2. The discernment of the angels saw the immense glory of His humiliation.

  3. As it was our Master's glory, so is it ours.

IV. Now enter the cave.

  1. The shepherds, humble men, adoring their new-born King in humble simplicity.

  2. Joseph, overwhelmed with pious humility as foster-father.

  3. Mary had won the Incarnation by humility; so now who shall tell how she abased herself.

  4. On that wisp of straw the Everlasting God!

Oh, my dear Brethren, we think too well of ourselves. We are less happy than we should be, because we are less humble. We do not advance, because we do not keep ourselves down. We do not love God as we desire, because we do not despise ourselves. Oh, it is so delightful a thing to be humble, so full of joy, and peace, and love: let it be our practice now. It is a devotion in which we can make no mistake, in which we can never go too far. Let us keep to the side of

U.

our Infant Lord, and sink with Him out of the sight
of men and of self, into those depths of dear humility
which will gently leave us at the last, not in the poverty of Bethlehem, but in the boundless riches of our
Heavenly Father's house above.

III.

CHRISTMAS DAY.

FOR THE CHILDREN.

Bethlehem is more wonderful than a fairy tale.
The persons in the cave.

I. Jesus.

   1. Eternal God: so disguised.

   2. Beauty of His Body and Soul.

   3. He saw this chapel of His foster-father, and longed
      for our little love.

II. Mary.

   1. No other of God's creatures is like her.

   2. The unutterableness of her joy.

   3. She is our own Mother, and it is part of her joy
      to be so.

III. Joseph.

   1. Joy of God in the love of His Son—this was St.
      Joseph's joy.

   2. His familiarities with Jesus.

   3. His love of all children for the sake of Jesus.

IV. Shepherds.

   1. Simple-hearted and very reverent.

2. Jesus thought of them first.

3. What they must have felt when they heard the angels sing.

V. The Wise Men.

1. Nobody wise but those who come to Jesus.

2. We must give Him our best when we come to Him.

3. But, oh! what will not He give us in return?

Love each other—let the houses love each other—you shall both be together, happy, peaceful, bright, at the feet of our dearest Jesus for ever!

IV.

NEW YEAR'S EVE.

I. The view which the saints take of the world as a howling wilderness compared with the view ordinarily good men take of it: the latter view stated.

1. The pleasure in living, especially if we have health.

2. The pleasure of doing good, and being kind to others.

3. The pleasure of relationship and love.

4. The pleasure of earth's sunshine, and the world's pastimes, especially society.

5. The pleasure of sorrow, when it is blunted.

6. The pleasure of past adventures, and of memory.

7. The pleasure of the dead we possess as ours in another state.

II. If to ordinarily good men the world is such,
wherein does it fail?

1. In not keeping its promises.
2. In not coming up to its own standard.
3. In its continual changing.
4. In having nothing to satisfy an interior want,
whose hunger increases as the soul loves God
more and more.

III. The Rest and the Soul.

1. What we thought last New Year's Eve, and how
we have been balked.
2. Have we the heart to ask no more of the coming
year?
3. What our soul is and what its destinies are.
4. The world at its best estate compared with the
soul.
5. What it is to be from home—we have never seen
our home.
6. Our home is in the Bosom of God, amid the
assemblage of His Attributes.
7. The Infant Jesus was at home as soon as He
was conceived: Mary's lap—the Bosom of the
Eternal Father.

He starts His Years—so let us start ours—and
with Him—and keep close by the side of our Elder
Brother: but what of the past? Aye, what of the
past? Let us go to Mary, and ask her what we are to
do with that. To-morrow our Brother sheds blood for
the first time; let us go to the temple, and ask to be
touched with it, and like a lightning flash the past is
done away!

U.   ℞

V.

THE EPIPHANY.

No history in the Gospel more strange, more singular, or more apart.

Lesson.—God will lead the most unlikely people in the most unlikely ways to Jesus, rather than that they should miss the salvation of their souls.

Yet though so singular a mystery, there is none which describes more faithfully what has happened or will happen to every one of ourselves.

I. We are to be led to Jesus, the end of our creation: how sweetly our Father cares for each of us.

II. We were unlikely people; alas! who more unlikely?

III. We were afar off; oh yes: how very far—by sin, by coldness, by ignorance, by relapses.

IV. We were led in unlikely ways—look back on life—how strange is all that God has done—and how plain, when we are far enough off to get a good view of it! Yet all in *one* way, which is the true faith.

V. What is all life but stars of Bethlehem? this is the meaning of everything.

1. Every sorrow is a star to lead us to Jesus.

2. Every joy is a star to lead us to Jesus.

3. Every change in life is a star to lead us to Jesus.

This is the simple view of life: what is life without God, without Jesus? How it passes away in joy; how it lingers in sorrow; how perilous, how anxious, how doubtful it is when it comes to end in death!

Oh! poor, poor life of man! it means nothing but one
only thing—Jesus Christ and Him crucified, the Son
of Mary, the Babe of Bethlehem!

VI.

THE EPIPHANY THE FEAST OF
CONVERTS

The Three Kings the first fruits of the Gentiles—
glory of the wideness of the Church. Epiphany a time
of prayer for the conversion of the whole world; also
a time for those who have had the grace of conversion
to reflect upon the past.

Parallel between the kings and converts.

 I. The life of the kings before they saw the star,
    seeking the true God among the starlit rocks
    of Arabia, and by the shores of its melancholy
    murmuring sea; seeking yet uncertain; trying
    to attach themselves to their home, and rest
    there, and yet God would not let them.

 II. The star rises—they hardly know why they trust
     it—but their heart tells them to follow: it is
     but a star, and yet so little: a glimmer—those
     who love them blame and wonder, expostu-
     late and weep—yet for them the glimmer is
     enough.

 III. They lose it—in Jerusalem—in crowds—even
      when so near: yet enquiry is quickened by the
      very withdrawing of the light.

 IV. They had false counsel given—to go back and

tell : now, they must first mind their own souls, and go home another way.

V. The star comes out again, and stands over Bethlehem—over Jesus and Mary: they hardly know whether it is the Mother or the Son they saw first.

VI. They were, for the most part, allowed the kiss of Jesus—sensible sweetness, or undoubting faith, or heaven awhile made plain.

VII. They had to offer the costliness of affections, of worldly goods, and of sufferings both inward and outward—gold, frankincense, and myrrh.

VIII. Now, what is left but that their lives must be lives of faith ?

The great grace of conversion is enough for them to feed upon: that one first sight of Jesus and Mary is a living vision in their hearts, and onward they go, into the unfading light of that more perfect vision, whose truth and beauty, satisfying joy and deep tranquillity, abide for evermore.

VII.

THE EPIPHANY.

The mystery narrated in detail.

I. The three kings an example of faith in their long journey. How much more sure are we : yet how do we act ?

1. In coming to mass.
2. In coming to confession.

U.   ℞

3. In putting ourselves out of the way in coming to
    Benediction.

II. Their journey a pattern of the pilgrimage of life.

1. In constant change, letting us have no abiding
    home.

2. In dangers and difficulties.

3. In disappointments, as when we lose our star.

4. But our end is the same—Jesus.

5. And we have a better star—even Mary.

III. What did they do all this for, and consider them-
    selves well paid by?

One sight of Jesus, one kissing of His little Feet,
one look, one conversation with Mary—and they waited
patiently thirty-three years for baptism, and shed their
blood in martyrdom, so deep had the loveliness of the
Infant Jesus passed into their souls. We have not
kissed His feet once only, but even received His Blood
in penance, Himself in communion—how many, many
times—and an eternal vision of Jesus before us! Ah!
see the difference between those who love, and those
who love not, my dearest children! Oh why will you
not love Jesus more? Is life so sweet, is earth so
peaceful, that you need no better home, no dearer
friends? You know how you look lovingly, and yearn
over your little babes when you rock them to sleep
in their little cradles—so take the Infant Jesus into
your hearts, let every beating of your hearts be like
the rocking of His cradle; let no rude word, no rough
oath, no loud immodest word awaken the sleeping
Babe; let no angry tempers, or evil deeds, cause Him
to cry with pain when He awakes. Mary will come
and teach you how to be a mother to her little Jesus,
in sweetness, and humility, and chastity: and oh the

thought that He of whom we speak so lightly, and so playfully, this pretty Babe, is none other than our God!

VIII.

. FEAST OF THE NAME OF JESUS.

The Name of Jesus—(1.) the greatest power on earth—(2.) the greatest miracle—(3.) the greatest happiness—(4.) the greatest attraction—(5.) the most common of all the Divine Mercies. What the name means · Thou shalt call His Name Jesus, for He shall save His people from their sins.

I. Without Him there could be no salvation.
  1. Men could do nothing with all their penances and .sufferings.
  2. Nor angels with all their merits and holiness.
  3. God wills to do it only through Him.
  4. The misery of the earth without Jesus.

II. With Him is " copious redemption."
  1. The faith of the Church.
  2. The abundance of grace.
  3. The abundance of the sacraments.

III. With Him salvation is easy.
  1. The little he requires from us.
  2. The facilities of pardon.
  3. His own interests in our salvation.

IV. The whole is done by Him.
  1. He is beforehand with us in Baptism and in grace.
  2. Our merits are all by His grace.

U.   Ꞁ

3. He gives us His own merits besides.

4. Our perseverance is His own gift.

V. How He has been a Saviour to each one of us.

  1. His knowledge and love of us in His thirty-three years.

  2. The time past of our lives, full of mercies and graces.

  3. The time present all is from Him.

  4. The time of death will be His choosing, and the best for us.

  5. All our future glory is from Him.

And all this is ours for a little generous love: nay, He seems to count Himself as under some obligation to us if we will only accept it. Let His name then be our tower in which we dwell, a safe refuge, a happy home!

IX.

DEVOTIONS FOR THOSE WHO WISH TO LEAD AN INTERIOR LIFE.

IN HONOR OF THE EIGHTEEN HIDDEN YEARS OF JESUS.

I. To the silent eternity of bliss which God enjoyed before He created anything, in order to gain detachment from creatures.

II. To the nine months of Jesus in the womb of Mary, to impetrate a love of the hidden life.

III. To the agony in the garden, to impetrate fortitude in interior pains, and in repugnances
•in prayer.

IV. To the life of Mary in the house of St. John,
to impetrate continual recollection of Jesus
and union with God.

V. To the holy Angels, especially our own guardian, to impetrate the union of inward recollection with outward duties.

VI. To the Blessed Sacrament, to impetrate the
grace of holy abjection.

VII. To the Holy Ghost, as the minister of the marriage of our souls with Jesus.

VIII. To the souls in purgatory, to impetrate conformity in suffering.

IX. To St. Joseph, to impetrate interior peace.

X. To St. Philip, for the gift of tears, and tenderness at mass.

XI. To St. Ignatius, for the love of concealment.

XII. To St. Teresa, for the gift of mental prayer.

XIII. To the interior life of Jesus, to obtain a thirst
for the glory of God.

XIV. To the priesthood of Jesus, to obtain the spirit
of sacrifice.

XV. To the infancy of Jesus, for simplicity and a
love of helplessness.

XVI. To St. Paul, for a special devotion to the
Eternal Father.

XVII. To St. John, for a devotion to the Sacred
Heart.

XVIII. To St. Clare of Montefalco, to obtain a special
devotion to the mystery of the most Adorable
Trinity.

X.

THE PERSON OF JESUS CHRIST.

Now this is eternal life: that they may know Thee, the only true God, and Jesus Christ whom Thou hast sent. St. John xvii. 3.

I. Beginning of Lent, troubled clouds of past sin, penance, &c.—now amid the clouds comes out clearly the person of Jesus Christ, He Whose Passion we are called upon to commemorate.

II. No mathematical God—idea—or form of words— but a living Person, two Natures—this is the *solid* of Catholic devotion: all else is from this —Blessed Virgin Mary—Real Presence—feasts of the year.

III. The one grand object of the Church is to make the Person of Jesus Christ better known and better loved in a forgetful world; this in its measure presses upon every Catholic of every age, rank, or ability.

IV. Now, in Lent, we have also to reconcile ourselves to Him, or to engage ourselves more deeply in His service, or to pledge ourselves more solemnly to Him.

V. What sort of a Person was He? (1.) A Child flying to Egypt. (2.) Sitting at the well of Jacob. (3.) Refusing to accuse the adulteress. (4.) Defending the Magdalen. (5.) Trying even in the garden to save Judas. (6.) Father, forgive them, for they know not what they do. (7.) Feed My lambs.

Wonder that men do not love Him! Look at what He has done for *you* in past life: we, when we grow old, weary of sin: He wearies not in pardoning. Come then, give Him a Palm-Sunday entry into your hearts—and while the thrones of the ancient earth are tottering, enthrone Him more firmly, more honorably, aye, and above all, more lovingly than ever, as King over you, over all you are and all you have, and all you can suffer for His sake. Oh, what a day will Easter-day be, if thereon you solemnize the coronation of our dearest Jesus in your hearts!

———

XI.

OUR LORD'S CHOICE OF POVERTY.

The Holy Ghost was called *Pater Pauperum:* so were the saints also: so was Jesus: love of the poor is a characteristic of true holiness, as well as of the true Church. The poor you have always with you, but Me you have not always. This shows how completely they came to occupy His place, even more than direct texts.

I. The choice of Jesus.

  1. He being the Eternal Wisdom, chose poverty.

    (1) As the state fittest for His great end.

    (2) As the one in which He could raise His Sacred Humanity to heights of Holiness.

  2. How consistently He kept to His choice through the three and thirty years.

U

3. How it satisfied the longings of His Sacred Heart and His Divine Compassion.
4. The result of this fact that Jesus chose poverty is that the poor are made authentically the favorites of God.
5. Hence in the Church.
   (1) Voluntary poverty, and
   (2) Sacrifice for the poor.

II. The blessed effects of this choice of Jesus, to *all*, rich as well as poor.
1. The abundance of holy charity and liberality.
2. It rebukes the spirit of the world in us, and so raises us to perfection.
3. It likens us to the Sacred Heart, and so makes us dear to God.

III. Consolations of the poor: for there is no dignity or poetry about poverty, as about other suffering.
1. God has been a *poor man*—tried it all—scant food, hard lying, trust in alms, labor: those that are sick even have no such consolation: many an evening darkened in—where was He to lodge?
2. Not wrong to feel, and feel keenly, the privations of poverty.
3. New and supernatural motives for patience, supplied by the choice of Jesus.

What then is your riches? The Sacred Heart of Jesus. What have you but love of God? How foolish not to take what is yours! What have you else to make you happy? O blessed Poverty, if it drives you into the Sacred Heart—this is its one blessing, in which are all blessings. Forfeit this, and you are the dull thing the world pronounces you to be.

U.   ℞

XII.

POVERTY THE CHOICE OF JESUS.

I. Discontent of a poor man—his comparison of his
fortune with that of the rich and noble—the ill
temper which results from that comparison—the
childishness and uselessness of it all.

II. Let him turn his thoughts another way.

  1. Jesus was God, and might by His power have
chosen any state—yet He chose poverty.

  2. He was infinite wisdom—yet He chose poverty.

  3. He came to do His Father's work, as we do: and
He chose poverty.

  4. He chose it of the hardest and most continual sort.
Comparison between His poverty, and the comforts of poor men in general.

  5. The love He bore to the poverty He had chosen.

III. Privileges of the poor.

  1. Absence of temptation.

  2. Penance for sin.

  3. Special promises of the Gospel.

  4. Easy deathbed—so little to part with.

  5. Companionship of Jesus.

However dark your way may seem, however multiplied your hardships and your woes, you are what
Jesus chose to be, and is not that fortune enough to
make you richer than all this poor perishing world
can give?

XIII.

OUR LORD'S PRAYER.

Many things about our Lord are wonderful—none more wonderful than His prayer.

I. What prayer was in Him.

    1. It combined all the eminences of His soul.

    2. It was the abundance of the treasures of the Sacred Heart.

    3. It met and saluted all the Divine Perfections.

    4. It did to each of those perfections what was necessary for us.

    5. Its thanksgiving, intercession, and congratulation mysteriously peculiar.

    6. It was the prayer of true Man.

    7. It was by an awful mystery the prayer of true God.

II. Characteristics of His prayer.

    1. Lifelong.

    2. Principle of all He did.

    3. Recorded ways and times.

    4. Its efficacy.

    5. Its lastingness in the Church.

    6. Its privacy—public only once.

    7. Intense reverence of it—He was heard because He feared.

III. Our Practice.

    1. The thing most needed to imitate in Jesus.

    2. The thing most perfectly imitable.

    3. The best prophecy of our final perseverance.

    4. The most sure relief from present difficulties.

5. Prayer brings all other holiness along with it.

6. It is like nothing else in the world.

7. But a life of prayer is the only true prayer.

No prayer is unheard, none is wasted, there is none that we shall not meet again in the world to come. Oh when we die, how bitterly shall we mourn that we have prayed so little, prayed to negligently; ah! we shall see then that life was hardly life, when it was not also prayer!

————

XIV.

THE MYSTERY OF JESUS BEING THOUGHT MAD.

I. The Mystery of the Eternal Word being thought mad.

1. As the Passion is a marvellous disclosure of the creature's treatment of the Creator, so is this mystery of the look which the Creator when visible had to His creatures. The Passion discloses their will, and this mystery their understanding.

2. It was a witness borne to His ways being above our comprehension.

3. It was a terrific measurement of the distance which the world had drifted from Him.

4. It should be a continual subject of trembling sorrow, and of frequent acts of the most tender and respectful reparation.

5. And it was, of all the Three Persons the Eternal *Wisdom* who was thought *mad !*

II. The lessons to be learned from this mystery.

    1. The world, even the good and kind ,part of it, does
        not comprehend supernatural principles—it was
        His own who laid hands on Him.

    2. It is the cross which the world cannot take into its
        calculations, and so blunders.

    3. How hidden must Jesus have been—so then also
        must we be!

    4. How this mystery is realized in the saints: this is
        half the wisdom of the Gospel—we should lay
        it to heart, and make it thoroughly our own!

    5. What a contempt it ought to give us for the world
        —so foolish in its wisdom that it thought its God
        mad: one trembles to say the words: surely the
        very angels invisibly shrink around us.

Oh adorable foolishness of God! how shall we worship our own honor and reputation, when He so annihilated Himself, and stripped Himself of His? So let us be thought mad :—

    (1) In our faith by heretics.

    (2) In our holiness, even by our own people.

O Jesus! dearest Lord! give us the heart which was in our father St. Philip, the heart not to be wise with men, but to be mad with Thee; and of the world too we have one thing to ask which it will not be slow to give, that as it made wild sport with Thee in the court of Herod's house, so it may for Thy dear sake make sanctifying sport of us.

XV.

THE WEARINESS OF JESUS AT THE WELL.

I. The Creature would desire to see—to have a long steadfast undazzled look at the Creator of all this Universe—to look—to learn to love—to worship: look at Jesus sitting on the broken wall of Jacob's Well: He made that cold sparkling water far down, and now He asks it of His sinful creature: the weariness of God made Man ; awe-spiring yet consoling also.

II. Weariness of Jesus.

  1. With our sin and ingratitude.

  2. With His own toils for us.

  3. With the fervor of His love, which parched Him on the Cross.

III. Consolation for us.

  1. As sanctifying our toils for Him, even our bodily fatigues, and the aching of the sleepless head, the throbbing of the footsore limb.

  2. As showing how he forget Self to save a soul, whereas she left her picture and went to the city forgetting His thirst.

  3. As rule and model for us in trying to convert others.

He made, I say, that cold sparkling water far down, and now He asks it of His sinful creature: so it is in all things : He gives us hearts, He gives springs of love to flow there as into a well, He sits and looks down with a sweet thirsty envy, and we will not give Him drink !

U.

XVI.

EASTER SUNDAY.

The three points of the world at the midnight of Easter were the Soul of Jesus in Limbus, the Body of Jesus in the tomb, the Mother of Jesus in the house of John.

I. The Soul of Jesus in Limbus.
   1. Enjoying as it ever had done the Beatific Vision.
   2. Imparting it to others, and so making Paradise.'
   3. Freed from the interior agonies of the Passion.
   4. Delighting in its present conquests of grace.
   5. Still full to overflowing of love for men.

II. The Body of Jesus in the tomb.
   1. The silence around the tomb.
   2. The angels watching.
   3. The guards sleeping.
   4. The seal set upon the stone.
   5. The adorable Body in its grave-clothes, all seamed with wounds.

III. Mary in the House of John.
   1. Her dolors accomplished, as well as His Passion.
   2. She is supporting the apostles.
   3. She watches in prayer, as at the Annunciation.
   4. Her Heart holds the Faith of the whole Church in it.
   5. She keeps adoring the Body and the Soul of Jesus in spirit.

IV. The Mystery of the Resurrection.
   1. The angels collect the Precious Blood, and worship it.

2. The soul of Jesus comes to the tomb, and enters.
3. The retinue of angels and Souls that are with Him.
4. He opens the tomb, and discloses His Body, pointing out the Wounds.
5. Adam and Eve, Abraham, Moses, David, St. Joseph, the Baptist, and the rest adore it.
6. The grave-clothes are unfastened, and laid in order on one side.
7. Jesus by His power as God, and at the word of the Father, resumes His Body with the Blood.
8. Its instantaneous life and beauty; yet retention of the Five Wounds.
9. Just as the light dawned upon the hill-tops, He with His retinue enters His Mother's room, and strengthening her heart, He shows her His everlasting Godhead, the surpassing beauty of the Person of the Eternal Word.

Thus it was, O beautiful consummation! that He who died for our sins, rose again for our justification.

XVII.

THE VICTORY OF THE RESURRECTION.

The hour of weakness and of suffering was past—the triumph come—the dawn of the morning was the time—to the eyes of Mary first of all the victory was proclaimed. Emancipation proclaimed to a whole nation of slaves, what it would be like! The resurrec-

U

tion was the emancipation of the world.   The slavery
of men — the slavery of Jesus in His Passion — here
it ended.   Easter dawn is come, and with it man's
victory.

  I. Victory of the Flesh.
    1. Its weakness, pains, ignominies.
    2. The prison house of the soul, almost forcing it to
       sin.
    3. The veil that blinds our eyes, and darkens us.
    4. The glory, beauty, power, brightness, new self of
       the resurrection.
  II. Victory over sin.
    1. Sin has done its worst to Jesus.
    2. Sin does its worst to us.
    3. Sin separates body and soul.
    4. Resurrection the reunion of the two for glory.
  III. Victory over death.
    1. The empire of death.
    2. The cowardice with which men crouched under it.
    3. How faith comes and sets us free from this das-
       tardly bondage.

The extreme beauty of a disembodied soul in a state
of grace—its return as a conqueror to reanimate the
body—God's care of the precious particles of the body
for that great day — the entry of the soul into it —
heralded by angels into the Presence of the Face of
God!

XVIII.

THE EASTER JOY OF JESUS.

I. There are no marks of the Crown of Thorns upon His brow—yet He looks more than ever a King! The placid sunrise is beautiful, but there is not half so much quiet beauty about it as reigns over that incredibly sweet face. What maturity and yet what youth! Oh look into His eyes, what a depth of love, what a tenderness of love, yet what an overwhelming *power* of love. That smile upon His lips, so royal and yet so wonderfully familiar, how human it is in its gentle winning gravity. What a light of unspeakable expression shines over His whole face, glows like sunshine on His beautiful Hair, and runs down like an unction into His comely beard!

II. But He must not speak: if He speaks our hearts will break with love. It is true He will speak to us the very first time we see Him: but He must not speak now. Jesus Risen! What think you? Is that beauty the old beauty of dear Bethlehem? or is it the look of the boy at Nazareth? or the sweetness of the preacher and miracle-worker of Galilee? It is all of them and it is none of them. It is something of its own. Somehow the Human Soul fills all the features marvellously with a most human loveliness; and yet His Divinity shines through with a masterful majesty, and with a gladness so bright that it makes us worship to look at it.

III. I interpret His Easter look to be an immense joy
—human joy carried to its utmost limit—the joy
of His Godhead made visible by His Human
Soul overflowing His Glorified Body with an
incomparable jubilee.

IV. His Easter joy was one of a constellation of His
joys—let us think of them.

1. His joy at the moment of the Incarnation.
   (1) His delight in the worship of God at that
   moment.
   (2) His delight in His Body and Soul.
   (3) His delight in the sweet sanctity of His
   Mother.

2. His joy at His first sight of Mary.
   (1) He gazes, and reads each feature; rejoices in
   His likeness to Her.
   (2) She was His own creature.
   (3) He exulted in Her ecstatic delight at seeing
   Him.

3. His joy at her first Communion.
   (1) Like the Incarnation over again.
   (2) The graces He found in her, and the new
   ones he gave.
   (3) The joy of her joy at this fresh ineffable
   union.
   These three joys met now, were all blended, and
   were surpassed by the Easter joy.

4. His joy in seeing her now; Mary, so familiar with
   all His old beauty, is struck with His Easter
   brightness and loveliness.
   (1) The joy to His human eyesight, as if long
   years had parted them, such vast mysteries
   had they both traversed.

U.

(2) Her fresh beauty from her dolors.

(3) His ecstacy in filling each abyss her woes had made in her heart, with fresh love and grace.

V. Dearest Lord! He had yet another Easter joy! He thought of us and of our salvation, of each one of us by name and look: He will have it over again when we see Him first; it is little, yet nothing is little to Him, nothing little to love, while nothing of His is little to our exceeding littleness—to Him and to us it will be like His first apparition to His Mother.

1. His joy at this particular judgment in passing a favorable sentence.

2. His joy in being our Redeemer.

3. His joy in His mother's gladness at our salvation.

4. His joy in the beauty and sweetness of our souls.

5. His joy in our unutterable joy.

Oh Easter is a happy day: but I think our true Easter will not be till we look that first time on the beautiful welcome of His Easter Face.

XIX.

DIES QUAM FECIT DOMINUS.

Can there be light after such a darkness? Can there be day after such a night, peace after the death of God, joy after the passion of our dearest Lord? What is Easter like? Like the beginning of eternity, like the dawn of God's endless day! Easter has come with its thousand thoughts, its thousand doctrines,

its thousand graces : how can the Church express it?
With that sublime simplicity, with that artlessness of
a child which is close upon the wisdom of an angel,
she sums it all up in one word—*Hæc dies quam fecit
Dominus*—This is the day which the Lord hath made.

I. *Quam fecit Dominus.*

　1. This is the one joy of all things — that God
　　made them.

　2. It is our joy that *we* are created by God and by
　　such a God.

　3. So we congratulate all creatures that they have
　　the happiness of having been made by God.

　4. But He makes some things specially, and keeps
　　a special royalty over them.

　5. Easter Sunday is one of these things.

II. But did He not make all days, and cause all suns
　　to shine? Oh yes! but never a day like this—
　　the sunrise of the Everlasting Saviour!

　1. Because from it comes the blessing of all days.

　2. Because the glory of Jesus was so infinitely dear
　　to the Father.

　3. Because He is the true sunshine of the earth.

　4. And His glorified body the sun and moon of
　　Heaven.

　5. And He is a sun who has no setting—oh the
　　joy of this to us! He is a day which is all
　　morning, fresh, pure, grateful, full of sweet
　　light and of sweet odors.

III. The Resurrection.

　1. The sun is not yet above the hills: in the pearly
　　dawn we see St. Mary Magdalen looking down
　　into the sepulchre : why does her face shine so
　　brightly if the sun is not risen? It is from

the two angels in white sitting in the sepulchre: how her tears glistened in the light!

2. Dear loving Magdalen! is it the memory of the Passion that makes her weep? The angels, beaming with gladness, say, Woman! why weepest thou? Who has any right to weep at Easter? Because they have taken away my Lord, and I know not where they have laid Him. Earth without Jesus! no! that could not be. So Jesus had said about her brother Lazarus—Where have you laid him?

3. When she had thus said, she turned herself back, and saw Jesus standing, and she knew not that it was Jesus. Did she not feel, or was she so engrossed in seeking Jesus? Her eye was full of that wounded Body on the Cross. She turned herself back—what were even angels when she was seeking Jesus? Jesus, as if to have time to drink in her fond faithful love, as if it was so great an Easter joy to Him, saith to her in a feigned voice, Woman, why weepest thou? whom seekest thou? O dearest Lord! thus to play with her grief and love, to ask Thy servant such a question — whom seekest thou, as if Magdalen could seek any but Thee. She, thinking it was the gardener—poor Mary! truly He was the gardener—the gardener who had once planted the paradise of old—saith to Him, Sir, if thou hast taken Him hence, tell me where thou hast laid Him: and I will take Him away. What! in thine arms like a child, Mary? as thy great namesake carried Him at Bethlehem and in the Wilderness? I will take

Him away—oh beautiful—as if He was hers, as if He should not be a charge to any one but her, as if she was hostess of Jesus by office, now and for ever. Then she seemingly turned her face to the sepulchre. Did not the empty sepulchre remind her of His words to Martha, her sister, I am the resurrection and the life? If any word is like the last trumpet of the archangel it is *Ego sum resurrectio et vita.*

4. Jesus saith to her, behind her, in *that* voice, Mary. Does she live, or has that one word broken her heart with the abruptness of its jubilee? She turning, oh with what speed, with what surprise, with what unmanageable ecstasy of love, said, Rabboni, which is to say, Master. Oh in the long history of the world how many sweet surprises has love contrived for love—but was there ever any one half so sweet as this?

5. Joy says short words and few ones. Her beautiful bright face may have told the apostles all when she met them, for her face had been sad enough for days past; but as for her tongue, she could only say—I have seen the Lord! and these things He said to me. Oh happy, happy Mary! help us to our Heavenly Easter, to that morning when Jesus our Judge will have spoken a few words to us; it is only a few years distant now, and then we can come to thee in Heaven, and repeat thy simple but all-sufficient words, I have seen the Lord, and these things He said to me.

XX.

THE RESURRECTION A MYSTERY OF CALMNESS.

The peace around the tomb—the peace of Mary's desolation: we almost fear lest the notes of holy triumph should break a spell so sweet, so calm, so heavenly, so beautiful; for peace is more like God than anything else on earth.

I. The Mystery of the Resurrection.

1. The sunrise a type of its exceeding calm, its tranquil glory and effulgence; light makes no noise.
2. The soul of Jesus, not fluttered, not elated.
3. Calm adoration of the souls by which He is accompanied.
4. Calmness of the Adorable Body lying separate in the tomb.
5. Calmness of the Body and Soul in their joyous union: witness the grave-clothes, and the rolled stone, and the sleeping guards all unwakened.
6. Calmness of the bodies of the dead which rose and walked the streets.
7. Calmness of His immense and unperturbed Divinity.

How unlike the world is all this!

II. Peace and calm the gift, the special foremost gift of Jesus Risen.

1. Exemplified in His apparition to His Mother at the dawn.

U   ℗

2. To Magdalen He reveals Himself gradually, so as to leave her calm, and by His *voice*, which stilled the seas.

3. To the disciples going to Emmaus.

4. On Easter evening to the disciples—*Pax vobis*—breath, priesthood of peace and calm.

5. On Low Sunday to St. Thomas—*Pax vobis* again.

6. This peace displayed in the subsequent conduct of the apostles.

7. Persevered in by our dear Lord all the forty days.

III. All this because He was God, for God is the God of calmness and peace.

1. The unworldliness of it all in itself is a proof of His Divinity.

2. Calmness is His spirit, and a token to us how far that spirit is on us.

3. Calmness of God in His Incomprehensible Self.

4. Unutterable calmness round about His throne.

5. Into that calmness we are day by day being drawn, by prayer, by sacraments, by the silent stealing away of life from under our feet.

O heavenly Jerusalem, city of light and of the Lamb, our true home, our real country, when will our exiled spirits pass from all this sound and noise and fatiguing distraction, into that joyous, boundless, endless peace of God of which the great apostle himself can only say that it surpasses all our understanding?

XXI.

SUNDAY WITHIN THE OCTAVE OF CORPUS CHRISTI.

I. One of the greatest surprises at our judgment will be the sight of what we might have done for God and have not done.

1. Natural talents unused.

2. Graces neglected.

3. Inspirations slighted or culpably unheard.

4. Opportunities wasted, and supernatural providences unperceived through want of a sense of the presence of God: amazing loss of souls through idleness alone.

5. Faith not converted into practice.

II. God the opposite of all this.

1. Full of the most considerate love of us.

2. Minute in His legislation and arrangement for us.

3. Marvellously faithful to His promises.

4. Economical, even while abundant, in His giving of grace.

5. Setting an immense value Himself on the least of His graces, because it cost His Son so much.

III. Example of all this in the mystery of the Blessed Sacrament.

1. The wonder of the Mass, yet our infrequency and indevotion.

2. The miracles of communion, yet the little change they make in us.

U.　　　　　　　　　　　　　　　ℬ

3. The potency of Benediction, yet how cold, how uninfluenced are our hearts.

4. The facility and opportunity of His presence in the Tabernacle, yet how unused, or how little used, or how badly used.

5. The reiteration of all these things makes our life an almost incomprehensible miracle: and yet we perversely manage to make it trivial, commonplace, childish, and *undivine.*

Yet Jesus is not a *little* grace! He is the eternal riches of the Father. He has been His Father's fascination and delight from all eternity. He has been the gladness, the glory, and the most dear treasure of the Holy Ghost, from all eternity, as He is at this hour. His own delight, oh unspeakable, unintelligible taste of a Divine Person! is to be with the children of men— and we treat Him as we do! The Father and the Holy Ghost follow Him to the altars of the Church, while He comes to satisfy His insatiable longing for human love by haunting the company of men. And *we* meanwhile? Do we lavish our riches on Him, give Him our time, put Him foremost among our occupations? Do we lavish our love even upon Him, our reverence, or our fear? A Catholic without enthusiasm for the Blessed Sacrament! Oh what manner of Judas is he? Ah, my brethren, you know, each of you in your hearts, how you treat the Blessed Sacrament. Jesus does not look you visibly in the face now; He shrouds His face in the white veils of His dear Sacrament. But if we saw His look, would it not be a look of reproachful sadness? Oh, can you not picture to yourself the piercing look of tenderest reproof which He will cast upon us, as He reminds us

of all this at the judgment? Truly if we go straight
to heaven, it will be no little purgatory to pass into
the gates of the Golden City under that dear and
intolerable look!

XXII.

THE LENT EXPOSITION OF THE BLESSED SACRAMENT.

The days of pilgrimage and sanctuary, with all their
peculiar graces, are renewed in the Exposition of the
Blessed Sacrament. But no sanctuary is equal in the
spiritual magnificence of a real presence to the Catholic
altar. Let us then prepare for this great gift by
renewing our faith in the presence of our dearest Lord.
Who is it that comes to us? Who is the Blessed Sacrament, who this Guest, upon whose created robes of
childlike white we are to gaze?

I. It is our Creator.

    1. The immensity of the world—the wisdom required
        to plan it—the power to put it into execution.

    2. The end of all creation was His own glory in
        obtaining our love.

    3. He knows our weaknesses—He has known us
        from all eternity—He seeks our love—He
        values it above ten thousand stars.

Think of Him during the seven days—think of Him
when choosing our souls out of possible souls—think
of Him burning the world up at the last, and saving
not our souls only, but our bodies also, from the conflagration.

U.

II. It is the Son of Mary.

1. Of like nature with us, not the less the Creator, though part of His own creation.

2. All Bethlehem, and Nazareth, and Calvary, are there—the memories are in His soul—the wounds are in His hands.

3. We had a place in that Sacred Heart during the agony, we have a place there now—He woos us to enter more deeply in.

We are men met together to worship our fellow-man, who is our God as well.

III. It is the Eternal.

1. He is coming who never had any beginning, who leans on none, has none to lean upon, unchangeable, and yet unspeakably changed.

2. He loved us eternally—there was never a time when we did not exist in His love: how overwhelming is this thought! He loves each one of us in Church, and changes not, though we have done so much to forfeit His exceeding love.

3. Now He desires to have us to spend the rest of eternity with Him—He comes to give graces —for the simple end of giving graces—He for that object is about to spend forty human hours of His long eternity in a special way with us, to fit us for our eternity with Him.

Oh sweet thought! Oh comforting sustaining truth! The years, as they go by so quietly and swiftly, are drawing us fast into His eternity, when He will welcome us to His own home, and press us to His Heart, and put aside His veils, and show us His face, and take the sight of it away from us no more.

XXIII.

THE LENT *QUARANT' ORE.*

The business of our sanctification is carried on by two sorts of opportunities, those which we impose upon or make for ourselves, and those which the Church in her office as mother is careful to supply us with; and these last advance us most because there is no self-will in them, and we have the Benediction of the Church.

I. God's choice of times and places.
    1. This is a feature in God's manner which is very much to be observed.
    2. Old Testament examples of it.
    3. Christian pilgrimages and seasons.
    4. Miraculous shrines and apparitions.
    5. The end of these is not only to confirm faith, but to destroy sin and increase holiness.

II. Lent is one of God's times.
    1. Apostolic institution: supernatural vigor of the Church all the world over.
    2. It is far more than the great feasts of the year.
    3. It is the spiritual rudder of the year.
    4. Fasting is a means, prayer the end.
    5. Those who cannot fast are the more obliged to prayer and interior mortification.

III. Church is one of God's places, especially at the time of Exposition.
    1. Exposition is a substantial part of Lent nowadays.
    2. More than La Salette, Loreto, or Palestine.

U.   ℞

3. Angels are amazed at the graces ready, and which only need our reverent taking.

4. What one Exposition could do if fervently corresponded to.

   (1.) For self. (2.) For the Church. (3.) Robbing Hell. (4.) Purgatory. (5.) Glory of heaven.

5. Oh for fervent persevering prayer! whether mental or vocal, with book or without, what matters; only let us pour out our whole souls in prayer.

XXIV.

THE SACRED HEART.

To-day's feast as refreshing as a cool wind in the wilderness.

Need of consolations in these times: nowhere to be found but in the Sacred Heart.

I. The Sacred Heart itself.

1. It is not a mere emblem.

2. But lives a human life this day.

   (1) In heaven.

   (2) In the Tabernacle.

   (3) It has been in us at Communion.

3. Its power, science, love, for He is God.

4. The touchingness of the devotion.

5. And He Himself revealed it.

II. What it is to us.

1. No other real shelter from the world.

2. Nor consolation in sorrow.

3. Nor home so kind.

U.   𝔇

4. Nor welcome so sure and sweet.
5. Nor such fulness of satisfaction.
6. Nor such abounding love.
7. Nor such assurance of heaven.
8. Nor such dear mercy when we have fallen.
9. Its maternal character—Mary-like.

III. It is so utterly our own.

1. The empire we exercise over it is like Mary's.
2. The place, a particular one, we have always occupied in it.
3. Its fidelity, and rewarding of little services.
4. The identity of its will and interests with our own.
5. Yet it is the cabinet of the treasures of the Godhead.

How hidden is this treasure! Comfort to us that it is hidden; for the world takes all from us that it can.

XXV.

THE SACRED HEART.

I have given them Thy word, and the world hath hated them, because they are not of the world.—St. John xvii. 14.

Earth is a rehearsing for heaven: yet the world forces us abroad; it will not let us face God and duty and the thought of eternal things. It is in this very thing that we must beat it down—be bold in the love of Jesus—and assert our liberty. Yet here is the secret of the Christian life. How shall we be in the world,

U.

yet out of it, upon the flood and riding safely on it, in the heat, but under shadow; in the storm, yet sheltered from it? By living in the Heart of Jesus. Ah! let us invoke the gentle St. John to get us grace to dwell continually as hermits in that sweet hermitage, as doves in the cleft rock. always in charitable activity, yet always in contemplation.—The Sacred Heart of Jesus—our model—our love—our sanctuary.

I. Its perpetual intention:—to glorify God—always speaking of it in St. John's Gospel—thirsting after it—the first great end of the Sacred Humanity.

II. Its interior occupation—(1) adoring, (2) annihilating self, (3) oblation of self, (4) incessant grieving for sinners and at them.

III. Its secret suffering: a secret consuming tormenting fire caused by love and sin from His Conception to His Cross, only the depths of that profound abyss may be poorly fancied from the few echoes that came up to the surface during the anguish of the Passion.

IV. Continual unbroken calm, putting away of all pleasing of self, and assuagement, as though He were in love with sorrow and interior bitterness. This is the mystery, this the long lesson of the Cross.

V. Horror of maxims of the world—He was Eternal Wisdom.

World.	Sacred Heart.
1. Esteem of greatness and glory.	*Quod altum est hominibus abominatio est ante Deum.*
2. Care of reputation.	*Saturabitur opprobriis.*

3. Spirit of policy and management.	*Columbæ—parvuli.*
4. Attachment to wills and ways.	*Subditus illis*—pleased not Himself.
5. Pursuit of pleasures.	United in itself all body and mind most shrink from, and that from choice.
6. Worship of comfort and conveniences.	Stable — flight — poverty — hard work — houselessness—benediction of the poor.

Ah! we have much to learn! but shall we sit down in idle despair?—O paradise! bright—beautiful—eternal —how strange sound the words of thy wisdom on this distracted earth : we have but to love—to love Him whom it is so hard not to love, so wonderful all men do not love—we have but to love, and all that is ours— thy brightness, thy beauty, thy eternity. Oh false and miserable and cruel world—this day we break faith with thee, solemnly and forever.

XXVI.

PERPETUAL FRESHNESS OF JESUS.

A deep changeableness in our nature—often against our will—making things grow dull to us easily, and making it hard for us to be faithful.

I. How even religious things grow wearisome.

1. Prayer, which was once so sweet.

U.

   2. Books, which it seemed we could feed upon all our life, and never want new ones.

   3. Services, so full of unction to our souls.

   4. Even sacraments, so fresh and exhilarating.

   5. But Jesus Himself never: He is always fresh.

II. The freshness of Jesus.

   1. He never tires us.

   2. He is always equally loving;

   3. Or rather each time more loving than before.

   4. Always the same, so far as regards fidelity.

   5. Always new, so far as regards His charms.

III. Experience of this.

   1. Christmases: He seems really newly come.

   2. Changes in life—He suits Himself to them.

   3. Sunshine—He makes it passing bright.

   4. Sorrow! ah, He is a new Jesus, so full of delightfullest consolation.

   5. We have left Him and returned—how do we find Him? Quite the same, yet altogether new.

IV. Experience of all things else.

   1 The world, its promises and its fulfilments.

   2. Our own will, its plans, wishes, enterprises.

   3. Pleasure, its transitory feverish excitement.

   4. Age—always looking onward—brings nothing like Jesus.

   5. Even religious changes—nothing satisfactory but Jesus.

And death—what think you death will bring? It has but one alternative, either everlasting darkness, or Jesus to be eternally old, everlastingly new, in His own bright land above.

· XXVII.

THE LIFE OF JESUS A LIFE OF LOVE.

What it is to love! and what to lead a life of love!
I. The life of Jesus a life of love.
   1. Love seemed to be His very life—His whole life.
   2. It was unintermitting.
   3. Deeply hidden, yet for ever flashing out.
   4. It swallowed up all other characteristics of His
      life.
II. His love's characteristics.
   1. Its utter disinterestedness.
   2. Its propensity of self-abasement.
   3. Its excesses, and its being given to excess.
   4. Its mixed character of human and divine.
   5. Yet evidently following some deep laws, not
      appreciated or understood by us. it reveals
      God to us. For this is the life most like the
      life of God.
III. His loves.
   1. Of God.
   2. Of His Mother.
   3. Of sinners. He seems to sacrifice the other two
      to this, as (1.) My God! why hast Thou forsaken
      Me? as if He so clung to men and loaded Him-
      self with their guilt, that the Father was com-
      pelled to forsake Him. (2.) Our Lady, whom
      He martyred for our sakes.
   4. It is our joy that we had even then a distinct and
      recognized share of that love.
Our lives must be copies of His.

U.

XXVIII.

OUR LORD'S LOVE OF US.

As the Father hath loved Me, I also have loved you.—St. John xv. 9.

Is there any sight in all creation we should so much wish to see as the place we occupy at this moment in the Heart of Jesus? We know that He really loves us, and immensely loves us: but how much, and with what kind of love? His own words quoted above answer this question. He loves us as the Father loved Him.

I. Now how did the Father love Him?

1. He loved Him eternally, with an untiring love, vehement yet peaceful, a love that was an immense joy to Himself, a divine love. Think what it is for us to be loved with a divine love!

2. He loved Him with an enormous love, an unimaginable love. It is hard to picture an ocean without a shore, or a world without an end. Yet this is the figure of the Father's love of Jesus, and therefore of the love of Jesus for us.

3. An eternal love, a ceaseless love, must necessarily be a love of undistracted detail; so that those words of Blosius come true, "He would not even allow a cold wind to blow upon His elect, unless He knew it was expedient for their salvation." *

4. But the most striking of all the features of the Father's love of Jesus, is that He loaded Him with crosses, cares, and sorrows: so will Jesus do to us.

* Institutio Spiritualis, cap. viii.

(1) Because His Father did so to Him.

(2) Because it is His longing to conform us to Himself.

(3) Because it is what is best for our souls.

Now, are we prepared for this? Do we take this view of our troubles? Alas! to strive against our cross, is to try to make Jesus love us less.

———

XXIX.

COME UNTO ME, ALL YE THAT ARE WEARY.

I. The intense happiness of Jesus in the Blessed Sacrament.

1. Because He is God, Whose life is everlasting joy.

2. Because of the abounding joys of His vast human Soul.

3. The intense pleasures of the senses of His glorified Body.

4. His joy in His Mother, the angels, the saints, and the Church on earth.

5. His joy in the hiding-place He has invented for Himself in the Blessed Sacrament.

Why then does He seek sinners as if He needed them? Can we, or such as we, be a joy to Him?

II. The life of sin. Have we not all once lived it?

1. All we break through to begin it—baptism, grace, faith.

2. Its poorness of pleasure.

3. Its rapid satiety.

U.

4. Its discomfort of remorse.

5. The chilling prospect of its consequences.

III. The invitation, Come unto Me, will be some *one* day sounded in our ears.

1. Can we believe our senses?

2. But to such great sinners as we are?

3. If to Jew or Pagan, still can it be to us who have fallen from Him.

4. His authority to speak, and His power to fulfil His promise.

5. The proofs of His sincerity are in the Blessed Sacrament—He has not tired these eighteen hundred years.

IV. The interview: Lord! what wilt Thou that I should do?

1. What penance?—only be sorry.

2. What reproof?—absolutely none.

3. How long a process is forgiveness?—momentary.

4. What forfeit?—none.

5. As if He was the obliged person, not we.

Is not all this incredible except to the strength of faith? Does not it baffle all understanding, and transcend all explanation? It is said of heaven, Eye hath not seen, &c.; is not the same true of the forgiveness of a sinner? It is the first step to heaven, an earnest that He means to give us heaven, only let us hold fast and persevere. Heaven will soon be here; it will steal upon us almost before we are aware; and life with all its trials will be like a speck in the distant past, the memory of which will be almost forgotten in the beautiful delights of our celestial home. You and I, brethren, have seen many here in darkness and in struggle, in sin, in repentance,

U,   Ɖ

in the fight of poverty, the coolness of the world's neglect, and the achings of a comfortless and hard sick-bed,
who now are in the Bosom of Jesus in heaven, so bright
and glorious, so radiant and beautiful, that we should
die if we beheld them. O dearest brethren! only love
Jesus, and what an unspeakable eternity is ours.

XXX.

THE TEARS OF JESUS.*

Man is never so like God as when he is consoling
the afflicted; and this is one of the functions of the
Confraternity; it reaches it by prayer; so consider—

I. The tears of Jesus.

  1. Angels beholding with wonder the first tears of
    Adam and Eve.

  2. They look up to the Eternal Word—they will one
    day see Him weeping man's tears.

  3. The tears of Bethlehem, for Himself, for sin, for
    sorrow, for us.

  4. At the grave of Lazarus—in sympathy with the
    sorrow of the sisters.

  5. On the Mount of Olives over beautiful Jerusalem
    —over sin and sin's punishments.

II. The lessons of those tears.

  1. The nature of sorrow.

    (1) It is an angel from God.

    (2) If it is punishment, it is that we may escape
      punishment in another world.

     * After the battle of Inkerman.

(3) To make our hearts soft and gentle to others.

(4) To conform us to the likeness of Jesus: how He loves those in sorrow.

(5) Grief is no imperfection: tears of resignation are sweet to the Eye of God.

2. More confidence in Jesus.

(1) What confidence means, and how little we have when proved.

(2) Sinners, why He loved them most of all.

(3) Littlenesses and meannesses of spiritual persons. Oh He knows them so well and feels for them so compassionately.

(4) We are inclined to despair because of temptations—why, your own mother will not guide you so gently as Jesus will.

(5) The *Name* of Jesus is our trust—Thou shalt call His name Jesus: for He shall save His people from their sins.

XXXI.

WITHOUT JESUS IN THE WORLD.*

I. My dear brethren! what should we do without Jesus in the world? We have to live, we have to die, we have to be saved. Oh what should we do without Jesus in the world? Dearest Lord! you see I am going to dare to speak of Him to you in His own presence.

* Lent Exposition of the B. Sacrament, 1856.

U.　　　　　　　　　　　　　　　　　　　Ⓡ

1. In sorrow what should we do without Jesus?
2. Iu illness and pain?
3. Iu poverty and hardships?
4. In the loss of those we love?
5. In the hour of death?

II. Jesus—because He shall save His people from their sins.

1. Look at heathen, what if we were like them?
2. Look at sinners, what if we were like them?
3. Those outside the Church, what if we were like them?
4. Ourselves in past years, what if we were like them?
5. Without Jesus, where should we be now?

And can we ever spare Him—now? in death? in judgment? after that? never, never.

III. And the Blessed Sacrament is our own very Jesus.

1. The Jesus who loved the poor.
2. The Jesus who wept over His dead friend.
3. The Jesus who consorted with sinners.
4. The Jesus who comforted the sorrowful.
5. The Jesus who feels more anxious that we should be saved than we do ourselves.

And what is the Blessed Sacrament a sign of? His unspeakable fidelity. He yearns over us while we stay away: He implores us while we ungraciously refuse His love: He clings to us even in our sins: He longs to take us in His arms, and bear us away to heaven, and to have us with Himself for evermore. Our beloved Brother! and shall we refuse to go? Oh no, no! let us pour out our hearts before Him—let us tell Him how deeply, how dearly we love Him—let us beg Him to save us in spite of our own selves,

U.   ℞

and to make us love Him more and more and more, and to bear with us a little longer, and we will serve Him better, and die in His arms, and then go with Him to His Father, and be at rest forever.

———

XXXII.

THERE IS NOW THEREFORE NO CON-DEMNATION TO THEM THAT ARE IN CHRIST JESUS.

Many words of wonderful beauty have been uttered in the world which have lived on for generations like music that could not die—but few more beautiful than this, which came to St. Paul while making tents at Corinth, and which he wrote to the Romans.

I. No condemnation!　Is not this just what we want?

  1. Feeling of people who are on trial, as we are: it is just our business as creatures to be judged.

  2. Conscience judges us within, and the world without: we fear the stern truth of the inward judge, and we chafe under the invariable unkindliness of the outward one: all happiness and unhappiness depend on these judgments.

  3. But God, Who knows all, understands all, sees the secret truth of all, and is unutterably holy.

  4. To be condemned by God; it is very easy, very likely; all merit it: to know that we should be saved—is it not heaven beforehand?

  5. Well, there is now therefore no condemnation to them that are in Christ Jesus.

U.　　　　　　　　　　　　　　　　ꞕ

II. But who are in Christ Jesus?

   1. Those who have the true faith and practise it.

   2. Those who have a great sorrow for their sins.

   3. Those who love others for our Lord's sake.

   4. Those who are *trying* to be holy even if they are not so yet.

   5. Those who *wish* to love Jesus, though they do not *feel* as if they loved Him yet.

Ah, my dear brethren, you may have many years to live yet; many temptations, much unkindliness, much sorrow, much pain, many unworthy and simple imperfections; but through it all you can truly keep saying to yourselves, as men murmur songs they love, those beautiful song-like words of our dear St. Paul: There is now therefore no condemnation to them that are in Christ Jesus.

XXXIII.

THE FIRST SIGHT OF THE FACE OF JESUS.

Seek ye My Face! Thy Face, Lord, will we seek! What it is to have Jesus with us; how it increases our longing to see His face; what joy and light and life would that veiled Face pour into our very inmost souls!

I. Our first sight of Jesus.

   1. We shall actually see Him, and it cannot now be very long.

U.

2. But we must go through grave and solemn things to reach this sight.

3. St. Simeon's long years and then his *Nunc Dimittis*—is it a figure of our lives?

4. We must die, and are daily nearing the time.

5. The more we love God, the more real must be our fear of death.

6. The act of death—the first moment of the separate soul.

7. First sight of Jesus—judgment begins. What will our thoughts be? Saints have said they should be almost distracted with the sweetness of that first sight of His Face. Alas! I shall tremble, and be first ashamed, and then afraid.

II. We lose sight of that Face again

1. Judgment is over—wherever we go, shall we ever forget the beauty of that Face?

2. If to Purgatory, it is no light thing to dwell among those fires.

3. The pain of parting with that Face; for long years we may perhaps see it no more.

4. And yet it will haunt us like a ray of light in our punishment.

5. Yet is Purgatory inevitable?

6. No! To avoid venial sin, to break with the world, to have an abiding sorrow for sin, to be patient—these are ways of avoiding Purgatory altogether.

7. Perhaps a particular devotion to the presence of Jesus in the Blessed Sacrament may have a peculiar power to avoid or shorten Purgatory.

Oh let no one be without hope of escaping Purgatory.

It is less hard than many think. The punishment itself is fearful—the delay of being with Jesus is intolerable to a loving heart. Oh after a weary life, is there still to be another weary waiting for our deliverance and our rest? If we must burn, let it be with the fire of love now, not with the fires of chastisement hereafter!

Part Second.

THE SACRED HUMANITY OF JESUS.

SECTION II.

THE PASSION.

I.

*CALVARY.**

CHAPTER I.

THE PASSION; ITS HISTORICAL, DOCTRINAL, AND MYSTICAL CHARACTER.

I. The darkness of an eclipse—it gradually lightens—the white towers of a city not far inland at the end of the Mediterranean—slowly being disclosed against the darkness is the Body of Jesus hanging on the Cross, facing the grand west, disfigured by suffering; and a broken-hearted mother standing beneath the Cross now wet with blood.

1. This is the fountain of all supernatural things, and flows both before and behind.

2. Henceforth the history of the world can never get from under the influence of this.

3. The sorrow and happiness of each individual soul starts at the foot of the Cross.

4. It is the only earthly object of any real abiding value: all is dross compared to it; it is the marriage of heaven and earth.

5. Its effects are eternal and unspeakable.

* The twelve following chapters are the sketch of a proposed treatise.

169

II. The Passion considered as a history.

   1. The congruous end of the Thirty-three Years of
the Incarnate Word.

   2. The Supper Room.

   3. The Garden.

   4. The City.

   5. The Mount.

     On earth we can get no higher idea of God than
that which the Passion gives us.

III. Considered as a doctrine.

   1. The two Natures and the one Person.

   2. The accomplishment of Redemption: a different
idea from the Incarnation—(1.) Of glory. (2.)
Of suffering.

   3. The Sacraments come out of it.

   4. The daily sacrifice is a continuation of it.

   5. The unnecessary suffering in·it an abyss of
divinest doctrine. It is also remarkable that
our Lord's satisfactions were not in voluntary
penances, but in things which came on Him
through His Father's will—this is a characteristic
of His sanctity—the consolation of it to us.

IV. Considered as affecting the ritual of the Church.

   1. The Blessed Sacrament the living Lord.

   2. The connection of the Passion with the
Blessed Sacrament—mass, communion, use of
the Blessed Sacrament as reparation—Holy
Sepulchre.

   3. In the Calendar—The Church nowhere drama-
tizes so much—then there are memorial feasts
all the year round.

   4. As a devotion characterized by (1) Its abiding-
ness; (2) Universality; (3) Connection with

other devotions; (4) Variety, Stations, Wounds,
Words, Trials, Blood, Dolors.

5. The calm grave endless thought and memory of
the Passion by angels and souls even amid the
joys of Heaven.

V. Its mystical character.

1. It produces a whole inward life of its own, on
peculiar supernatural principles.

2. To effect this more abundantly God has poured
abundant revelations of its details into the
Church through the contemplative saints.

3. He has also impressed the Passion on them in
physical and moral miracles.

4. He has strewn over the world the instruments
and relics of the Passion. Just think what it
is to be in the same room with a piece of the
true Cross.

5. All holiness, high and low, is imitation of the
Passion, while the Passion has and communicates a substantial virtue which enables us to
imitate it, and exercises a mysterious attraction
over us.

The fervor of the primitive Church was owing perhaps to a livelier memory of the Passion. The days
of creation—their wonders—these days were more
wonderful, Thursday, Friday, and Saturday: the
Triduo of the Passion was the creation of an invisible
world.

. II.

THE EXCESS OF THE PASSION.

The beauty of sorrow—its poetry, romance, philosophy, and literature—the pathos of God's world—none like to the Passion—it is a very world, the flowers of suffering made beautiful by the innocence and also the divinity of Him Who bore it: we must get a view of its extent.

I. The Thirty-three Years up to the Passion were a Passion in themselves.

   1. Sufferings of the first twelve years—poverty, weariness, use of· reason, prevision of Passion, view of sin.

   2. Sufferings of the Hidden Life—the same, with toil and Joseph's death.

   3. Sufferings of the three years' Ministry, homelessness, disciples, persecutions, fatigue, failure.

   4. Steady, incessant, vehement, energetic view of the Passion throughout.

   5. His Mother involved in the same law of suffering, although exempt from the law of sin.

Thus the Passion is not one separate mystery, but the blood-stained diadem of all.

II. The Mystery of unnecessary suffering in the Passion.

   1. Why it was so long, and not done all at once.

   2. Infinite value of each one of His satisfactions.

   3. Prodigality of everything—pains bodily and mental, shame, all exhausted—it is hard to conceive of more.

4. It cannot have been really unnecessary—this is a profound mystery.

5. Probable reasons, at least on the surface.

    (1) Because being God, He would do all things in the most excellent and superabundant way. We do not sufficiently look at the Passion on God's side. It is a many-sided mystery.

    (2) In order to make a more royal satisfaction to the justice of God.

    (3) To give us a deeper and more dread view of the horror of sin.

    (4) To exhibit the illimitable excesses of the divine mercy.

    (5) Because it was all for love, and of love.

    (6) That God's glory in creation, and that in the Sacred Humanity alone, might far surpass the curse of sin.

    (7) To show what manner of service *we* should render to Him, and to take away our hardness of heart, which nothing short of omnipotence can soften.

III. The Deep Sea.

1. The number of the sufferings—count up from the Garden to the Cross. The *unknown* sufferings, like the unknown perfections of God. There is a sort of *secrecy* in the Passion: half is not told; men could not bear the details; the revelations of saints disclose now and then these secret depths in the Passion.

2. The variety: every affection of the heart, every faculty of the mind, every sense and nerve of the body.

3. Intense degree of them—in themselves—from the circumstances—and to Him.

4. Concentration of them in a short time—no respite to collect self, &c.

5. Aggravating circumstances of them—site, time, company, presence of mother, spectators, and their malice.

.6. Inward circumstances—mental perturbation and oppression, shame, injustice, view of each kind and class of sin for which He suffered. ·

7. The indifference of those for whom He suffered —this was unbearable to His Sacred Heart. They were inflicting, and did not know it, a most dreadful outward Passion on One who had already an unspeakable Passion within.

8. Aggravation from those who afflicted Him— (1) Rude Romans, (2) His own Jews, (3) Powers of Hell, (4) Mary, (5) Eternal Father—think of Him with these five enemies hemming Him in in seeming appalling alliance.

9. The horror of that for which He suffered, viz., sin.

10. The love with which He suffered was of itself an indescribable martyrdom.

11. Augmentation of suffering from the exquisiteness of His Human Nature.

12. Augmentation of it by His Divine Nature— (1.) What it withheld, and so contrast. (2.) Strengthening Him to bear. (3.) Adding something peculiar to each torture. .

IV. Results.

1. All martyrdoms as nothing to His sufferings (against Suarez).

2. All human suffering, inclusive of seven dolors, far outstripped by them.

3. In intensity they exceed all the pains of purgatory because of His Soul.

4. In sensible pain they possibly exceed in intensity all the pain of the lost, and of their bodies after the resurrection.

5. He Himself could of God's absolute power have suffered more—this is all we can say.

6. Only His Divinity without alleviating any enabled Him to bear all.

7. We shall perhaps never understand them—St. Jerome says that what our Lord suffered on the Thursday night will not *all* be known until the doom, when the Father will reveal it according to the prophecy of Nahum, *Revelabo cunctis regibus et gentibus ignominiam tuam.*

What a scene! God out in the darkness of that night, amid the mountainous billows of that storm—where all humanity and all angelic nature would have foundered and gone down: God! God! the Eternal God! That night, in that dark sea, with that affliction and fatigue, my soul was saved!

———

.

III.

THE BODILY PAINS.

The *Ecce Homo!* a worm and no man: His beauty crushed out of Him: the nature almost trodden out of Him; life held in that mangled wreck by simple power.

U.

I. The bitterness of bodily pain.
  1. Our own experienced inability to bear it.
  2. All generations have made their punishments out
     of it.
  3. The way in which it afflicts the soul.
  4. The revolution it works in our characters.
  5. The amazing merits and crowns of martyrdom.
  6. Purgatory and Hell.
  7. By this pain was redemption to be effected.
II. General view of the Bodily Pains of the Passion.
  1. Their length—some eighteen hours—but especially
     long to the swift operations of His Soul.
  2. Their variety, and their being constantly inter-
     mingled; and all over His Body. Revelation
     to the V. Paola Maria Scalza, that the Wounds
     and Disfigurements of our Lord's Body were
     above all that had been said, written, or
     thought.*
  3. Their keenness, from their severity and rapidity,
     and from His sensitiveness.
  4. Their all being violently contemporaneous one
     with another.
  5. Without respite, or refreshment, or time to collect
     self; save only visit of angel in the garden.
III. Their kinds.
  1. Stunning, aching bruises, Cedron, up the hill, the
     Via Dolorosa.
  2. Stricture of ropes.
  3. Flesh wounds down to the bone, and all over.
  4. Dislocations, with ropes, of jaws when struck,
     and stretching on the Cross, and hanging
     from it.

* Vita, pp. 289, 290.

5. Excessive bleeding—intense anguish caused by it, no repose allowed.
6. Stabbing through nerves with thorns and nails.
7. Flaying, with the two strippings.
8. Tearing flesh off, as martyrs had, at the scourging.
9. Cold, Cedron, the night.
10. Fatigue to its uttermost limit of throbbing, dull, seemingly impossible pain.
11. Hunger all those hours, and with such nervous suffering.
12. Thirst after the loss of blood.
  N.B. Breaking of bones and fire were the only two pains not applied.
IV. His Sacred Limbs.
1. Head—blows, hair, crowning.
2. Eyes—filled with clotted blood, inverted lashes —blows.
3. Mouth—swollen with blows, teeth loosened, lips cracked, tongue swollen.
4. Face—blows, spittings, thorns half down the brow.
5. Shoulders—raw with scourgings, laid open at stripping.
6. Arms—ropes, bruises, scourges, out of joint.
7. Hands—blood from under nails with ropes, nails on the Cross.
8. Breast—torn with scourges, painfully distended to cracking.
9. Sides—bones laid bare with scourging, bruised and livid with blows of staves.
10. Knees—broken with falls, skin hanging down, as in various revelations.

U

11. Feet—bleeding, sore, nailed, dislocated, wrung
   into unnatural positions.
12. Heart—fever, anguish, bursting, fainting, irre-
   gular spasms.
V. The instruments of His Passion.
   1. Ropes.
   2. Gauntlet.
   3. Scourges.
   4. Thorns.
   5. Reed.
   6. Spears to prick Him with in the Via Crucis.
   7. Hammer and nails.   .
VI. His five Blessed Senses—mixed bodily and mental
   sufferings.
   1. Hearing.
      Blasphemy—denial—Mary's sighs—awfulness of
      the cries of a crowd.
   2. Seeing.
      Sin—Mother—instruments of Passion—absence of
      apostles—wicked faces.
   3. Smelling.
      Odors of sin, which sickened the saints—corrup-
      tion of Golgotha—the well on Thursday night.
   4. Tasting.
      Gall, blood, mud, spittle, hunger, thirst.
   5. Touching.
      Scourge, thorns, nails, men's rude hands.
VII. His death.
   1. Not the gradual failing of power, so as to be
      easy.
   2. The horror of the position to die in.
   3. The combined unity of all the pains mounting to
      one head and crisis.

4. The loud cry, so unlike Him.

5. It has been said that the greatest pain in the Passion was the act of death, because of the inexplicably perfect union of His Body and Soul.

Oh the tranquillity of the Dead Christ on Mary's lap; we breathe now, like men just saved from shipwreck, after this roaring sea of horrors, which has stunned and bewildered us, has gone in its great ebb far down the beach. This is that sweet stillness round the tomb, that fatigue in tranquil rest recovering its bruised heart and scattered mind, which makes the peace of Holy Saturday almost a dearer gift than the joy of Easter.

IV.

THE MENTAL SUFFERINGS.

The feelings of Jesus, when for the last time, whatever day it was, He woke from sleep before His Passion.

‑I. The mystery of our Lord's sleep.

1. Not suspending the use of reason, nor the capability of meriting.

2. Peopled with the prevision of His Passion.

3. Scantily taken through all the Three-and-thirty Years.

4. Yet a real rest to His Sacred Humanity, the more so from His sinlessness, and perfection of Body.

5. But His waking was not a gradual dawning on Him when He cast off drowsiness; clear as an

Asiatic landscape, defined as a Greek sea-view, lay His Passion close at hand.

II. Mental sufferings.

1. Mind has much greater capabilities of suffering than the body, in variety, acuteness, depth, so that there is hardly any limit to mental suffering, except physical death.

2. And by His divine power that limit in His own case was miraculously thrust back.

3. In purgatory and hell the pains of sense are incomparably below those of mind.

4. The way in which apprehension magnifies coming evils, and is a more real suffering than the actual endurance.

5. But who shall estimate rightly the capabilities of His Soul and Heart, or the wonderful torture of wounded feelings and violated sensibilities in Him?

III. The mental suffering of the Passion considered generally. •

1. Fear. Intense pain of it. (1.) Foresight. (2.) Faces of multitude. (3.) Their cries. (4.) Being hated. (5.) Eternal Father. He was like a hunted animal, yet was the great God omnipotent.

2. Horror. (1.) Of the Passion. (2) From the vision of sin. (3.) From the excesses of un-appeased justice.

3. Feeling of defilement. (1.) Clothed in all sins. (2.) Stuck close to Him. (3.) Burnt into His Soul.

4. Shame, as if He would have hidden Himself in nothingness; Adam's shame was nothing to His.

U.

5. Sadness for the lost, for all sinners; for all that sin should make any of us suffer.

6. Compassion, for each and all of us in our lost state. St. Bonaventure thinks His Compassion was a greater suffering than His Passion, not only for each soul lost, but for each pain of the elect: it was co-extensive (1.) With the Blessed Virgin Mary's dolors. (2.) All martyrdoms. (3.) All griefs. (4.) All voluntary austerities. (5.) All our own private sorrows and pains.

7. Love as it were barbed and poisoned every shaft that strung Him.

IV. The Agony was the Crucifixion of His Soul, and may be taken as a specimen of these Mental Sufferings. Look at the process of the Agony, and see how the pains took possession of His Soul progressively for three interminable hours.

1. Fear, with its alarms, unsettlements, shadows, panics, chills.

2. Disgust, as if it was all so loathsome that He could not persevere.

3. Weariness, so that all power to make head against the commonest sorrow was gone.

4. Drenching bitterness, so that He had no vicissitude, no relief of posture in His mind, no refuge in Himself, no privacy in His own Nature.

5. Fight in His Human Nature, the novelty of it, and the vehemence.

6. Tightness, or narrowness, and anxiety, as if He was pressed in some spiritual instrument of torture.

7. Desolation, deep darkness, accumulation and

acme of interior trials and anguishes, all void
and vast around Him, with nothing to lean
against.

8. Crushing oppression, as if all His faculties were
squeezed into one immense sort of suffering.

9. Exhaustion, such as would have made death
sweet, such a mixture of restlessness and the
loss of all power of exertion.

10. Rush of love into this wounded Nature, like
drenching a wound in spirit or in acid; it was
like goads. St. Bernardine says that the alter-
nate charges of fear and love against each other,
and with all the power of His Soul, caused the
Bloody Sweat.

11. Loss of blood and consequent increase of all the
former mental tortures left a complete wreck.

12. Aggravating circumstances. (1.) Multiplicity of
the objects which distracted Him. (2.) The
vehemence of the impressions they made on His
Soul; angels could not have borne it. So that
His Will seemed to totter: one angel, Michael
or Gabriel, comes to comfort Him. If Michael,
can that be the Word for whom he fought in
heaven his grand battle? if Gabriel, he thinks
of Mary on Annunciation night, the same 25th
March.

V. The revelations to Battista Varani are like an
insight into the character of our Lord, and his
personal feelings as Man; this is their special
beauty.

1. First Dolor. From the view of those who
should be lost eternally: like dislocation of
limbs—the eternity of the separation, *quel mai*

U.   ℞

mi cruciava: but as separate from Him, their torments after death did not enter into this woe.

2. Second Dolor. From the sins of the elect, and all their pains, penances, persecutions, and temptations. As if He had millions of eyes, and each eye in the insupportable agony which the eye can feel. As not separate from Him, the pains of purgatory did enter into this woe.

3. Third Dolor. From His Mother's sufferings. This was the one alleviation, the only one He did crave for, that His Mother should be exempt from suffering. With filial tenderness and many tears did He pray His Father for this. It was like all His Passion a second time on the crushed Soul and sore raw Body.

4. Fourth Dolor. From the grief of Magdalen. Except His Mother, none grieved as she. He had told John secrets which supported him. John would have crucified Him himself to get the good which, when leaning on his Master's Bosom, he learned was to come from the Passion. This upheld him; but Magdalen knew nothing of this. Heaven and earth seemed gone to her; as her glorious love was without order or measure, so was her woe. This was why He appeared to her at the Resurrection.

5. Fifth Dolor. From the dismay and desolation of His Apostles and disciples. His grief in His last sermon to them on Thursday night.

6. Sixth Dolor. From the treachery of Judas, after all He had done for him. "When I bent over to wash his feet, My long hair fell over My face,

and when I pressed his foot to My mouth and kissed it, I bathed it a second time with hot tears of love."

7. Seventh Dolor. From the ingratitude of the Jews. All the old history, and then, Crucify Him, crucify Him! That Thursday night long centuries ago, the Exodus of the chosen people from Egypt, and now the Exodus of all Humanity through the dry bed of our Lord's Soul out of the darkness of the land of the shadow of death.

8. Eighth Dolor. The ingratitude of all creatures. To each of us He has done what He did to Judas, to each of us what He did for the Jews, and yet we love Him as we do. B. Battista Varani,* when she saw Him in such a "hell of amorous pains," almost doubted His being God : but rather the very excess of the love, .o far beyond either the reason or romance of earthly love, might have shown her that it could be God alone who could love in such a way.

* * *

V.

THE SHAME.   ·

Look at that figure in the streets of Jerusalem, the unresisting Captive; men are pulling His beard, spitting in His face, and kicking Him, as if they were driving some stupid ox to slaughter, while then as ever count-

---

* See Battista's postscriptum about devotion to interior and to exterior pains, in the French life of her, p. 155.

less angels, awe-smitten and in ecstacy with the beauty
of His holiness, are singing *Sanctus, Sanctus, Sanctus,*
round His throne!

I. The Worship of the beautiful Incarnate Word.

    1. In heaven, since the trial of the angels, and all
through the Three-and-thirty years.

    2. The dignity of His Sacred Humanity, and the
inconceivable glory prepared for It.

    3. It was both sun and moon to the whole enormous
heaven : one spark could lighten all the earth.

    4. To Him belongs the right of judging all men ;
He has ere now judged the smiters and the
spitters.

    5. To see Him is to be happy eternally : it needs no
more.

II. Phenomenon of contempt of God.

    1. It is earth's lowest depth of sin—the stupidity
of earth is necessary to it—hell is too intelligent
to have it.

    2. It combines hatred and indifference about God in
one act.

    3. It only comes out in great sinners ; and seems
to rise round saints, as if their exceeding holiness drew it out of the most pestilential part of
our corruption.

    4. In our degree we all misjudge God ; it is the
grand grief of those who love Him.

    5. Hell swallows up contempt in fear ; contempt is
earth's own peculiar affront to God.

III. Contempts and insults and shame of the Thirty-
three Years.

    1. His poverty and obscurity and dwelling place.
Can any good thing come out of Nazareth ?

2. His wisdom. Is a devil and is mad. (John iii.)
How doth this man know letters, having never
learned? (John vii.) We know God spoke to
Moses, but as to this man we know not from
whence He is. (John ix. 29.)
3. His doctrine. Called a Samaritan and a heretic.
4. His power. His miracles were attributed to the
devil and to magic.
5. His innocence. Called (1.) A sinner. (2.) Glutton
and wine-bibber (Matt. xi.) (3.) Seducer of the
people (Luke xxiii.) (4.) Prevaricator of the
law. (5.) Blasphemer (John ix.)

IV. Shame and indignities of the Passion.
1. Words—the opprobrious acts doubtless not half
recorded.
2. Actions—blows, kicks, pulling hair, spitting,
mock homage, *Ecce Homo.*
3. Thoughts—cowardice, vile magician, stupid fool.
4. Manner—Annas, Caiphas, Herod, Pilate, all
others: death by crucifixion, thieves.
5. Circumstances—His triumph on Palm Sunday,
the feast and multitude.
6. From whom it all came—His Jews, those whom
He had fed and healed, those who had cried
Hosanna.
7. Sheer barbarities, hell-inspired blasphemies—
scene at Herod's court.*

V. What was wounded by this shame.
1. His love—contempt is the hardest of all things
for love to bear—and then it was such love and
such contempt.

* v. page 132.

2. The gracefulness of His patience—He felt how this aggravated their sin.

3. His honor and reputation—how nature feels this, and His nature most of all, as being most sensitive.

4. His venerable dignity—He had always been so mature and grave, and unseemliness was torture to Him.

5. His intellectual perceptions—of what was right, and due to Him, and base in them.

6. His modesty—especially ·in the stripping, both for the scourging and the crucifixion.

7. His holiness—by coarseness, rudeness, sin, scurrility, blasphemy, insolence.

8. His Divine Majesty—who can tell the horror of this to His Holy Soul?

VI. The mystery of what shame was in His Soul.

1. In us shame is chiefly the undue revelation of our true selves, of that which we most wish to keep concealed.

2. The intense suffering of shame.

   (1) Its keen penetrativeness into every recess of our nature.

   (2) Its nervous raw feeling, becoming unbearable, like touching the quick of a wound.

   (3) The way in which it prostrates all our powers.

   (4) It makes everything around us an instrument of suffering.

   (5) It drives us from our kind, into a mental solitude.

   (6) It surrounds us with darkness, deluding, puzzling, bewildering us.

   (7) Its confusion is the painful death of all that

U.

is most sensitively alive within us. And
yet, for the most part, all this comes from
the laying bare of our true selves.

3. Its office.

   (1) The shame of the Passion is dwelt upon in
Scripture as an essential element in it.

   (2) Its presence in all holiness: all saints are in
their measure made by shame.

   (3) What it was in His Soul we can only guess.
He doubtless had shame from many things
which we are too obtuse and coarse to
understand.

4. We may guess that in Him it was.

   (1) A false imputation of what was not due to
Him, and the mere imputation of which
was suffering to His pure Soul.

   (2) It was an accumulation of opprobrious and
vile and ludicrous positions in which He
was placed, which to His keen sensibilities
were inconceivably more so than they could
be to us.

   (3) It was like the flaying alive of the unimaginable modesty of His Sacred Humanity.

   (4) It was the glare of publicity, to shyness
which eyes looked through as if they were
swords.

   (5) It came upon Him when weakened and
crushed by tortures both of mind and body.

   (6) It was a violence to the tranquil depths of
His Humility, digging them deeper all the
while by its outrages.

   (7) It was immensely heightened by the sense of
injustice.

    (8) *Glory* was as it were the natural life and
        repose of His Soul because of the Hypo-
        static Union.

    (9) His Divine Person may have been in this
        respect a source of suffering to His Holy
        Soul.

The shameful Way of the Cross, His Mother bathed
in shame: the blasts of the Roman trumpets in the
streets reminded Him, if He ever needed His self-
collection reminded, of the angelic trumpet of the Day
of Doom—that day when all creation, even its holiest
heights, shall be put to shame, and God's lovely purity
gleam unspeakably bright above us, through the holy
Soul of our dearest Lord and Judge.

VI.

OUTWARD DEMEANOR AND INWARD DISPOSITIONS.

The rough men of sequestered Nazareth, when they
were sad, used to say, " Let us go and see Mary's Son!"
This was revealed by our Lady to St. Bridget. We
have treated of the bodily sufferings and mental sufferings, and the shame; now all these three things affect
outward demeanor and inward dispositions : we must
bear those three chapters in mind now, and see how He
bore up under them.

  I. The external beauty of our Lord.

    1. Everything about Jesus was full of living grace:
       nothing was merely exterior.

2. His beauty and venerable appearance, breeding holiness, yet attracting sinners.
3. It was the reflection of His holiness, and even the working of His Divine Nature.
4. This beauty was part of Mary's love of Him.
5. It is part of the joy of heaven at this hour.
6. How it added to the pathos of the Passion amid those harsh voices and dreadful faces.
7. While it was defaced, it still remained venerable and attractive as a spell.

II. His manner during the Passion.

1. His unselfishness, and unobtrusive considerateness, as Let these go their way; also His words on the cross.
2. Voluntary obedience, as in the garden when men fell before Him.
3. Kind words, and grave pitiful tone of voice, never changed or quickened or heightened.
4. His look under the worst indignities was full of mild forgiving sorrow.
5. The beauty of His patience was so imperturbable and winning.
6. His silence was the more wonderful because of His eloquence, and His exquisite sense of injustice, which last so rouses our nature, even in reading history. .
7. Yet He was neither stunned nor stupefied, but collected, sensitive, attentive, observant, prompt to the last. And all this with such natural grace that we hardly come to think of it until we meditate.

III. His demeanor to those who came near Him.

1. To St. Peter—in the supper room—when sleeping —after the denial—then, as if He carried His

loving thoughtfulness unbroken through cross, and death, and limbus, and resurrection, He says, Go and tell Peter.

2. To St. John—on His bosom at supper—in the garden—at the foot of the cross.

3. Judas—making three attempts to soften him, one in the supper room, eating out of the same dish; yet the others were not surprised; this shows how usual this courtesy was.

4. Jews—He wept over the city from the hilltop—in the garden His gentleness—women in Via Crucis—no reproach—no anger at the cry of *crucifige*—prayer on the cross.

5. Pilate—sent his wife to Him—admission of less fault.*

6. Herod—His silence with the excommunicated sinner—His dignity overawing any but a brutal mind, combined with the sweetness of childlike unresisting humility.

7. The thief—sweet words—instant forgiveness.

8. His mother—in the Via Crucis—on the cross—with less sweetness, as if He were in full intelligence with her, and treated her on a sort of equality.

9. To us—with our sins and waywardness—His thought for all—His Sacred Heart almost smiling on us with encouragement and welcome through the dun eclipse on Calvary.

IV. The inward beauty of our Lord.

1. Interior beauty compared to exterior—not the natural gifts of all angels are equal to one poor soul in the lowest state of grace.

* John xix. 11.

U,

2. Not all saints' and angels are equal to Mary, nor countless Maries to the soul of Jesus.

3. Wherein it consisted—union with God—merits acquired—sublimity of dispositions—their intensity.

4. All this was heightened by the illumination of His faculties, the capacity of His affections, the order of His appetites, and the serenity of His sensitive nature.

5. Then there was the glory of His Divinity which was shed so sweetly, softly, fittingly over all : the point of contact of His two Natures, riveted together, yet unconfused ; this union, or junction, is itself the most unsurpassed of all created beauties.

6. To us all this is more beautiful, because it is for us.

V. His interior dispositions.

1. The most unbroken peace.

2. Unspeakable conformity of will with the Father.

3. Inconceivable horror of sin.

4. Incomparable tenderness and allowance to sinners.

5. Undistracted love of each one of us.

6. The royalty of His spirit of sacrifice: restraint of consolation, &c.

7. His thirst for suffering.

8. The keen presence of every natural human feeling : no insensibility, nor loss of humanness such as *perhaps* some saints had.

9. His intense adoration of the justice and sanctity of God.

O my beautiful Lord! Like the moon on wild nights, the clouds of Thy Passion crowded round Thee, and thou movedst on in Thy heavenly gentleness,

U.   ℞

softening and silvering all things around, so that Thou
art still concealing what Thou hast done for us, Thy
very beauty making Thy Passion seem less a Passion
than it really was!

———

VII.

THE SOLITARINESS.

In the vastness and crowdedness of Creation there
is something overwhelming in the Unity of God.—
The Trinity seems to *suve* the solitude of the Unity—
so also in the haunted darkness and wild clamors of
the Passion, it is terrible to think of the loneliness of
Jesus, the one Mediator between God and man.

I. Solitude:—the solitary saints are the fewest in
    number—the most unknown—have the highest
    vocation.

1. How it ties our nature down to its deepest depths
    and brings up strange things.

2. Impossibility of not leaning on things to love,
    and in this life on created things.

3. Desertion and estrangement are hard to bear,
    because of the loneliness they bring.

4. The solitude of being misunderstood, and being
    out of sympathy with those around.

5. The loss of friends desolating and diminishing
    our circle—leaving fewer to love us, fewer for
    us to love.

6. Old age is a kind of solitude—only insensibility
    tempers it, and God is perhaps more with us.

7. Sickness is a drawing of us into still farther
    solitude—yet kind ministries are round.

8. Death is a very lonely action—yet we have priest and sacraments and a personal visit from our Lord.

9. Judgment is swift, but fearfully lonely, yet even there is our Guardian Angel, and the Human Heart of our Judge.

II. The outward Solitude of the Passion.

1. His Mother absent during part of the Passion.

2. His disciple whom He loved was gone.

3. Of those whom He had fed and healed not one came nigh Him.

4. The usual kindlinesses shown to the worst criminals were not shown to Him.

5. In all the steps of His Passion He was alone, in the garden, well, guard-room, Herod's court, streets.

6. The solitude of His silence—no one to speak to: except the women of Jerusalem.

7. The angels seemed withdrawn—at least so far as their presence comforted Him.

III. The inward Solitude.

1. None could appreciate His horror of sin, nor the multitude of sins He had to bear.

2. None could understand His pains, not even His Mother.

3. Where the eye looked for consolation, there was aggravation, in Mary, John, and the Apostles.

4. Accumulation of the burden on Him alone.

5. The abysses He saw before Him of (1) the divine anger—if one sin deserved hell, what must all the sins of the world have deserved? And it was just that which He suffered. (2) Hungry justice—(3) breathless suffering:—these were

all like so many huge unpeopled creations which
He had to traverse alone.

6. His Human Nature *as it were* deserted by His
Divine; the torture of this, as if Hypostatic
Union was going to be broken.

7. Thus left, It was beset with the usual assailants,
fear, sadness, wish to escape, fainting, all the
wild beasts of our own terrors let loose on His
exhausted strength.

IV. The presences which deepened His solitude.

1. The angel comforting Him, as lightning deepens
the night; it also showed that the solitude was
intolerable, one ray of light had to break in.

2. Mary: her Immaculate Conception was to be paid
for then.

3. John, whom He so intensely loved.

4. The crowd, which always intensifies solitude. He
had stilled the stormy lake, but as He looked
over the wild sea of stormy heads, He was silent
and alone; His power lay by His side like a
paralyzed arm, unnoticed or restrained.

5. The external hurry of being dragged about from
place to place.

6. The distractions of trials and questions, each
making His loneliness more painfully sensible:
distracted loneliness is peculiarly painful.

7. A raining tempest of momentarily diversified
physical sufferings, attempting to dislodge His
self-collection.

V. The Dereliction of the Father.

1. Fearfulness of spiritual trials, evidenced by the
writhings of manly souls under them.

2. Horror of even great saints at the temporary

hidings of God's countenance, which they can hardly bear. God justified even Job for his words.

3. Usually solitude from creatures brings to us a more intimate presence of God.

4. No interior trials were like those of the Soul of Jesus, because no soul had so enjoyed His presence, and none probably was ever left in an abandonment so nearly total, or so complete.

5. The Father abandons Him: we have no line to fathom this depth of the Passion. as if the Unity of the Trinity were going to break up; creation opened under Him, and He sank, oh horror! He cried out piteously, and that moment the angelic songs were all thrilled into mute amazement! it was as if He were slipping out of creation—the Creator losing Himself in the depths of a Created Nature, as if He had trusted Himself to a spell, and was now spellbound, and could not help Himself.

Let us turn away, or we shall go wild. Look at Him on His lonely Cross: He hangs there as it were till the end of the world: but men fall off from the crucifix, like a crowd at a fair tired of some exciting show: all are busy, in the fields, or on the roads, or keeping the feast at home, or clustered like Sunday idlers at the city gates. Jesus is left upon His mount alone!

———

U.   ꟼ

VIII.

THE CIRCLE OF EVIL.

Those who have a devotion to the Passion must to some extent share in it, especially in its want of repose, and in the irritating presence of repulsive horrors and violent images. We must beware of false delicacies in this respect.

I. The presence and overshadowing of evil.

   1. The keen and various suffering which it is to us increasing with our holiness.

   2. The fear which great sinners, murderers, and even drunkards, inspire into men.

   3. The acute torture of coarseness and vulgarity to extreme sensitiveness.

   4. Dread of extreme cruelty joined with great power.

   5. Horror of lawlessness; multitudinous clamor, when justice and fairness seem unrealities, or out of reach.

   6. The loathsome presence of the wicked in hell is one of its most exceeding tortures to the wicked even.

   7. What all this was to the sensitive and holy Soul of our Blessed Lord.

II. The representative wickedness of all ages gathered round Him.

   1. The High Priests—falsehood, injustice, rage, conspiracy, hypocrisy.

   2. Herod — loathsome sin, sensual brutality, rude blasphemy, daring to tempt to miracles, the base violent pride of mere overbearing power.

U.

3. Pilate — the cruelty of weakness, contempt of worldly indifference, paltering with conscience, which was sacrificed to love of popularity.

4. The Jews—possessed, surges of howling passion, natures transfigured, irresponsible fury.

5. The Roman soldiers—debauched ruffians, offscouring of all nations, sinful hands, stench of sin.

6. Even women:—as the one who made Peter fall: children are not named—perhaps they kept to their Hosannas: children crying after Him would indeed be earth's rejection of Him.

7. Judas: — treachery, avarice, hardness of heart, stupidity in not seeing beauty and truth, contempt of great graces, personal dislike of the Saviour, despair, which rightly considered is a sort of personal dislike of God.

8. Impenitent thief: — low base sin, vulgarity and meanness consummated in impenitence close to our Blessed Lord's dying bed, so that He is almost in contact with the damned.

9. Invisible legions of evil spirits—each of whose history, and the horrible interior foulness of whose spirit, during a long and crowded biography of thousands of years, were known to Him—an agony of desolation to His Soul, which was shaken to its centre.

10. And where was the good? It had fled, forsaken, denied Him, was ashamed of Him, doubted Him, as at Emmaus the disciples did, or at best followed Him afar off. There was no fidelity anywhere but in His Mother, and she drew John after her to represent us all beneath His Cross, and have His last breath which was to

U.   ℞

be our new life, breathed upon us in the person
of that dear Apostle.

III. The Creator's visit to His creatures.

1. He comes with His eternal love, laden with gifts,
   and beautiful exceedingly.

2. The holy intelligent stupor of the angelic creation.

3. He comes with a created nature on Him, and
   that nature is man's.

4. With what love will they not receive Him? for
   they are captives, sick, hungry, thirsty, naked,
   cold, homeless, condemned criminals—runaway
   slaves with inevitable arrest before them—and
   He is *all* to them.

5. The understandings of men not only cannot
   understand Him, but so misunderstand Him
   that they have a plain view that He is mad.

6. Their wills are so corrupt that eternal freshness,
   beauty, and truth are to them tiresome, ugly,
   and unpersuasive.

7. All that is most divine about Him, viz.. His
   doctrine, patience, absolution, miracles, and
   Divinity itself, is just what is most repulsive
   and hateful to them.

IV. The phenomenon considered.

1. He had doubtless mysterious reasons for choosing
   the time and place.

2. His presence drew out the evil by some hidden
   law, as good always seems to do.

3. Every nation and blood was perhaps represented
   there.

4. The world may possibly have been less wicked
   since, just as Satan has been more bound.

5. Satan had now found out the Incarnation, and it was the great battle, greater than St. Michael's of old.

6. The extremity of iniquity hunted and brought to bay the extremity of holiness as its prey. Oh, how men hunt in packs like winter wolves!

7. Human nature, around the Sinless Humanities of Jesus and Mary, because half devil and half beast, and was the fittest of all natures, because of its double capability of spiritual and material wickedness, for the awful insurrection of matter and spirit combined against the Incarnate Creator.

V. The Creator in the power of His creatures.

1. The ring of evil drawn closely round Him in one city in four-and-twenty hours.

2. It was made up of, (1) rage, (2) hatred, (3) scorn, (4) indifference, (5) disgust, (6) weariness, (7) petty spite, (8) political jealousy, (9) foreign disdain, (God a foreigner!) (10) national faction, (11) persecution of false doctrine, (12) unreasoning cruelty, (13) malicious cruelty, (14) inventive cruelty, (15) imitative cruelty.

3. And all this was at once triumphant, and outbursting in barbarities and indignities, which one human life could not have had concentrated in itself without the aid of omnipotence.

4. The phenomena are inexplicable except on the supposition of the heights of human guilt being topped, and its energies reinforced, by the awfulness of demoniacal possession. This makes the Passion part of the sin of the angels.

5. The tempest is at its height. in the streets of

Jerusalem—awful end of creation, the creatures triumphant, crowding in on their Creator, treading on His heels; God is in their power, and the wickedness of all generations is charging down upon Him, to trample Him beneath their feet: they will pull Him down as if to worry Him.

6. God's ordinary control over corruption is apparently withdrawn: awful unboundedness of the freedom of sinful wills.

7. In the midst, almost trampled out of existence, was a young man of three-and-thirty, well nigh disfigured out of human shape, staggering under a cruel instrument of punishment, and falling with a dull sound upon the street, and a weak woman, the victim's heart-broken mother, flung almost under the feet of the mob and the hoof of the centurion's horse, with her blue mantle stained with mud. That young Man was God!

Has not evil won the battle? Is there one hope left of triumph for eternal love?

IX.

HIS DIVINITY IN THE PASSION.

Listen! the noise of frantic Jerusalem has died away, or sounds faint and far off: and there are the soft strains of celestial music with calmest rapture and most penetrating melodies winding around the throne of the Eternal Word, and dying down into pauses of the most profound and restful silence.

U

I. Devotions to the Incarnation, and especially to the Passion, require a constant remembrance of our Lord's Divinity.

1. He is Himself that *Ecce Homo*, the Everlasting God, in all things equal to the Father and the Holy Ghost, no faintest shadow of subordination falling on the measureless waters of His Divine Nature.

2. His Person is the Second Person of the Most Holy Trinity, and so the truth, beauty, and wisdom of the Father.

3. His Advent and Passion are equally the act of all the Three Divine Persons.

4. It was His own free will to come, and to be sent by the Father, and to rejoice in His Mission, which in no way encroached on His Equality.

5. No created holiness, singly or collectively, could have merited His coming.

6. It need not have been with such profusion of suffering and shame; that was His choice with a view to our enthusiasm, loyalty and love—and perhaps, for other mysterious reasons, to slake the celestial thirsts of His dear Human Nature.

7. His Sacred Humanity claims fullest divinest worship, because of its union with His Person and Divine Nature.

II. How this affects all the mysteries of Jesus.

1. It even seems to make them more human: as His own Creator, He understands His own created nature, and like one skilled in a perfect but difficult·instrument, draws out new and enchanting sounds, in marvellous entrancing combinations.

2. It gives an unerring beauty to all He said and did; everything is a model, a type, an ideal.

3. It throws a tenderness over all His mysteries, like the revealed love of the Father, not like any thin human love.

4. But especially it gives the uttermost pathos to the Passion.

5. It is the only true basis for our real intelligent horror of Sin, which must always be measured not by the weakness of our nature, but by the Divinity of Him who made the expiation.

6. It alone gives a light strong enough to reveal the depths of His love for us.

7. It alone can nourish to its gigantic proportions our love of Him by infallibly persuading us of the immensity of the value which He sets upon our love.

III. What His Divinity conferred in the Passion.

1. His omnipotence enabled Him to live to suffer more.

2. His wisdom enabled Him to penetrate the revolting abominations of sin.

3. By it He could fathom the anger of the Father, and know what it meant to have an angry God, and how beautiful is the imperturbable dread glory of anger in the Divine Nature.

4. By it He could pierce the darkness of hell, and estimate sin's punishments.

5. By it He could foresee the comparatively few who would appreciate His Precious Blood, the low esteem of It in those who should love Him best, and the almost forgetfulness of those whom It would save.

6. By it He was enabled to feel all the torments there and then unconfusedly, and with indescribable reality and vividness, both His own and those of His elect.

7. It flooded His lower nature with a light, in which it grew unspeakably refined and sensitive, and which made shame an unspeakable stabbing, sharp, deep, fiery, to a *quick* which other men have not.

IV. What His Divinity withheld.

1. It withheld the joy-bringing effects of the Beatific Vision from His sensitive nature; and probably also restrained His intellectual nature from comforting and illuminating and restoring His sensitive nature, at least to some degree.

2. It froze up all the joys of the human Nature, except the point of the Soul, where the Vision was.

3. It did not alleviate one single pain, or make it less intolerable.

4. Neither did it console one single mental agony.

5. It did not let loose its omnipotence, which, seeing how it loved the suffering nature with which it was so intimately united, was a sort of constraint and loss of liberty.

6. It doubtless withheld other mysterious influxes of which we know nothing, but which had to do with the living communion of the two blessed Natures.

V. The use of His Divinity in the Passion, so far as it regarded ourselves.

1. By it we know that we are separately and distinctly before Him in all that Passion.

2. It teaches us not to shrink in thought, as it did not shrink in fact, from the distressing horrors of the Passion, as modern weak faith and fastidiousness are fain to do. Oh, if it rends our body and soul asunder, let us not be so irreverent as to shrink from fathoming the terrible things into which and through which we ourselves actually thrust Him.

3. His Divinity teaches us that love alone can repay Him, for love alone approximates to the infinite.

4. It intensifies our spirit of adoration.

5. It tries, stretches, invigorates, and gives new capabilities to our faith, like exercise and mountain climbing to the muscles.

6. It discloses in all its real grandeur the copiousness of our redemption, each of those countless pains being simply infinite expiations.

7. It shows us that part of our own deification must be imitation of the Passion, nay, more than imitation, even true participation in it.

Oh then let us kneel down before the Divine Nature of the Eternal Word, and feel our thoughts and imaginations travelling away far beyond our reach, and the fires of love burning with unconsuming heat our holiest affections, and the deep, deep spirit of dreadest speechless adoration taking possession with its calm strength of our soul and flesh, and let us so love that illimitable Nature in its pale, bleeding, disfigured, crucified tabernacle, that we shall cease to pine on earth for heaven, because earth contains what we most desire in heaven : for Calvary is changed to Tabor, because of the Divinity of Him who with sweet tones like His Mother's is speaking His beautiful words upon the Cross.

X.

THE SPECTATORS OF THE PASSION.

Around that marvellous mystery were gathered such spectators! The whole universe was there to see; the angelic creation; past generations whose eyes had been fixed upon it, and were now in limbus, purgatory, or hell; and all generations to come; probably representatives of all peoples were actually on the spot; and more than that, the Uncreated, God Himself, was there to witness.

I. It was a trial—

1. Which decided the greatest interests.
2. Which exhibited the highest sublimities.
3. Whose effects were to be for ever.
4. Which wedded temporal and eternal as never had been done before, and up to the limits of what is possible.
5. Which involved the deepest and most numerous mysteries.
6. Which resolved more of God's secrets.
7. Which was more wonderful than even the surpassing pomp of the world's last day.

II. The Spectators: what they saw, and how it looked to them.

1. God.
   (1) The beautiful accomplishment of eternal decrees.
   (2) The exhibition of the most surpassing excellence of created sanctity.
   (3) The completest worship which ever satiated His hungry glory.

U.   ℞

(4) The greatest event in the history of creation.

(5) The furthest stretch of love out of Himself. Oh what a mystery that it could not increase His love of the Eternal Word, already immutable in its Uncreated Excess!

2. Mary.

(1) She so penetrated each horror, that even the prevision of it had taken nothing out of it.

(2) She saw each as the price of her own graces.

(3) She saw the redeemed Church in dusky shadowy magnificence rising like a grand and endless procession out of the tumult of noise and blood and shame.

(4) Her heart was in completest union—1. With her Son. 2. With the Saviour. 3. With her own martyrdom. 4. With sinners. 5. With the Apostles. 6. With the Eternal Father.

(5) Even to her it was like a new revelation of her Son's beauty and sanctity.

3. Angels.

(1) A fountain of heavenly amazement, which they looked into with intense desire, yet which even their vast intelligences could not fathom.

(2) It gave a new character to their devotion.

(3) Their having to be neutral, being bidden to stand back.

(4) It seemed a new disclosure of God to them, far more than the mere foresight of it could be.

(5) It taught them in a more excellent way the science of loving men.

U. ·

4. The Apostles and Disciples.
(1) It stunned and overwhelmed them.
(2) They were simply supported by their Master's prayer and their Queen's example.
(3) It explained to them so much of the past.
(4) Their faith in His Divinity took root in all this shame.
(5) They, like the angels, began to learn the true science of loving men—instinct for souls: souls were in the world of the Passion what bodies and hearts are in the common world.

5. Evil Spirits.
(1) A terrible bewildering amazement.
(2) An intensification of their misery.
(3) A piercing fear which loosened and made faint all the compactness of their strength.
(4) An excitement of their rage and envy against men: increased fury as fighting a losing battle.
(5) Yet an actual diminution of their power.

6. The Jews.
(1) Everything indistinguishable in the first fury of their possession.
(2) A source of aching misgivings when excitement evaporated.
(3) A national shame, and a corporate sin not to be retracted.
(4) The end of their history in a second Exodus, when they would not cross: Titus was only wanted to burn up the ruins.
(5) Yet a curse, and a living energetic stigma, which they had evoked like a spirit out of its awful depths — they branded them-

selves with the Precious Blood like Cain's, and the world watches them.

7. Gentiles.

(1) It lay before them like the great sea before an idiot, an unmeaning commonplace expanse.

(2) Not of more consequence than to be the talk of the guard-room for a day or so.

(3) It was their first actual contact with God since the Fall or the Flood.

(4) The Roman empire really the servant and lacquey of the Passion.

(5) It transferred to the Gentiles the divine empire of the world.

8. The rest of the world at the time.

(1) A piece of news flying without much excitement along the Roman roads.

(2) In some places combined with various frightening phenomena of nature.

(3) Like God's great works generally, it did not disturb the ordinary current of affairs.

(4) Yet there was not a nation there, whose future light was not to rise out of that darkness.

(5) For each one apart, and with diversified special application, that Passion is suffered.

9. Subsequent generations.

(1) A perfect revolution of ideas: strength of weakness, wisdom of folly, glory of shame, &c.

(2) New standards of moral excellence, forgiveness, patience, silence, &c.

(3) The deep imbedding of the supernatural in the natural.

(4) The irresistible mould of their future litera-
    ture, history, art, law, and even falsehoods.
(5) At once the creator and the destroyer of their
    successive civilizations.
10. Ourselves.
    (1) The deep in which to drown our past lives.
    (2) The buoyant waters of the harbor where our
        present rides at anchor securely.
    (3) Out of which all hopes and successes for the
        future are to come.
    (4) Its shores are our sole terrestrial home in the
        life of grace, exiled from which we pine and
        die.
    (5) The literal Red Sea through which must be
        our Exodus to our eternal home.
III. Let us look again.
1. There is no tranquillity anywhere but in Jesus
   and Mary.
2. Hurry, precipitation, noise, frenzy, mental darkness, moral delirium—no one thinks or sees what
   it all means, but He and she.
3. Oh the unsuspicious impetuosity with which men
   accomplish God's decrees for Him.
4. Jesus still beautiful in His patience, venerable in
   His sufferings, though sunk almost out of sight
   in the depths of woe.
5. The quietness which follows round Calvary, the
   new Sabbath after this second terrible creation
   of the world. The second Adam has been the
   Creator, and He lies cold and still in His desolate garden, and the dark night falls on the
   second Eve, driven with her broken heart in
   that desolate wilderness of the cruel city.

U.   ꟼ

The green hill of Calvary—all the ages of the world beat at its foot, and fling their surge over its base; the ages before our Lord flooded darkly up, and sank back, rolling the stones down the beach with hoarse murmur, like the vain efforts of an ebbing tide. High above all c.vilizations rises the green hill, with the sun upon its sides, and the beacon of the crucifix, far-seen and radiant, and in the dark night giving out unobscured light —it is the sole harbor of tempest-tossed humanity, its sole safe anchorage, where anchors never drag, and the rolling billows fall back from its base, as if tamed on the instant by a spell!

XI.

THE SHADOWS OF CALVARY.

It is more hard to think of God within us than of God without us, yet it is the best way of practising His Presence: so it is hard to think of the Passion, not as an historical fact or a mystery accomplished, but as a living surviving thing, a power, a piesence a divine energy; yet this last is the true view of it.

I. The Passion living on in the Church.

   1. Really in the Mass, which is the continuation or renewal of the same sacrifice on ten thousand altars daily; and thus the abiding presence in the tabernacle is through the continuation and memory of the Passion.

   2. In the sacraments, whose living efficacy in each case is the application of the Passion to the soul.

U.   ℞

3. Martyrdoms are deep real shadows, nay, true participations of it.
4. All the sufferings of the elect are sanctified and made meritorious by the shadow of the Passion.
5. All the spiritual realities of inward and outward mortification shadow forth the Passion, and they are innumerable daily.
6. The shadow of the Passion on men and things is the badge of Christ's ownership.
7. The hearts of the saints, like sea-shells, murmur of the Passion evermore.

II. The Passion an attraction.

1. Our Lord's prophecy that it should be so; If I be lifted up from the earth, I will draw all things to Myself.
2. Its attraction to sinners from the plentifulness of its redemption
3. To those who are simply world-wearied, like the restful darkness of the welcome night.
4. To those who love God and are aiming at perfection.
5. Even to little children, who as yet hardly understand sin.
6. It satisfies the doubts and cravings of all hearts by reassuring them.
7. There is something quite supernatural in this attraction over and above the beauty of the mysteries.

III. The Passion in the active life.

1. The grand fountain of unworldliness, and supernatural principles.
2. The daily works of mercy endlessly flowing out of it, all over the Church.

    3. Holy Week a sort of universal retreat to the whole world; one use of the functions is to make it unlike all other times.

    4. The stimulus of missionaries, and the converting persuasion of nations and sinners.

    5. Power of endurance of the calamities of life.

    6. Excessive sweetness and mutual forbearance all over society.

    7. The constant occupation of the mind of Christendom.

IV. The Passion in the contemplative life.

    1. With most contemplative orders the Passion is the chief thing, and expiation the basis: some are founded on the Passion.

    2. Individual contemplative souls are brought by attrait into some peculiar relation to the Passion.

    3. The way in which it out-tops with them all other mysteries.

    4. How it fixes the gaze of the contemplative soul.

    5. It becomes at last a kind of sacred possession.

    6. It is life-long, and runs the year round, deepening in Passiontide.

    7. Its process is firstly compassion, then imitation, then actual participation in the Passion.

V. The Passion working inward similitude.

    1. The spirit of sacrifice and expiation.

    2. Love of suffering independent of the idea of expiation: thirst for it increasing with the amount of it.

    3. Supernatural horror and sadness, because of the sins of others.

4. Efficacious desire to expiate the sin of others, thus passing beyond the sins of self.
5. Suffering in silence, and abandoning with unearthly discretion all self-defence.
6. Inward trials distantly resembling our Lord's with mysterious operations of grace in the soul, mixed up of deep joy and intense suffering.
7. Transformation of the whole man, intellect and will, who views and feels towards all things as He did then: the world gone out of sight, hardly realizable even to the imagination—in strange thick oblivion, so that the powers of thought cannot advance in that direction.

VI. The Passion working outward similitude.
1. Revelations: constant increase of knowledge poured into the Church through contemplatives.
2. Visions, both intellectual and imaginary; hardly a saint is without them.
3. Pilgrimages either outward like St. Bridget's, or inward like St. Lidwine's.
4. Inwardly feeling the actual pains of the different mysteries, sometimes of the whole Passion successively.
5. Stigmatisation — partial — complete—visible—invisible—gradual — instantaneous — transient — perpetual—recurring.
6. Postures of body, acting out in ecstacy a real drama of the Passion, called Mystical Stations.
7. Supernatural states, having reference to the Passion—either habitual, or in sympathy with

the Christian calendar; even martyrdoms of
saints shine forth through other souls.*

 VII. Conclusion of all this.

1. The greatness of the Passion, and so the duty of
   steadfastly contemplating it all.

2. Its ever-living power, fresh as the first day and
   multitudinously reduplicated.

3. The mysterious way in which it works in soul
   and body, like plants and flowers shaping,
   coloring, and scenting themselves by hidden
   chemistry.

4. How Jesus clings to it, thus renewing it in the
   Mass and the saints, and keeping His Five
   Wounds in heaven.

5. How it is a great deep world underlying all
   common holiness, which is overarched above it,
   with saints perpetually working through it, and
   all perhaps doing so in their death agonies.

6. It is not therefore an historical fact done and
   over.

7. It is a perfectly furnished world, with *creatures*
   of its own, and a way of life, and standards of
   practice, and ideals of beauty, quite unearthly,
   not formed on earth's life, but as if creatures
   and life of some other planet.

Thus everywhere is the vast Church resounding
with the Passion; over its rich and populous lowlands
lies forever the Shadow of Mount Calvary, and all
things good grow beneath its cool defence: in its
highest mountains its mystical echoes sound strangely,
from noon to midnight, and from midnight back to
noon, fearful and beautiful for us dwellers on the plain

* Gorres, Mystik. 1. iv. c. 20.

U,   Ꞃ

to hear, while its rivers that wind everywhere amid
the close woods and peaceful fields, and through great
cities, bring down the plentiful Blood that was shed on
Calvary, from altars where the real Sacrifice, the very
Calvary, is transfiguring earth with its transcendent
truthfulness in the daily mass; so that our sights and
sounds, the supernatural odors on our river banks,
what we touch and taste, and feed upon, feeding with
mouth no less truly than with mind, is all from Calvary
where those rivers rise—and the mouths of those rivers
are the harbors of eternity!

XII.

THE ABYSS.

O Tabor! Calvary is far better than thou art, for all
thou didst catch such a flush of glory once from the
open heavens.   It is far better to be with John on Calvary than with our great father St. Peter upon Tabor;
and Peter thinks so too now, and thought so upon
his inverted cross at Rome, when he found his Calvary
so near the Vatican.   But now is the great three hours
on Calvary.

   I. The Seven Words. St. John's word about silence
      in heaven for half an hour: so now is there
      silence and a beautiful darkening of the world
      in the hearts of millions of God's creatures.
      The whole Church is as it were gathered on the
      top of the platform of Calvary, to receive into
      its heart the last words of its dying Lord.

U.

1. First word. Father! forgive them, for they know
   not what they do. Its circumstances. Elevation of the cross, blast of trumpets from the
   temple below, insults, many minutes as if dead,
   then the voice of the Creator heard.
   (1) The beauty of its being the first thought.
   (2) It sums up all the Passion — He breaks the
   silence in behalf of sinners.
   (3) The power of that word going on to this very
   day.
2. Second word. Amen, I say to thee, This day thou
   shalt be with Me in Paradise. Dismas and
   Gesmas, the two thieves—darkness grows—birds
   and beasts hushed by the eclipse—men whispered only—Mary prayed for the thief—then
   came the word of the Incarnate Word.
   (1) No single soul was forgotten in the multitude;
   but the thief was a happy type of multitudinous souls.
   (2) Exulting abundance of omnipotent grace,
   going beyond the thief.
   (3) Oh! when we come to die how that word will
   make music in our ears.
3. Third word. Woman, behold thy son;—behold
   thy Mother. Not *Me*, but thy new son — He
   looks at her, as if to thank her for her prayer
   for Dismas—the whole history of the world in
   His look, and oh! the love of it.
   (1) This is her second Annunciation.*
   (2) How He sanctifies thereby the holy solicitudes
   of domestic love.

* v. Foot of the Cross, p. 302.—(in the Fourth Edition, p. 321.)

U.   ℞

(3) The grandeur and sweetness of the legacy He left us.

4. Fourth word. My God! My God! why hast Thou forsaken Me? There is trouble in the city—He is like God in the cloud of Sinai.

(1) He has given away His Mother: now His Heavenly Father leaves Him.

(2) Momentary revelation of the depth to which our sins had sunk Him.

(3) Yet He will approach His Father rather than us: not one word against us was wrung from Him.

5. Fifth word. I thirst. Light glimmers—His whiteness red-streaked — His voice beautiful, but faint.

(1) Revelation of His true Human Nature.

(2) He thirsts for more suffering.

(3) He thirsts for more souls, and is disappointed with the scanty draught; so few, and those so ungenerous.

6. Sixth word. It is finished. Vinegar and gall— the sweat—St. John wipes His feet—coming of death—voice very faint.

(1) We repay His love with vinegar and gall, and thus our malice is finished.

(2) The work His Father gave Him is finished; think of Him in the temple at twelve years old.

(3) Our redemption is finished: oh! the joy of this as in His Sacred Heart He saw each one of us.

7. Seventh word. Father, into Thy hands I commend My Spirit. Silence—His Wounds grow

red—He lifts His weary head—earth quakes, rocks are rent, air is darkened, and in the midst of all that the great God's *loud* cry.

(1) He is going home—it is to His Father—so creation after all is no home for the Creator; yes, there is still the Blessed Sacrament.

(2) He is the more homeless, as He has just given His Mother away to us.

(3) The model of deathbeds: trust in God is the last of all things, and the whole of all things.

II. Death is drawing nigh; watch

1. The fountain of salvation bleeding away in human blood.

2. The eternal ending, Life unbeginning succumbing now to death.

3. Omnipotence engulfed in the weakness of the last faint of mortality.

4. The King of kings the slave, with all men and all things for His rightful owners.

5. The Creator held to die by His creatures, by nails through Hands and Feet.

6. The perfection of beautiful love pressed and tortured to death by unmitigated diversified hatred.

7. The All-holy indistinguishably confounded among sinners—it is hard to identify Him.

III. Death lays hands upon Him.

1. Creation is first silent, then broken up; its material horror; what was it among angels in the depths of their intelligences?

2. Angels are withheld, yet their forms are gleaming like bristling silver as they lean eagerly out of the gloom towards the cross; but the dead burst out of their tombs.

3. God—all signs of Him are absolutely invisible; the world was never so left to itself.

4. The sweet patience and excessive love of Jesus— His Heart all on fire that moment: oh! those flames shall one day burn up the world.

5. The depths of Mary's martyr heart, firm to receive the blow of the last faint breath.

6. Time and eternity come to take their law from His lips in death.

7.. Actual separation of Soul and Body. He bowed His Head, His Feet turned slightly on the nail that fastened them. Mary! thou art childless: the Babe of Bethlehem is dead, thy beauty, thy wonder, thy love. He is dead. The earthquake passed away, the darkness rolled off; there arose a cool fresh wind, which blew over the face of the earth, and round the cross, and stirred His hair. See! it lifts the few locks not matted with blood, and gives a momentary look of life to His Face. But the rocks of Calvary, the ears of John, the Heart of Mary, nay, the very silence of the air, still rung with the Creator's cry; nay, at this moment the world over many a Christian deathbed is faintly, sweetly echoing back that word, Father! into Thy hands I commend My Spirit!

IV. The thought which at the foot of the Cross overwhelms the individual soul.

1. A God is dead for me: the occupation of all holy souls on earth.

2. A God is dead for me: the ravishment of the angels in heaven.

3. A God is dead for me: the endless despair of the lost.

4. A God is dead for me: and ready to die for me again, and as many times in number as my sins are numerous, rather than that I should be lost.

5. A God is dead for me: and I know myself to be what I am.

6. A God is dead for me: and He knows what I am in His sight, so much more than what I am in my own.

7. A God is dead for me: and for this was needed (1.) A God's wisdom to plan it. (2.) A God's power to execute it. (3.) A God's love to suffer it. (4) An incarnate God's mind to conceive it. (5.) A supernatural gift of faith to be able to believe it. (6.) An inability on the part of all creation to repay it. (7.) The hardness of a reprobate heart not to be touched by it. He was the Man of Sorrows because He was the God of Love!

V. Forthwith the soul under the pressure of that thought, a God dead for me, begins to sink out of its depth—the seven descents of the soul in the deeps of the Passion.

1. Wonder—which is part of contemplation and of the Beatific Vision, arising from the thought of Who suffered, what He suffered, how He suffered, for whom He suffered.

2. Exultation—that it is so divine a work, so much our concern, so abundant, oh! such a grand glory of God.

3. Liquefaction—all dispositions running into one, barriers melting down—it was all with such intense love of us, and so pathetically, so beauti-

fully done, so unparalleled, and simply like Himself.

4. Conflagration—heart growing hot, each affection ready to ignite, each faculty of mind getting hot as if it were an affection, in an outburst of fire, consuming world, sin, self, and even imperfect goodness.

5. Foolishness of love—fire like wine, wine too strong for the soul, half involuntary gestures and exclamations, holy indiscretions,—yet wisdom of much of the seeming folly—like foreign ways which men laugh at, heaven the foreign country from which they come.

6. Contemplative Union—annealed, steadfast, fixed gaze, supernatural tranquillity of will, close union, —real contact with Christ calms weak transports, and effaces previous signs of mortal want of self-collection, and of inebriation,—strong efficacious languor, like the weakness out of which His *loud cry* came.

7. Possession—the Passion wholly possessing mind, heart, will, even body; Jesus possessing the soul, the soul in another sense possessing Jesus,— espousals, mystical marriage, the boundary of heaven and earth worn indistinguishable by fretting flames of love.

Each of these seven descents has been like a fall from the starry heights of heaven, and yet far down and down and down I see angels in the darkness, just visible by the light they shake from off their wings, and as they rise, they tell me they are faint with their long breathless fathoming, and they have seen no end, they verily believe there is none, to the ABYSS.

U.   ℞

II.

CALVARY.

CHAPTER I.

THE PASSION:

ITS HISTORICAL, DOCTRINAL, AND
MYSTICAL CHARACTER.

JESUS CHRIST and Him Crucified—this is the object of
our present contemplations. In an age of abounding
knowledge, this is the knowledge which concerns us
most of all. It was the one sufficient science which
St. Paul desired to know. We grow older; and, as age
comes upon us, it seems as if the very years as they
passed drew us closer to the Cross Life extinguishes
its own lights one after the other, until the darkness
of Calvary is brighter than the obscurity of a world,
which has first played us false, and is now deserting
us. As we grow older, we set a greater price upon
fidelity; and where is there such faithfulness as in the
Cross? Devotion to the Passion is at once the surest
sign of predestination, and the shortest road to heaven.
Happy are they whom the cruelty and treachery
of life have driven to the Cross! But happier far
are they the chivalry of whose youth drew them there

223

in early days, and who have spent their lives in its mysterious sanctuary! In the cloister and in the world, to young and old, to rich and poor, for clergy and for laity, the Passion is the grand object of devotion. Its intensity was the characteristic of primitive times. All that was beautiful in the Middle Ages shaped itself pre-eminently upon the Passion. It has been the especial work of modern saints to propagate and heighten this devotion. The Church herself is perpetually adding feast, and song, and pensive commemoration, although it seemed long since as if she had left herself no fuller means of honoring the Passion of her Spouse. All this is a warrant for another devotional treatise on the Passion. There is nothing new to be said of it; but every man has his own way of saying old things, by which he reaches unexpected places in the hearts of men, and kindles fresh varieties of love. Let us ask St. Mary Magdalen to lend us her heart, while we wade as far as we dare into the depths of the Passion. Let us study the science of Jesus Crucified with her for our mistress, whose name and memory perfume the whole Church with the balm of the Blessed Passion. It is a science wherein we learn by prayer, and in whose deep places our hearts see further than our eyes. It will give us what in these days we want most of all, the old simplicity of faith. What is progress but an entanglement? What is the breadth of literature but a distraction from God? What are the endlessly successive theories, each in its turn claiming to be final, but a weariness, under which we grow reasonably impatient? What are the vaunted discoveries of science, but either lights which blind by night, or

heights from which the horizon of our ignorance is for
ever widening? What are material prosperities, but
a slavery of increasing wants increasingly dissatisfied?
There is no grandeur in our work, there is no heavenli-
ness in our repose, except through the old simplicity
of faith.

There are many ways in which we may treat of the
Passion. The majority of books lead us through the
mysteries in detail, from the Last Supper or the Agony
in the Garden to the Burial of Jesus or His Resurrection. Upon the whole, this is the best way to
consider the Passion, because it is the most necessary
to the devotion of the faithful. Every mystery has
its own lesson to teach, and contains its own treasures
of prayer and contemplation. We can never understand the Passion, unless by repeated meditation we
have mastered it in detail. If then this successive
consideration of each mystery is not the only way of
handling the Passion, it is at least the method which
is most indispensable. We can do without other
methods; we cannot do without this. But there are
so many books which follow this method, that it is not
my intention to add to them by this treatise. I pro-
pose to treat of Calvary after the same fashion in
which I have treated of Bethlehem. The Passion, like
the Sacred Infancy, is not only an assemblage of divine
mysteries, united to each other by a similitude of
spirit as well as by the order of time. It has also a
·unity of its own as a whole. Like the Hidden Life
at Nazareth, or the Three Years' Ministry, it admits of
being regarded as a constellation apart. It sometimes
happens that, by exclusive meditation on separate
mysteries, we lose sight of many important truths.

U   ℞

We have a less distinct understanding of our Lord's Three-and-thirty Years. We do not appreciate, even so far as we might, the magnificence and the loveliness of the divine works. Nay, we do not even do such justice, as it is in our power to do, to the separate individual mysteries, because their connection with other mysteries, or their position in the constellation to which they belong, assist us in no slight degree to the right understanding of themselves.

The way, then, in which it is proposed to treat the Passion in this volume, is to look at it as a whole, not to follow it in order of time, nor to break it up into its component mysteries, such as the Scourging, the Crowning, and the like, but rather to break it up into its characteristics, characteristics which enter as ingredients into each of its separate mysteries. For instance, we shall have to consider the Excess of the Passion, its Bodily Pains, its Mental Pains, its Shame, our Lord's Outward Demeanor and Inward Dispositions, His Solitariness, the Circle of Evil which surrounded Him, His Divinity in the Passion, the Spectators of the Passion, the Shadows of Calvary which are cast over the world at this hour, and the Abyss which the Death of God opens to Contemplative Souls. These eleven subjects will furnish us with as many chapters, as soon as we have considered in this preliminary chapter the Passion generally, in its historical, doctrinal, and mystical bearings. By this means we shall get a different view of the Passion from that furnished us by meditation on its separate details, and at the same time a view which will give to our subsequent meditations a light, a force, and a touchingness beyond what they had before.

Let us begin by making a simple picture of the Passion for ourselves, one which shall not distract us by any multiplicity of detail. We stand upon the low top of Calvary, that Calvary which in so many senses is the highest mountain in the world. There is a preternatural darkness, like the luminous gloom of an eclipse, all round us. But it is preternatural, no mere eclipse. There is silence there, only mingled with a few sounds, there were some people in the darkness stirring, yet only stirring as if afraid to move. It gradually grows lighter. The white roofs of a city, not far inland at the eastern end of the Mediterranean, become visible. As the light waxes clearer, sounds increase both in number and in loudness. Slowly disclosed against the darkness is the bloodless Body of the Son of God, indescribably venerable in the excess of its disfigurements, hanging on the Cross, facing the west as if in prophecy of its grand Christian future. Standing beneath the Cross, now wet with blood, is the broken-hearted Mother, Mother of God, and now also Mother of men. There also is the Virgin apostle John, with such impassioned calm upon his woe-worn features as his knowledge of the secrets of the Sacred Heart would be certain to imprint upon them. Among all the sons of men there are few so great, so holy, so privileged as he who by his beauty took captive the Human Heart of his Creator. There also is the glorious Magdalen, the brightest trophy of God's love, which men take heart when they look upon, a very picture of the uttermost forlornness of human sorrow transfigured by the radiance of adoration into more than angelic beauty. O Magdalen! thou art there to tell how the hopes of all men may be so bold as to take refuge upon Calvary.

U.

This is the Passion, the Passion consummated.
This is the grand event in the world's history, giving
the law to all other events whatever. This is the
visible impression made on the decrees of the Creator
by the free will of the creature. This is the incredible
revelation of the Divine Perfections, which an angel's
intelligence could never have imagined, and even now
is unable to fathom. Incredible, even when revealed,
unless also a supernatural gift be given with the
knowledge, whereby we may be strengthened to believe
it. That mystery on the hill-top, which we express by
the name of Calvary, is the fountain of all supernatural
things, flowing both before and behind. That darkness
has illuminated forty centuries of time already, before
it actually overspread the green sward of the suburban
hill. That blood has inundated all the children of those
centuries, with innumerable graces, while it was still
unshed itself. There has not been a grace in any
human soul from Adam onwards, but it came from the
foresight of that Calvary. In all those dark, dreary,
lagging ages, there has been no lightening of any human
burden, no brightness in any human destiny, no
possibility of virtue, no struggle of manful hearts
against overwhelming evil, no birth of infancy, no death
of age, which have not been full of anticipations and
prophecies of Calvary. Even the inanimate creation
had some sort of consciousness that Calvary was the
centre of the world, when, as old tradition held, the
waters of the Deluge drifted thither the body of Adam,
and entombed it in the yielding soil.

But if the whole history of the world previous to the
Passion is filled with presentiments of it, nay, is wholly
unintelligible except by the light of it, much greater is

U.   ℞

the influence of the Passion upon the history which
follows. Henceforth the annals of the world are little
more than the chronicles of the Passion. It has im-
planted new ideas in men's minds. It has worn deep
traces upon their language. It has renovated their
philosophy. It has given another form and a different
spirit to their literature. It has enlarged their moral
instincts, while it has also refined and quickened them.
The victory of defeat, the triumph of self-abasement,
the divinity of suffering, the magnificence of shame, the
power of silence,—all these are ideas from the world
of the Incarnation; and they have supplied men with
weights and measures, which, if not in all respects
literally new, are practically new from that irresistible
authentication which the Passion has conferred upon
them. As time goes on, the Passion will give out from
itself, as its own creation, a peculiar civilization. Great
social institutions shall be based upon it. Govern-
ments shall acknowledge it as their authoritative guidance. Peace and war shall often become questions of
the Passion. It shall shape and fashion private life.
Henceforth, from the day on which the mystery is
accomplished, the world shall never get from under
the influence of Calvary. Civil history shall more and
more tend to merge itself in ecclesiastical. Even when
the outward monarchy of the Holy See shall appear to
have passed away, or rather to have cast aside its
mediæval insignia, when the days of Concordats shall
have come, and it shall be the ambition of states,
especially of those which are destitute of ennobling
traditions, to stand apart from the Church, when the
empire shall dream that it is glorifying itself anew by
working itself clear from the priesthood, when diplo-

macy shall have had most cause to congratulate itself on the unity which the balance of power, its own invention, has brought about, when earth shall seem more visibly man's because it is less visibly God's—even then, more than ever, shall civil history become religious. Alliances, instincts, sympathies, literatures, philosophies, the temper of cabinets, all these shall grow not only more religious but even positively theological. Christ has been crucified; and every event in the world shall draw from this fact more or less of its significence. The world, as it gets further from Calvary, shall become more personal in its hostility to Christ. The dominance of heresy is but Satan's protest against Calvary; and when the world comes to its worst, and to its end, it shall be so influenced by Christ that it shall instinctively concentrate itself into an Antichrist. It is travelling thither daily, and in this day it would appear to be attaining its end with more than usual celerity.

But from the great outward world let us come to our own secret selves. The sorrow and happiness of each individual soul starts at the foot of the Cross. However remote our generation may be from the era of the mystery, whatever our lot may be among the seemingly inexhaustible diversities of human fortune, however far off from Judea our home may lie, and however deeply hidden we may be in the indistinguishable obscurities of private life, our darkness and our light come from the top of Calvary. It is well or ill with us according as we are in harmony with the Passion which was accomplished there. To that hilltop centuries ago came every grief and joy of ours, every word and work and thought, every sin and every temptation, every secret shame and every undisclosed design. They came there clearer than objects in the noonday. They were seen by the inward eye of our dying Lord. They were understood as a whole, as composing one consecutive biography. They were weighed in detail. Nothing escaped Him. Grace was apportioned to each of them. His Precious Blood was offered and accepted for each. Sorrows were sanctified beforehand, and joys came out of the pure superfluous mercies of the Passion. Every excess of His torments was bidden to do its part, as a motive of more fervent love within our hearts: and there were colloquies between the Son and His Eternal Father, as if our single soul were the exclusive cause of all that happened upon Calvary, the one engrossing interest regarding which the Divine Perfections came to reconcile themselves upon that mountain-top. Our eternity was negotiated there, if we may use of these divine things those figures of vulgar commerce which God Himself by His apostle has condescended to make use of. Thus it comes to pass, that, even when our life is thickest and widest, there is no earthly object of any real abiding value to us compared with the Passion of our dearest Lord. All is dross compared with it; nay, all is dross compared with the knowledge of it. It is an earthly object and yet a heavenly one as well. It is the peacemaking, or rather the nuptials, of heaven and earth. In the uttermost distances of our eternal life, where in truth there are no distances, it is the Passion which will still support us, the Passion which will still keep the Vision open, the Passion out of which the inebriating torrents of God's splendors will still renew our souls.

U.   ⋑

Thus the Passion rules the history of the world, the history of the world before the Flood, of the world of the patriarchs, of the Israelites, of the heathen, before the coming of our Lord, and in a still stricter sense is it almost itself the history of the world from the Crucifixion to the Doom. Thus it is also the secret of all biographies of individual souls. All their ruin comes from their disloyalty to the Passion. All their holiness in time, and their glory in eternity, are the consequences of their loyalty to the Passion.

.　　.　　.　　.　　.　　.

III.

MEDITATIONS ON THE CRUCIFIX.

1.

THE HEAD AND EYES.

Introduction. Jesus All in All. The crucifix is a revelation. Our Lord said to St. Gertrude, that as often as a man looks tenderly on the crucifix, Jesus looks tenderly on him. Blessed Bernard of Caroline wanted to learn to read it. St. Philip Benizi called it his book, kissed it and died. Consider St. Alphonso at seventy-seven looking at his crucifix, and writing his meditations. Why should earthly lovers have the poetry and romance all on their side? Now come, let us learn Jesus. Mary will help us—how well she knew His blessed Features. St. Peter too, with his devotion to our Lord's Face. Seek ye My Face; Thy Face, Lord, will we seek.

U.   ℞

1.

THE HEAD.

The voice of my Beloved knocking: open to me, my sister, my love, my dove, my undefiled: for my head is full of dew, and my locks of the drops of the night. His head is as the finest gold: his locks as branches of palm trees, black as a raven.*

I. No golden crown! how is this? He is King of the world.

II. Crown of thorns—mud—blood—handfuls of hair gone—Head swollen—bruised—aching.

III. Our hearts the garden where those thorns were grown—blame not the innocent earth or its guiltless fields.

IV. That head which Mary nursed, the hair she smoothed, the brow she washed, and then dared to kiss.

V. Watch Him! He droops His head to die—He droops it to us as a father to his children, that we may kiss Him.

VI. Look upon Him once again, and now with the eye of faith, and not of sight—bright upon His throne, flashing in the light; Mary is wrapt in exultation, wondering angels worship, saints rejoice: Jesus, dear Jesus! we would see that: we would go thither: ah! sweetest Lord! Thou canst do this for us, and Thou wilt!

* Cant. v. 2, 11.

U.   ℞

2.

THE EYES.

I. Once the joy of Mary, and the wonder of Joseph; the sunshine of Bethlehem and Nazareth, the light across the wilderness; the revelations their looks made of the joyous secrets of His Sacred Heart.

II. The vigils they kept for us.

III. The tears they shed in infancy, for Lazarus, and over Jerusalem.

IV. The looks upturned to Him in prayer

V. The wistful look on the young man, and the converting look on Peter.

VI. The scene before Him on Calvary.

VII. The blows, spittle, and blood: yet it is He who gave sight to others.

VIII. Sun and moon darken as His eyes fade.

IX. His eyes turned to Mary on Easter morning; in heaven now, they are turned on us.

Oh shall we one day see them, and live and love in their sweet light? Mine eyes have failed with weeping*—His eyes are as doves upon brooks of waters which are washed with milk and sit beside the plentiful streams.† Oh my Jesus, give us the gift of tears, affectionate tears, holy tears. Dearest Lord! we have not loved Thee; no! hitherto we have not loved Thee, but we will love Thee now: make us love Thee, make us love Thee more and more. Thy servants sometimes ask many things of Thee, but we will ask but one—Love, Lord, love, love, and then more, and then eternal love!

* Lament. ii. 11. † Cant. v. 12.

U. Ⓢ

3.

THE LIPS, AND MOUTH, AND CHEEKS.

I. Filled with earth and blood in the garden: once with the breasts and milk of Mary.

II. The spittle of the soldiers mingling with His own.

III. The blows breaking His lips, and making them deformed and swollen: sweet lips that spoke words of peace and love divine: His cheeks which Mary fondled.

IV. The kiss of Judas: the kisses of Mary.

V. The sighs that come from that sacred mouth upon the cross.

VI. The white parched lips, once red and plump at Bethlehem.

VII. The burning thirst, the vinegar and gall.
Evil words, detractions, impurities, oaths, &c.

4.

THE TONGUE.

I. A hidden member, sheltered from the assaults of blows, &c., and our teacher.

II. Why He kept it without suffering till the last, except His Heart (and that too was wounded inwardly): that He might with it penetrate the ear and heart of the Eternal Father, to pray for His murderers, to absolve the thief, to bequeath His Mother, to show the greatness of His woes, to proclaim His dear thirst of souls, to teach us what to say when we too come to die. Oh what love! For our sake He keeps it, not for His own.

III. His thirst—the bloody sweat the night before—
jaws dry—tongue swells—no- drop of water—
Mary cannot reach—see a dying man, when his
tongue is dried up! Ah! what suffering was
the drink they gave Jesus.

IV. Our tongues—how are they employed? they are
Mary's lap on which Jesus lies at Holy Communion—Oh awful sins of the tongues of men!

V. What is the tongue of Jesus doing now? what
will it say to us when the last day comes?

5.

THE FACE.

I. The appearance of It. (1) The forehead, (2) the
eyebrows, (3) the eyes and eyelids, (4) the
cheeks, (5) the lips, (6) the nostrils, (7) the
chin, (8) the beard, (9) the long flowing hair: the
horror of this to the angels, who knew that Face
to be the beauty, joy, and brightness of eternity.

II. How Mary looked upon that face when it was
small and infantine. Will she forgive me who
have now covered that Face with such a fearful
veil of shame and of confusion?

III. Implore the Eternal Father to look upon the disfigured Face of His only begotten Son. Jesus
offers it for our sins, offers it to obtain pardon
and grace for us.

IV. But see! the Face moves, the eyes close, it is no
longer uplifted heavenwards, it droops, it sinks
upon the breast, oh awfullest of all awful things

U.

that ever were on earth! Jesus breathes his last
—God is dead!

V. Now I will think of my deathbed—Oh may I see
that Face then, shining, beaming, smiling on me!
Say for ejaculation—Blessed be the beautiful
Face of my Jesus to all eternity!

6.

THE EARS.

I. The delicacy and tenderness of them. The misery
of noise to the sick and dying. The roar of
the blaspheming multitude, like a pack of cruel
howling wolves in the ears of Jesus. Noise,
cruelty, hatred, sin, all so many causes of pain.

II. The names they call Him:

1. Malefactor—He who has done all things well.

2. Imposter—He who was eternal truth, and kind
teacher of truth to all.

3. Guilty of death—He was life, and gives life to
us, and was that hour giving His dear life
for us.

So the streets, the judgment-hall, and Calvary
resounded—and how do we bear one word of just
reproof? Think too of the sins committed with our
ears.

III. There is a heart breaking at the foot of the Cross!
Oh the deep sighs, the stifled sobs that come from
it; they are darts of fire entering in at the ears
of Jesus, and piercing His Sacred Heart. Think
of the sighs of the poor in our ears.

U

IV. Where are the ears of Jesus now? (1) in heaven, hearing what we ask, and what Mary is asking for us, (2) in the tabernacle, drinking in the acts of love that we may make.

7.

THE ARMS.

I. What they suffered in the garden with the thick ropes—tied in front of Him, then at the scourging behind Him—swollen—torn—bleeding —weakened.

II. He opens them to embrace the Cross, while He kisses it most tenderly, and then takes it on His shoulders.

III. Those arms bound in swaddling clothes—twined round Mary's neck, as the ivy twines round a tree.

IV. Dislocated on the Cross—the whole weary weight of His Body hanging upon them with agony unspeakable.

V. Look well at those arms, omnipotence is in them: they are the arms of Him who made the world, and could move it from its place at this moment —they could loosen themselves from the Cross if they pleased.

VI. How those arms embraced Mary at her Assumption: us too He will perhaps raise up when we run and fall adoring at His feet at our first entry into heaven.

8.

THE HANDS.

I. The sweetness and the beauty of those Hands—little in infancy, working in St. Joseph's shop, all the beneficent miracles and works of the thirty-three years, lifted up in prayer for us, laid on little children's heads.

II. Handcuffed, struck with lashes, broken and wounded with falls, swollen fingers, bleeding: so they grasp the mock sceptre, and so the cruel Cross.

III. The nailing to the Cross, the agony of the redoubled blows, the dislodging of the nerves, the jostling of the Cross into its place, the burning wounds.

IV. Those Hands created me; those Hands elevated the Host at the first Mass; those Hands are above me in the confessional, though I see them not.

V. Those Hands—how beautiful and bright in heaven now, angels adore them, they put the crown on Mary's Head, oh ravishing sight!

VI. To be at the Right Hand is all our joy, our bliss. Ah! may we be allowed to kiss the shining wound on that Right Hand, when we are admitted to the peace and joy of Heaven!

9.

THE BREAST.

I. The Breast of the infant Jesus, rising and falling
—Mary's love of it.

II. St. John reclining on it, the heat he felt in it;
St. Philip, the beatings of the Sacred Heart.

III. How we look at the blue sky, and think of heaven
behind it; so at the white breast of Jesus—the
Eternal God there as in a treasure-house—how
frail a wall! yet who would dare to break it
through?

IV. The Breast of Jesus as it was seen upon the Cross
—outrages in the garden—stamping on it—
lashes of scourging—distention from outstretched
arms.·

V. The Breast of Jesus dead on Mary's lap.

VI. The Breast of Jesus now in glory—the Sacred
Heart beats there once more—rises and falls
with love of Mary and love of us.

10.

THE FEET.

I. Feet of the Infant Jesus—return from Egypt—
three days' loss in Jerusalem.

II. Feet of the Boy in Joseph's shop, or fetching
water from the well.

III. Feet of the Man—weary, sore, throbbing, cold,
hot.

U.

IV. Feet of Jesus with Magdalen kissing them, &c.

V. Feet of Jesus on the Cross—dragged down with ropes,—broken, wounded, nailed, the weight of the Body resting on them.

VI. Feet of Jesus ascending, leaving prints behind.

VII. Feet of Jesus in glory—shall we one day print a kiss of burning love upon them?

IV.

OUR LORD'S INNOCENCE.

Do we not feel how the love of Jesus is growing into us with our meditations on His Passion? If our hearts do not burn, there is something like burning beginning in them. That woe-worn Face is getting so worn into our hearts that we shall hardly love His Easter beauty.

I. Manifold views of the Passion—enough to distract the contemplations of an angel.

1. The awful profane wickedness and diabolical inspiration of it.

2. Its crowded and multiform cruelty.

3. The venerable glory of His everlasting Divinity.

4. The extreme human sweetness of His demeanor.

5. But there is another point, which I venture to think was exceedingly foremost in our Lady's mind, almost jealously prominent—His innocence. Rightly considered, it is the most heart-breaking thing about the Passion.

II. Innocence on earth.

   1. Its look of strangeness and of wonderfulness. We never saw any one who was quite innocent except the Blessed Sacrament.

   2. Its look of exile—there is something heavenly in slavery detained on earth.

   3. Its look of peril, yet of helplessness.

   4. Its look of exquisite reproachfully unreproachful pleading. There is some hidden sympathy between innocence and silence. It *ought* to be eloquent as an angel, but it is silent as God. And yet there is a look of guilt about its silence which is in reality the artlessness of its simplicity—or the holy trouble of its humility.

   5. The way in which Jesus and Mary loved it in each other, because it was their exclusive wealth on earth.

III. Innocence suffering.

   1. Horror of innocence suffering at all: *e.g.* a child, a baby in its agony.

   2. Innocence treated as guilt, yet it was the very artifice of love in his Passion to clothe the innocent with guilt.

   3. Innocence enveloped in rudest, maddest violence.

   4. Innocence tortured with cruelty.

   5. The peculiar agony of injustice to the delicate sense of innocence. Innocence is so gentle, so un-selfdefending.

IV. *Quid mali fecit?* Pilate certainly was not blinded by hatred as the Jews were: but yet what spiritual discernment had he?—imagine it— dream it—and yet he discerned His innocence.

   1. His face was piteous then, yet not wholly dis-

figured. Yes truly: what evil has He done? name it.

2. The miserable Pilate saw all His spotlessness in the silent face. Pilate forsooth falls in love with innocence, and says, *Innocens ego sum.*— St. Matt. xxvii. Oh, if we could but see that face in vision for one moment, could we ever sin again, or ever cease to love?

3. They chose Barabbas: I was going to say this was a wickedness without name—but we had best say little about it: alas! our choices have been the worst features of our life. Dear Jesus! how many Barabbases have we preferred to Thee!

4. Why does He not speak! One word, a tone, a sound, would have made that beauty irresistible: it would have calmed that raging sea of hatred, it would have cowed the multitude into adoring love. There were mothers in the crowd, yet no one saw what to Mary was so infinitely beautiful.

5. Yet, oh! do not speak, lest Thou shouldst clear Thyself—and then what should we do? oh, it is almost a relief to us, a joyous deliverance from our suspense, to hear that discordant *crucifige!* As in the agony in the garden, our salvation seemed for a moment to tremble in the balance —for they might have let Him off: but if His Father would not hear Him then, will He hear the Jews now?

V. *Nullam causam invenio.* A third time Pilate said, *Quid mali fecit?* Then, I find no cause. A third time—he could not believe the Jews would still

U.

persist—to him the face was *such* conviction. Yes,
the beauty of that face gave a kind of obstinacy
even to that weak and vacillating judge.

1. Are we getting frightened at the innocence of
   Jesus? at least we are eager to tell Pilate that
   he is wrong with his *nullam causam.* O Pilate,
   thou art blinded by His beauty!

2. All the sins of the world are on Him—is not that
   guilt?

3. He alone can expiate them—is not that *cause?*
   and cause of death also, for so only can He
   expiate them. Now again we are uncertain:
   will Pilate give way against his own conviction
   of His innocence? But they were instant with
   loud voices requiring that He might be crucified. And their voices prevailed, and Pilate
   gave sentence that it should be as they required
   (St. Luke xxiii. 23, 4),—and as we require, oh,
   yes! and as we require. Ah! if there is a necessity on earth, it is salvation.

4. Dearest Jesus! Yet His innocence so works in
   us, that in hot times of prayer, we feel as if we
   could almost sacrifice ourselves to save Him.
   But, no! O Mother Mary! be content. Jesus
   has made it a greater love in us to let ourselves
   be saved by Him than that we should save Him
   from the cross.

V.

THE FACE OF JESUS.

Passiontide veils the face of the crucifix, only that it may be more vivid in our hearts.

I. The face of Jesus in the Thirty-three Years.
1. The most beautiful of all the beauties earth has ever seen.
2. As predestined by God, and the model of all beauty.
3. The devotion of Mary and Joseph to it.
4. The devotion of Peter and the apostles.
5. In Infancy, Boyhood and Manhood.

II. His face during the Passion.
1. In the agony in the garden.
2. Before His various judges.
3. When He met His Mother.
4. On the cross.
5. In death, on Mary's lap.

III. What thoughts this gives us.
1. Hatred of our own sins which caused it.
2. A truer idea of the Father's anger with sin.
3. Intense love of our Blessed Lord.
4. Deepest compassion with His Mother.
5. A yearning to be more holy.

IV. His face now.
1. It is being seen in numerous particular judgments momentarily.
2. The saints have sometimes seen it as it is, and nearly died of ravishment.
3. It is the bliss and ecstacy of Heaven.

4. It is the most beautiful sight God sees outside
   Himself, and yet in so strange and wonderful a
   sense hardly outside Himself

5. It is there in the Blessed Sacrament, with the
   eyes, the mouth, the brow: most thrilling, most
   hushing mystery.

Oh, to look upon that face eternally, how sweet a
destiny! A humble, reverent, familiar, affectionate
devotion to the Passion is one chief sign of our predestination to see the face of Jesus for evermore!

VI.

THE DESERTION OF THE APOSTLES.

It is Passion Sunday; we must take our lesson from
the Passion.

We have a great deal to do to be saved: and God
does not save us without ourselves, *i.e.* we must do our
part, we must correspond to grace. Now here comes
a most important question: to what amount can we
trust ourselves, and what can we trust ourselves for?

I. Our salvation looks safer the longer we persevere
   in the spiritual life. Does this come from any
   change in ourselves; any change which we may
   safely trust? Grounds of trust are—

1. Strength of character, which may be partly
   natural and partly acquired.

2. Habits of virtue, which certainly make the exercise of virtue easier.

3. Great graces, which are not only signs of predestination, but inward revolutions.

U.

4. Perseverance in good, up to the silencing of temptations.

5. Amount of actual sincere love of God, which even humility must admit.

All this is true; but what I want to bring out is that it is not our own but God's, and more than this, that it is not a gift of God which we hold in our own dominion—it is not so much something done and over, as a present grace, depending upon grace—and therefore, while it is an immense reason for infinitely trusting God, it is no just reason at all for trusting ourselves.

II. I infer this from that most painful mystery of the Passion, the desertion of Jesus by His own Apostles.

1. It is probable, from what we know of the usual customs of divine grace, that they had beautiful natural characters to start with, and had led pure lives.

2. The grandeur of their vocations, next to the Divine Maternity.

3. Their novitiate with Jesus, its inexhaustible benedictions.

4. The bewildering amount of love He had lavished on them.

5. The immense enthusiastic love they had for Him —no saints have attained it.

III. Yet—the most melancholy incredibility we have ever been called upon to believe—they fell—

1. Fell after all those repeated miracles, after two in the garden itself, namely, the falling back, and the healing of Malchus' ear.

2. Fell at a *small* danger—for they were not aimed at—and at the *first* danger.

U.

3. Fell just when common love and loyalty would have called them forward, especially as it was all done through the treachery of one of their own body.

4. Fell after solemn reiterated warnings and solemn reiterated protestations of *all*. And in like manner said *all* the disciples (Matt. xxvi. 35).

5. Fell just after first Communion—and that the first Communion in the world, just as the first man fell, and the first among the angels fell. Merciful God! what then have we to trust to but His mercy?

Hence I infer that we can trust ourselves for nothing. O dear Brethren! that I could write this single truth so deep in your hearts that no length of years nor adventurousness of life should ever efface it, that in order to secure our salvation, life must be one long, unsuspended, unforgetting dependence upon grace!

VII.

JUDAS.

I. Jesus had a secret sorrow—Judas—He never alluded to the cross but often said, one of you shall betray Me.

II. Judas in childhood.

1. Winning ways.
2. A mother's love.
3. A promise dear to his mother.
4. Little faults may have preluded his great ones.
5. Unsuspectingness of his future doom.

U

III. Jesus with Judas.

   1. His first love of Judas.

   2. The fall of Judas began with taking scandal, *i.e.* at St. Mary Magdalen.

   3. How Jesus spares him at the supper, not naming him openly.   Dear Jesus!

   4. Washes his feet.

   5. Communicates him.

   6. That which thou dost do quickly.

   7. Then in the garden—horror of the words of Judas—*tenete Eum.*

IV. Judas' despair—ah, where is Jesus?   He takes the money back, and they jeer him—how unlike Jesus, who would have so soothed him—*where* is Jesus? (No soul so needed Him—because of the thought of Him no soul was so despairing as Judas was *then.*)   Gone to death by treachery.

Does not all this give me comfort?   Will He bear with me?   I don't know: I am worse than Judas, I fear.

Jesus was troubled in spirit, and the disciples looked one upon another.   (St. John xiii. 21, 22.)

V. If we love Jesus we hate Judas.   We should like to know what his character was like, whether it was like ours.   At least we have resemblances to him.

   1. He had a sweet and potent call from Jesus—so *we.*

   2. He once loved Jesus perhaps—so *we.*

   3. He got to know Him on familiar terms—so *we.*

   4. He began with venial sins and self-seeking—so *we.*

U   ℞

5. He did not know how hard his heart was getting —so *we*.

VI. See life of St. Joseph of Cupertino, which says that the loss of Judas was the worst pain of the Passion.

VIII.

HIS BLOOD BE UPON US AND UPON OUR CHILDREN.

Night over the valley of the Nile—destroying angel —doorposts stained with blood—so now it is night— this life is a night—incessant flight of the destroying angel in company with the angel of death—souls stained with blood. If the Blood of Jesus is not on us then, we are lost to all eternity. But how was this mystery of the Precious Blood proclaimed in the Passion?

I. The mystery.

1. Pilate washing his hands with water: the Jews were wiser who took blood. An act of the greatest human childishness done by the side of and in the face of Divine Wisdom—Jesus looking on, listening, silent as usual; His eyes look on the crowd, not with the piercing dignity of a judge, nor even the meek reproachfulness of a sufferer, but with the clear beaming of unmingled, unceasing love.

2. They saw Blood on Him, and thirsted for it like beasts, yet did not know *what* It really was.

3. They had reached now the height of the sin of

U.   ℞

putting the God of Abraham, Isaac, and Jacob
to death—*universus populus*—yes! *universus!*
what a sweet prophecy.

4. They were ready to be victims themselves, if only
they can make Him a victim: oh, what wise
theology, what Christian science in all this mad
blind sin. They threw their hearts wide open,
turned God's grandest blessing into a curse, and
took it in, and made it from that time forth
their life, a chained life, a life of most horrible
chaining and enchantment

5. The cry—so wild, so thrilling, so enormous, so
unanimous! like the cry from a ship going down,
or the cries at the deluge till Noe heard them
no more.

6. The silence after the cry, like the silence which
Noe felt, nay, heard above the turbid waters, for
there are silences which are so silent that they
can be heard more—the city so silent, their own
hearts so hushed by the panic of their own cry,
Pilate so astounded—it was a wonder that an
angel did not speak, if only to break the intolerable silence. Perhaps the angels thought God
would speak, as over the Jordan, and when the
multitude said it thundered.

7. Jesus in that silence—and the Holy Trinity.
God even then was silent: Oh that inveterate
silence of God! what an endless revelation it is!

II. The Saviour! We look on that furious crowd—
on the blue vault of sky filled with the noiseless
shining of the sun—on the silent buildings—how
dumb they look in their brightness,—on the cower-
ing Pilate, on the blue mantle of Mary—then on

U.

THE SAVIOUR OF THE WORLD with the morning
sun shining whitely on Him.

1. His look—how could anguish be so beautiful
   when it was visibly so bitter? lips goldened as
   it were by the heavenly words He had for
   years been uttering.

2. His silence—He had not sentenced them, it was
   themselves. He had thought of this hour, when
   He was weeping over Jerusalem!

3. His thoughts—angels adored His wisdom, could
   come nearer to fathoming that than to fathoming
   the bitterness and yet the sweetness of His
   thoughts.

4. His Heart—its love, its exultation, its faintness,
   its pang, its augmentation of love for them. It
   rushed out upon this crowd in augmentations of
   love which were like new creations for impetuosity and magnificence.

5. It was a wonder they did not *see* He was God.
   Aye, see with the very eyes in their heads that
   He was *God!*

III. The pain of that cry.

1. As an immense sin—and to Him a gigantic ingratitude. How ingratitude crushes tender and
   affectionate natures.

2. As coming from those He so specially loved—
   and the love of whom was communicated to
   His Human Nature by His Divinity.

3. As a true prophecy of their future misery—
   another wandering than that glorious one in
   the wilderness, and with quite another sort of
   melancholy miracle about it. Homeless, un-
   sanctuaried people!

U.

4. The foreseen sacrilegious use of His Precious
   Blood—nay, was it not a torture to Him that
   the first use of His Precious Blood should be a
   sacrilege?—of His Precious Blood which He
   loved so amazingly, just as He was *turbatus
   spiritu* (St. John xiii. 21), from foresight of
   Judas' Communion?

5. As an intense sorrow to His Mother, because she
   loved her people, and because it was always an
   incredible surprise to her to see Him not loved.
   Dear Mother! she had been used to it from early
   days, and yet could not get used to it.

IV. The joy of that cry.

1. Because the last obstacle to His Passion was now
   removed.

2. Because all allusion to the shedding of His Blood
   was a delight to Him, just as a generous man
   rejoices in the abundance he has to give away.
   The cry roused Him as the trumpet rouses the
   warhorse.

3. Because of the conversion of the Jews at last—
   and of many now, *e. g.*, three thousand by the
   sermon of St. Peter, who is now hiding away for
   fear and shame.

4. Because of the fulness of the Gentiles: He
   saw the crowd of all men: He saw us with His
   Blood upon us; the thrones of *some* of us in
   heaven: nay, why should I say some, why not
   all? it is my want of faith.

5. Exultation at the immensity, continuity, completeness, and magnificence of His redemption.

There are two prayers which never cease from off the
earth; one the Lord's prayer, taught on a grassy hill of

Galilee notable for the thick tuftings of its grass, over-
looking the quiet lake, the other by a whole people in
the frenzy of their sin in the streets of the Holy City ;
the blasphemy and curse have turned into a blessing
and a worship, and a wild, wild prayer for the Precious
Blood! ˙All the day and all the night throughout the
whole earth the silent eloquence of Christian faith,
and the speechless song of Christian hope, and the
endless wistful sigh of Christian humility are for ever
rising to the throne of our Heavenly Father, beautifully and adoringly prolonging the cry of that dark
day of poor Jerusalem: His Blood be upon us and
upon our children.

IX.

HE SAVED OTHERS; HIMSELF HE CANNOT SAVE.

Is it not strange that such wicked works can be so
beautiful? Yet are they *not* beautiful? Oh, beautiful
as some fragment of an angel's song! He saved others:
Himself He cannot save.

I. What He looked like to those who saw Him on the
cross.

1. Description of Him all disfigured.

2. So changed from what they had seen Him in the
temple, or on Palm Sunday. He was not an
object of horror. Suffering can beautify with
a pitiable beauty. It can make reverend.
Even death can beautify. Its rigid repose can

U.   ℞

even be a more graceful thing than the supple
grace of life.

  3. At the least He was an object of pity: horror of
gibing the pitiable, and in the hearing of His
Mother! What a dreadful thing hatred is! and
such a hatred!

II. What He looks like to us.

  1. The Godhead shining through the disfigurement.

  2. His love of men beautifying the very disfigurement itself.

  3. Oh to us such an object of love, of pity also, yet
much more of love and of adoration.

III. He saved others.

  1. What! did they hate Him for *saving* men?

  2. But the fact, how true it is! He did indeed save
others, He saved us, perhaps them; some who
jeered, *e.g.* the good thief, are now with Him in
heaven.

  3. He did not care to save Himself, so long as He
saved us. He never thought of Himself: this
was His human character, He pleased not Himself: it was this which so touched St. Paul.

IV. Himself He *cannot* save.

  1. Can this be true? He is the omnipotent God;
angels are waiting His sign.

  2. Yet this *is* true. He *is* helpless; He cannot save
Himself; He cannot come down from the Cross.

  3. But what hinders? Oh such a might of love, of
love only, of love for us.

V. *We.*

  1. Did we then seem so beautiful? oh no! how far
from that!

  2. But we *did* seem so pitiable! He lost all pity

U.   ℬ

for Himself and for His Mother, because we
did look so infinitely pitiable.

3. And yet, even after it all, we can scarcely force
ourselves to pity Him; we can hardly strain a
tear, or force a sigh, because of the pains of our
dear crucified Love!

How much the Passion has saved us from! Out of
what a depth it has rescued us! Truly we can now
use those merciless words of the Jews in quite another
sense. We can take up our crucifix, and kiss the Five
Wounds with at least so much love as to grieve we
have not more love, and then looking at our Saviour's
Face we can say, Yes, my Jesus, my Lord and my God:
Thou savest others, Thyself Thou canst not save!

X.

OUR LORD'S COMPLAINTS IN HIS PASSION.

If one you loved lay dying, would you rather he
were silent or complained? Sorrow has many ingenious
questions to settle, but hardly any more interesting
than this.

I. The Doubt.

1. How much from one point of view silence on their
part enables us to bear the sufferings of those we
love! Our *heart* is less wounded, and our *mind*
estimates the suffering less.

2. One of the ends of the silence of Jesus was to
spare us. Had He complained we should have
sickened with sorrow over His Passion, with too
much sorrow to have left room for love.

3. Yet somehow we love the pain complaint gives us; if not a solace, it is a pain such as sorrow covets.

4. There is something graceful in the complaining of those who suffer: something which discloses the inward beauty of their souls: to me it seems of all human sounds not only the most beautiful but the most dignified and the most religious.

5. It is often an index of great conformity to God's Will; complaint is the voice of patience.

6. We cannot bear for long the silence of those we love: looks speak, and sighs speak, nay the silence speaks, but love craves *words*.

7. In memory how precious, like far off music, are the complaints of those we have lost.

II. Jesus complaining.

1. The mystery of God complaining: how this would strike a heathen in the Old Testament; it reveals God so marvellously as a God of love, as the God who out of love made us free, that He might *want* our love the more, and then is endlessly, pathetically, almost humbly complaining that He does not get our love.

2. The special mystery of the complaints of the uncomplaining Jesus; His whole life was so uncomplaining.

3. The taciturnity of the Word makes His words so precious, especially in the silent Passion.

4. The inexhaustible beauty of His complaints, so like Him and yet so unlike; somehow they increase our devotion to His silence by making us feel it to be so Godlike.

5. The extreme unexpected simplicity of His com-

`U.   ℞

plaints; unexpected because of their plain, artless, spontaneous humanness. The Human Nature united to the Divine must have had a singularly simple, translucent, guileless character.

III. The Five complaints; all of personal things and to persons. Simon, sleepest thou? Couldst thou not *watch one hour?*

  1. *What!* Could you not *watch one hour* with *Me?*

    (1) Said to Peter by name as the next was to Judas by name.

    (2) As if Peter had only just finished his protestations.

    (3) Surprise. *What!*—as if He had *believed* the protestations.

    (4) Disappointment.

    (5) Pain, but un-upbraiding. *One hour!* it was such a small thing to do—to keep awake for an hour.

  2. Judas! Dost thou *betray* the Son of Man with a *kiss?*

    (1) Judas by name.

    (2) The tone of the voice.

    (3) Its sweet gentleness, as if not angry but lovingly incredulous.

    (4) The word *betray.*

    (5) With a *kiss*—had the apostles ever kissed Him before, and on the *mouth?* if so, how terrible were Judas' memories, if not, how terrible was the familiarity!

  3. Are you come out as against a thief with swords and clubs?

    (1) Said to His dear Jews.

(2) *A thief*—as if the disgrace affected Him, and the sense of dishonor.

(3) Still more that His people should not have recognized His Godhead, Who thought it not robbery to be equal with God.

(4) *With swords and clubs*, when He had always been so gentle, and said, Look at Me, I am gentle and meek.

(5) As if it was pain to think that they imagined He was not ready to die for them without any violence; this last was the worst wound.

4. If well, why smitest thou Me? these words are naturally in St. John's Gospel, because of His devotion to the *Word*, who for words is now smitten.

(1) Said in the house of Annas.

(2) His sense of injustice.

(3) He remembers all His kind and beautiful words; now it is for His words that He is struck.

(4) Sense of inhumanity, the first out of the way violence.

(5) His sense of innocence—if evil, give testimony of the evil. He was being judged, and He thought of the justice and the indulgence of His own court of justice.

5. My God, My God, why hast Thou forsaken Me?

(1) Speaking no longer to creatures, but to His Father.

(2) In a loud voice, as if His Father was so far off, or was getting deaf to Him, as creatures were.

U.

(3) Amazement. *Forsake!*

(4) Sense of intolerableness.

(5) Yet somehow this is the most uncomplaining
   of the complaints, though the most heartrend-
   ing, because there is such adoration in it.

Note that all the complaints are questions—not
upbraidings but pleadings, unwillingness to believe
evil, the surprises of love at being wronged—their un-
rhetorical simplicity quite divine.

O dearest Lord! how sweet to us are Thy beautiful
complaints, the five wounds of Thy feelings! for we
seem to get nearer to Thee, or Thou to come nearer to
us, when Thou condescendest to complain!

XI.

OUR BLESSED LORD BOWING HIS HEAD UPON THE CROSS.*

Passage from mere Lent to Passiontide—from ex-
amining self to contemplating Him. Look at Him on
the cross, feature by feature. The drooping of a man's
head, when he dies sitting up; it is as if He were
pondering some difficult question, yet untroubled and
unperplexed.

The bowing of His head, His head crowned with
that cruel crown of thorns.

I. As if He was weary and would fain rest—and
   did He not grievously want rest? and what a

---

* The last sermon which Father Faber preached, Passion
Sunday, 1863.

comfortless deathbed we had given? Compared with this, there was luxury in the ashes on which saints have died. The Passion was more fatigue than creation. How His head must hvae ached! How the angels longed to hold it up!

II. As if He yearned to lean it on His Mother's ap.

    1. How sweet it had rested there at Bethlehem and in the wilderness! What she felt when she saw it move and droop.

    2. How it said to her (Cant. v.), Open to me, my love, my dove, my undefiled; for my head is full of dew, and my locks of the drops of the night.

    3. How afterwards she touched, and pressed, and kissed the dead Head beneath the cross.

III. In token of respect to His Father.

    1. As if His Father had spoken, and accepted the cross just then.

    2. As if now all was consummated—what an *All!* what a consummation!

    3. To give death leave to touch Him, Who was eternal Life.

IV. As though to welcome us and give us leave to kiss Him.

    1. The love He had for each of us at that moment.

    2. What is our love for Him? What our delighted worship of His Passion?

Dearest Lord! Why do we ever think of any one but Him? How can we manage to love any one but Him? Oh, may we come to feel and to know that we have but one faith, one hope, one love, one consolation in weary, painful time, and one reward in the grand, jubilant eternity—Jesus Christ, and Him crucified.

U

XII.

THE PASSION OUR DEVOTION THE WHOLE YEAR ROUND.

Seeming strangeness of speaking of the Passion at Eastertide.

I. The Passion is an abiding devotion.

1. Because in it redemption was accomplished.
2. Because the Sacraments come out of it.
3. Because Mass is a continuation of it.
4. Because it most safely suits our condition on earth.
5. Because it is a special antidote to hardness of heart. Examine this.

II. All holiness depends upon our hearts not being hardened; yet this is the great difficulty of life.

1. Because all that is seen (world so bright, people so kind and good), hardens the heart, while what softens it is unseen and supernatural.
2. Sin breeds sin, and so habits are formed which obscure the mind and harden the heart.
3. Low views of sin from the world's favorite notion that all duty to God is fulfilled in duty to our neighbor.
4. The very easiness of forgiveness helps to harden a wilful heart.
5. Natural corruption inclines that way, just as water gets cold if taken from the fire.
6. Because we pay so little attention to sins of thought.
7. Because we are so careless about venial sins, especially those of the tongue and untruths.

8. We have so little striving after perfection, and consequently little knowledge of our own vileness.

9. Because even good people act commonly from the sole motive of duty, without that of love.

III. Reasons why the Passion is so touching and heart-softening.

1. Because of the atrocity of the sufferings both mental and bodily.

2. The unparalleled heartlessness of the inflicters—there was every reason against *their* doing it.

3. The enchanting sweetness and patience of the Sufferer.

4. The thought that He was God.

5. That all these sufferings were for our sake.

6. That we have felt this a hundred times, and yet have so ill requited Him.

7. The fear that we might have acted as His executioners did, had we been there.

8. All the other circumstances of the Passion are so exquisitely pathetic. (1.) The betrayal. (2.) The Blessed Virgin Mary. (3.) The Last Words. (4.) The Centurian. (5.) Pilate's admission of His innocence.

9. Because from His Passion, as from a treasure-house of Divine Love, come

(1) All our hopes for the future.

(2) All our security about the forgiveness of the past.

(3) All the grace of our present life.

(4) The Presence of the Blessed Sacrament.

Hence the Passion is the daily bread of Christian souls.

XIII.

THE LEGACIES OF JESUS.

If sons, heirs indeed of God, and joint heirs with Christ. (Rom. viii. 17.)

Jesus, the poorest of earth's poor, leaves His legacies to His lovers: come to Calvary, come to the foot of the Cross: they are dicing for His seamless garment: we too must be there at that deathbed, to catch, if nothing else, the Seven last Words of wise and burning love that fall from His ever-blessed lips.

I. His peace:
   1. Interior mastery over self.
   2. Satisfyingness of our love for Him.
   3. Quiet certainty of our holy faith.
   4. Sweet inclination to judge well of and do good to all men.

II. His Cross:
   1. To make us carpenters for ourselves.
   2. To carry for Him, like Simon of Cyrene.
   3. To be nailed to, like Peter and Himself: and this
   1. In heart.
   2. In soul.
   3. In body.

Ah! who that has a loving heart will be cast down at such a legacy as this?

III. His Mother: as to St. John.
   1. Talk to her.
   2. Listen to what she shall tell us of Jesus: devotion to her opens mysteries.

U,   ℞

3. Defend her honor.
4. Beg her blessing as if she was in our house as she was in St. John's.

IV. Himself:

1. As the sweet Burden of Joseph's arms.
2. As on Mary's lap to make our hearts tender.
3. As in spices for sepulture in Communion.

Oh now with riches like to these that we would take heart and give ourselves utterly up to God. If life be bright and smiling, Jesus is the brightness and the smile—and how will He enhance that brightness. If our road lie through sorrow and through clouds, what a light ever shining is He. If our measure of life be wellnigh spent, ah what reparation have we not to make, and love alone can catch up lost time. If we be young, just leaving port in the gallant trim of youth with the bright flags of a hundred hopes flying at our masts, then with Jesus on board we shall be secure against wreck, and reach at once the haven where we would be. Oh that the mighty and Eternal Wisdom, the Eloquence of the Father, and yet the humblest of loving friends to poor venturesome sinners—Oh that He for the sake of these sorrowful mysteries and deep humiliations which we are all thinking of at this sacred season of Lent—Oh that He would speak one of His never-failing words in the hearts of each of us, and make us by a real conversion and a heavenly love His own, **His Heritage for ever!**

XIV.

SETTING UP THE STATIONS.

We are about to engage in an act to which the Church attaches great importance—is strict about—and enriches with quite unusual indulgences.

I. Devotions of the Jews to holy places—Jacob at Bethel, &c.—Also the heathen.

   1. It implies that we are in a state of exile, and that heaven is our real country.

   2. It is a means of reverence and adoration of God.

   3. It is an act of love and softens the heart.·

   4. It is a touching and eloquent witness to the world.

   5. Unusual grace and supernatural gifts often go with sanctity of place.

II. Devotion of the Stations.

   1. Beauty and naturalness of it considered in itself.

   2. Our Lady began it herself on Good Friday.

   3. How she continued it in after years in Jerusalem.

   4. Pilgrimages in the early and middle ages.

   5. The ardent love of Christians as it were invoked the holy places to their own homes, as St. Paula (so St. Jerome says), Blessed Columba of Rieti, and St. Lidwine of Schiedam visited the Holy Land bodily in ecstasy.

III. Fruits and benedictions of this devotion.

   1. It is an act of faith, of hope, and of charity.

   2. A thanksgiving to the Most Holy Trinity.

   3. An exercise most fruitful to contrition, penance, and humility.

U.

4. Most acceptable to Jesus and Mary.

5. Most supernatural in its effects on Purgatory.

The best way of making the Stations is to unite
    ourselves to the interior dispositions of Mary.

———

XV.

THE PAIN OF JESUS FROM OUR LITTLE DEVOTION TO HIS PASSION.

I. Have you ever been in great sorrow? Then you
    know how much harder to bear is want of sympathy
    than want of kindness. Kindness is a want with-
    out, sympathy a want within. Now with that
    thought come up Calvary.   .

  1. Did you ever see any beauty like the beauty of
     that dying Face?

  2. But is there not a look of surprise upon it? not
     that death is so hard; no! not that!

  3. And a look of being pained—not by physical pain,
     not by nails or crown; oh no!

  4. We each see that expression for ourselves—others
     do not see quite what we see.

  5. It is our Lord's pain at our want of devotion to
     the Passion: it is a pain we each of us have
     caused, apart from our causing the Passion
     altogether.

II. His pain at our want of devotion to His Passion.

  1. It was a separate pain for each one of us; for
     wounded love never repeats itself or its pangs.

  2. It was a very great pain, for love was just what

U   R

He was craving, and it was just the one possible consolation. We are too coarse to do justice to the mystery of the Passion; our lives are not sufficiently purified by penance.

3. It was a peculiar pain; and all peculiarity in pain is especially sensible.

4. It was a heightening of each and all of His other pains—want, ache, absence, feeling of wasted, unappreciated tenderness.

5. It was a separate thing for Him to *forgive*—yet not a sin exactly, and somehow this made it more intolerable to bear.

III. What we may reverently conceive to have been His dispositions about it.

1. Almost surprise—or what in any other human heart would have been surprise; *we* are surprised, indeed we cannot explain our own insensibility.

2. Intense sorrow—I had almost dared to say disappointment. The more intense because His own exceeding love made it altogether unreproachful.

3. An increased yearning for our devotion, as if its absence made Him hunger.

4. An increased passion to suffer, as if that might move us, and so get Him what He craves.

5. The pitiful pleading of His silence: in the garden He complained, what! could ye not watch? Yet on the Cross not one of His seven words was about it. But oh! how He intended that silence to speak, to speak in the hearts of His servants!

IV. What He *thought*, or rather what His silence said.

1. He had made His passion so various in order to

wound *all* hearts: I believe He meant some one touchingness of it for *each* heart.

2. He had run into all manner of excesses and enthusiasms, what could He do more?

3. Then He gave it all to each of us: He made what belonged to the whole world personal to each one of us.

4. His behavior and manner had all been so beautiful and gentle: angels even felt the sweet piteousness of His courteous love.

5. Then He had plunged His Mother in it, to break our hard hearts, because He knew with what intensity we should love her. Who can resist the piteousness of innocence suffering? and such dear innocence as hers?

I cannot go on multiplying thoughts: it is getting more than we can bear. O my Saviour! my Saviour! how I wish I could think He had had some consolation from knowing that I *should* be devoted to His Passion before I died!

XVI.

THE SEVEN JOURNEYS.

I. From the supper-room to Gethsemane.
   1. The departure of Judas on his accursed work.
   2. The presentiments of the disciples.
   3. The unspeakable calmness of Jesus.
II. From Gethsemane to the house of Annas.
   1. The violence of those who drag Him.
   2. The plunging Him in the brook Cedron.

U.   ℝ

3. His entry amid shame and abjection into the house of Annas.

III. From the house of Annas to the house of Caiphas.

1. The insults of His enraged enemies.
2. The disturbance in the dark streets.
3. The interior occupations of Jesus.

IV. From the house of Caiphas to the hall of Pilate.

1. The weariness and faintness of Jesus.
2. His confusion at being made over to the heathen governor.
3. The mingled feelings of those who see Him pass.

V. From the hall of Pilate to the court of Herod.

1. Increased faintness of Jesus.
2. His sweetness in suffering.
3. His patient charity.

VI. From the court of Herod to the hall of Pilate.

1. His submission to rude hands.
2. His acceptance of the humiliation.
3. His generous facing of death.

VII. From the hall of Pilate to Calvary.

1. His meeting His Blessed Mother.
2. His three falls.
3. His arrival at Calvary.

XVII.

THE FIVE TRIALS OF JESUS.

I. Before Annas.

1. Jesus justifies Himself.
2. He receives a blow.
3. His sweet patience and defence of Himself.

II. Before Caiphas.
  1. The silence of Jesus.
  2. The false witnesses.
  3. The adjuration.
III. Before Pilate and acquitted.
  1. The reluctance of Pilate.
  2. The modest defence of Jesus.
  3. Pilate's acquittal of Him and unlawful cruelty.
IV. Before Herod.
  1. Solemnity and severity of the silence of Jesus.
  2. His refusal to work a miracle.
  3. His being derided as a fool.
V. Before Pilate and found guilty.
  1. Pilate's human respect.
  2. The proposal of Barabbas.
  3. Jesus receives sentence.

Part Third.

OUR BLESSED LADY AND THE SAINTS.

SECTION I.

OUR BLESSED LADY.

U

L

DEVOTION TO MARY THE GREAT GIFT OF JESUS.

There is much in the world to make us sad, the present sorrows of the Church, and our own little love of God. Yet can we help a certain jubilee of heart in thinking that the Month of God's Mother has now begun, that each day of it is bringing more and more glory to God, and more and more help to the Church, because millions upon millions of souls, in every clime and of every blood, are daily growing in the deep reverence and the deeper love of the Immaculate Mother of God? Oh that the days were longer, and would pass more slowly, that we might fill them fuller of that sweet enthusiasm for Jesus, whose natural outburst is devotion to His dearest Mother!

I. The gifts of God.

   1. The pleasure of receiving gifts—huge pleasure to the generous—gifts from those we love.

   2. What then must be the pleasure of receiving them from God? yet all life is this.

   3. But our Lord says it is more blessed to give than to receive.

   4. How immense then the pleasure of God, and so in proportion His love.

   5. The wonderfulness of *our* receiving gifts from *God*.

the way it makes us love *Him* and humble ourselves.

II. The gifts of Jesus.

1. A peculiar sweetness in receiving gifts from Jesus.

2. He has one gift, an immense gift, of huge importance for time, and still more for eternity.

3. Not only an immense gift, but a choice one, one that He gives most of to His dearest saints.

4. One that was and is part of His own Heart and Character—and one which He is not so much ready to give us, as intensely burning to give us.

5. The gift is the grace to love His Mother! Oh if we did but prize and value this grace as we ought to prize it, as He Himself prizes it, we should be already half-way to heaven, because we should have half ensured our final perseverance.

III. It is the characteristic grace of Jesus: because He would give us such a gift.

1. As would make us love Himself most.

2. As would make us most like Him.

3. As would most honor His Mother.

4. As would be most advantageous to ourselves.

5. As would make Him love us most.

All these things are combined in the love of Mary.

What an intense joy it is in any way to resemble Jesus? How then ought we to cultivate and multiply this queenly grace of loving Mary! Oh, happy you who have it, happier you who greatly prize it, happiest you who are all on fire with it, for it is a fire which Jesus Himself has kindled in your hearts! The fair light of eternity, the sensible touch of God, the golden prophecies of a happy death, the cheerful securities of a joyous judgment are upon you. Happy, happy you! God be praised for your abounding happiness.

But oh unhappy souls, most unfortunate of men, most unfortunate at least of all men who are not yet the victims of the eternal prison, you who have not this devotion! There is much on earth, which bears, and rightly, the title of misfortune, but of all God's creatures upon earth, they are the most unfortunate who have no devotion to God's Mother!

Dearest brethren, there can be no repentance in heaven—else when we see Mary we shall wish we had known her better, prayed to her oftener, and loved her more; for we shall see brighter places than our own, further forward in the glory of heaven, where we might have been had we loved her more!

II.

MARY THE MOTHER OF SINNERS.

I. The dreadful condition of a man not in a state of grace.
  1. Cut off from God.
  2. Having no part in the redemption of Jesus.
  3. The sport of demons.
  4. Having already hell begun in itself.
  5. Chance of sudden death, and then eternal fire.
  6. Horror of the angels, and hatred of God, exemplified in the brand of Cain.
II. One thing is still left to him—the motherly

U.

solicitude of Mary. This is his hope—his treasure—his last resource. He goes about the
world linked to Heaven by this one thing.

1. Because she is the Mother of Mercy, not of
Justice.

2. Because God has willed it so, in love to her and
love to us.

3. Because experience shows that many who through
a sinful life have hung on to her by some little
devotion get grace at last.

III. How it is that, when she so approaches God in
His hatred of sin, she so perseveringly loves
sinners.

1. Because of the glory of God.

2. From a thirst to extend the harvest of Christ's
Passion.

3. Because all souls are the brothers of Jesus.

4. Because of her vehement enmity with the devil.

5. Because of her very hatred of sin.

6. Because she knows that Jesus saw each of us in
His sufferings, and specially suffered for each.

7. Because of her intense joy in beholding the
triumph of grace.

8. Because of her desire to exercise that peculiar
empire of mercy which God has entrusted to
her.

9. Because of the unspeakable tenderness of her
Maternal heart.

Address the hardhearted or the despairing, to have
unbounded confidence in Mary. You cannot better
magnify the love of God or show more welcome trust
in His mercy than by unlimited confidence in the
Heart of Mary!

III.

MARY THE SAFETY OF SOULS.

I. The opposite views which God and the world take
of men.
  1. The world's view according to science, or politics,
  or intellect, or wealth, or friendship.
  2. God's view, simply and exclusively as souls with
  one work to do.
  3. The difficulty of learning God's view and keeping
  to it: yet this is the very science of a Christian.
II. God's love of souls.
  1. The only treasure of His own creation He
  vouchsafes to set value on.
  2. The immense love of Jesus for souls.
  3. The whole Church simply a contrivance for souls.
  4. The way all heaven is engrossed day and night
  on behalf of souls.
  5. The characteristic of the saints is unforgetting
  enthusiastic zeal for souls.
  6. The value of the soul itself—death being better
  than sin—its unutterable penalties, its inconceivable rewards. Nay, God Himself is its only
  sufficient reward.
  7. The interests of the soul eminently unite the
  glory of God and the honor of Jesus.
III. What Mary does for souls.
  1. By what she suffered.
  2. By her example; the model of all ages, and
  simply a creature, simply imitable.

U.

3. By the conversion of sinners by missions, scapulars, medals, &c.

4. By the perfection of the saints.

5. By the religious orders she has founded either by vision or by love · and all they are doing at all hours all the world over, whether in the active or contemplative life.

6. By her peculiar winningness and familiarity as Mother of Mercy.

7. All she does for the Church and the Faith by her prayers is so much work for souls, as the peace of the Church is the salvation of the souls of the masses and multitudes.

8. The way she uses her angels on behalf of souls, and pursues them into Purgatory.

9. As the neck of the mystical body of Christ all graces pass through her.

IV. Conclusions to be drawn.

1. The little we can do for souls.

2. The immense privilege of being allowed to do that little.

3. The joy at the immensity which Mary does; this is another reason for loving her.

4. Also by our devotion we may continually get her to do more.

· Thus devotion to our Blessed Lady is an essential part of true zeal for souls.

IV.

DEPENDENCE ON MARY.

I. Our Lord is our example as well as our Redeemer.

  1. Hence the necessity of studying the four Gospels as our rule of life.
  2. In these things which seem the least fitted to His Divinity, He would seem also to be most our example;
  3. And these things are chiefly under the heads either of humiliation or submission.
  4. Instances: The Forty Days' Fast—His remaining in the Temple at twelve years old. I select these instances as on the surface least likely to be imitable.
  5. But above all, so much of the thirty-three years given to Mary, thirty out of thirty-three wholly, the other three very much.

II. His dependence on Mary.

  1. He waited her consent for His Incarnation, and fixed the time because of her.
  2. His infancy with use of reason, yet dependent on her.
  3. He seems to leave His Father's business and returns from the temple to Nazareth.
  4. The eighteen years—He was simply *subject* to her.
  5. The tradition that He asked her leave to go on His Ministry, and again to His Passion.
  6. At her word He anticipated His time for working miracles.

7. He perpetuated this dependence in the Church by transferring her to us through St. John.

III. Our dependence on Mary.

1. Her position to us is thus simply what it was to Him.

2. All true devotion to her is nothing but dependence upon her.

3. This dependence is based on—
   (1) Belief in her power.
   (2) Confidence in her love.

4. All good things which fail, fail because they have not enough of Mary in them.

5. We must put things in her hands, and look to her for results.

6. She must be imbedded in our lives, as she is imbedded in the office of the Church.

7. Holiness is impossible for us without Mary—for God has made it one consistent system, and she is part of it ordained by Him.

Oh if we would but throw ourselves more upon Mary than we do, with the whole weight of our love, with the whole weight of our necessities. She is loving each one of us at this moment with a surpassing love. No friend, no parent, no saint, no angel has ever been to us what she has been. It is wonderful what she has done for us without our asking, more wonderful still what she has done for our little asking, but most wonderful of all is what she can do and will do, if we will ask more, believe more, and trust more. Oh we who call earth our exile, and heaven our home, and Mary the Queen of Heaven, how is it we do not see that there can be no heavenly-mindedness which is not full of loyalty to heaven's great Queen?

U.

V.

MORE LOVE OF MARY.

Time goes differently with different people; and differently in different years even with the same person. Sometimes we live slowly; · sometimes we live quickly. But the years are always speeding, a quiet speed, but an incessant one. Are we speeding on the way to heaven? Speeding! yes! are we *speeding* on the way to heaven? It is a road on which nothing is safe but speed; nothing is prudent but impetuosity; nothing is cautious but bravery. What is age to the Christian eye? only this—more work, and less time to do it in. O Christians, how we dream! It was thus that I reproached myself the other day, and I awoke with a start, as if from sleep or from forgetfulness. More work and less time to do it in. This must be looked to; life must be put in order; I must be converted again, and at once, not to-morrow, but to-day, this very hour. Here is another year running round, the days are beginning to shorten again, we must quicken our speed both onward and upward. I thought I was getting hourly into God's debt; I sat down to teach myself a lesson, to preach myself a sermon, and reason with my own laziness and cowardice; and somehow it all went the other way, all my thoughts went into love. This was how it was; let us think the train of thought over again together.

I. The weight of our obligations to Jesus: what a delightfully hopeless debt it is.

U

1. All that He has suffered and done; let Him stand before us and show us His Wounds.

2. All His sweet patience lately, and at the pres-ent hour.

3. All the secret Love He has shown each of us, and which we alone know.

4. The intolerable misery of the little love we have for Him, and which we feel most when we love Him most.

5. We get hot; we rouse ourselves; we are deter-mined to love Him more, and to go and do some great thing for Him immediately. Worldly things are best done coolly, things for God are best done in a heat.

II. What is our great thing to be? We must do Him some *immense* service—but how?

1. He is God: we must adore His Divine Person; our adoration must grow more prostrate and more exulting every day.

2. But we want something special; just as His Incarnation was specially for us.

3. We must worship and love His created Nature, which He so intensely loves Himself, and which makes Him Jesus.

4. Prayer, austerities, work for Him: how little we can do in this way! No! He wants *imitation:* we must copy Him: we must copy His Sacred Heart. This, if I mistake not, is the work of all Christian life, and of Christians' lives, to widen the Sacred Heart of Jesus, to give it more room, to multiply its powers and faculties, its worships and its lives, and as it were add to it and broaden it by giving Him our own hearts to add to His

own and make it larger. Now what represents His Sacred Heart most both as God and man?

5. Then it dawns upon us like a revelation, like one of those almost frightening sunrises at sea, when the whole round sun leaps all at once out of the waters with a silvery suddenness. We must immediately love Mary with an entirely new love—with such a love as we never loved her with before, with such a love as nobody ever loved her with before—this is what we will do for Jesus. Dearest Saviour! Dearest God, how He will delight in this. Oh this is a sweet discovery—a most happy inspiration?

III. Measures of the love of Mary.

1. Our own greatest love, or all our love together? No!

2. All the Saints' love of her,—*e.g.* Joseph, Peter, John, and her particular friendship with St. James? No.

3. Her own beauty, goodness, and manifold dear offices? No.

4. Her own love of me? No! not even that.

5. The love of Jesus for her Yes that, precisely that, only that.

6. Alas! it is not enough; for we have more grounds for loving her than Jesus had: but we must be content with this measure.

IV. But I said to myself, it is impossible. Impossible! what does impossible mean? Does grace know of any such word? Impossible! Then I said, I will spend my life, and oh what a happy life it will be, in trying to accomplish this dear impossibility!

U

VI.

MARY MAGNIFYING GOD.

Is heaven far off, or near? We do not know: its songs are not heard, unless it be by the dying, or by saints as they are rapt in ecstacy. But then the soul's ear can hear far off. Still upon the whole we incline to think that heaven is near.

I. What is Heaven? It is the beautifulness of the outspread God.

  1. What angels think of this, and our own dear dead; it is all in all to them.

  2. Our want of appreciation intellectually, and the unmovedness of our affections.

  3. God is to us one of many things; hence our intolerably low views of God.

  4. Yet how stupid any low views of God must be: our own vexation with ourselves.

  5. To raise ourselves higher in this matter should be the one end of life.

II. Loving contemplation of Mary is the way to learn better adoration of God.

Blessed art thou by thy God in every tabernacle of Jacob: for in every nation which shall hear thy name, the God of Israel shall be magnified on occasion of thee.*

  1. This is her office. My soul doth magnify the Lord.

  2. She is the highest person in all God's creation, and nearest to the Divine Three.

* Judith xiii. 31.

U.

3. God has most incredibly communicated to her the splendors of His Perfections.

4. She has led the most wonderful life, and fulfils the most wonderful office, among creatures.

5. She has been more mixed up with God than all creation besides.

III. What she has been and is to God.

  1. In His Eternity before Creation.

    (1) Of all created persons, dearest and first.

    (2) His unutterable immense complacence in her, and endless desire of her.

    (3) He designed her as seemingly necessary to Him in creation, as the Mother of the Word.

  2. In the Kingdom of Nature.

    (1) Her perfections as a person the greatest in all creation.

    (2) Creation created subordinately to Jesus and herself.

    (3) The natural gifts of her body and her soul.

  3. In the Kingdom of Grace.

    (1) The highest sanctity of created persons is hers.

    (2) The Divine Maternity.

    (3) The Queenship of the Church on earth.

  4. In the Kingdom of Glory.

    (1) Her incomparable throne and exaltation.

    (2) The Queenship of the angels.

    (3) She beautifies even the unspeakable life of God by her exceeding glorious loveliness.

Oh Majesty of God, most dear, most mysterious, and yet so infinitely desirable! How shall we learn it more worthily, and worship it with more delighted awe, than by the contemplation of Mary? It will

U.

be well for us in time and in eternity to spend this month in intensest efforts to worship Mary with a more noble, more tender, more reverent worship. It is a matter in which there can be no excess; we cannot do too much: our most must be sorrowfully too little. God will leave us far behind in His love and admiration and complacency in her. Oh then, my brethren, let us worship the grand mother of God with every faculty of our minds: let us worship her with every affection of our hearts: let us worship her with a magnificent worship—and so shall there grow in our hearts the grand, broad, invigorating, exclusive, exulting, impassioned love of God!

VII.

MARY THE LIKENESS OF GOD.

How it would sweeten death, if when we came to die, we could feel that God had allowed us to increase in one single heart the love of our dearest Lady. I believe it would be a special joy for all eternity. Let us try now again to-day to inflame each other's hearts with this sweet love.

I. Astonishment is one of the chief joys of heaven.

  1. Caused by the immense incomprehensible beauty of God;

  2. And also by the inconceivable jubilee of all there.

  3. Always new, always as it were increasing.

  4. In saints on earth touches and glimpses of heaven bring ecstacy and rapture; but this is because

of their mortal weakness: it is not so in heaven.

5. The exquisite joy of astonishment, in mind, in heart, in glorified senses.

II. The likeness of God.

   1. It is difficult for us on earth to conceive what it is to have God all in all.

   2. He is so completely the one Object that all blessedness tends to become more and more one with Him, with an amazing oneness which will not be put into words.

   3. Our joy is that we remain separate selves, yet one with Him, and so can feel and enjoy our unity with Him.

   4. This union with Him is by becoming transformed into His likeness.

   5. All beauty therefore in creatures, and all joy, is in their likeness to God.

III. All creation is the likeness of God.

   1. Inanimate nature—in beauty of form—properties, &c.

   2. Animalcules — in *life* — fecundity — beauty — strangeness.

   3. Men like God.

   4. Angels like God.

   5. But Mary most of all.

     (1) Like the Father—in being the Mother of the Son, truly and naturally. What unimaginable likenesses to that dear and Blessed First Person does not this suggest?

     (2) Like the Son.

       1. In form and features, and human disposition.

2. In the character of her Immaculate Heart.

3. In mortal sufferings.

(3) Like the Holy Ghost.

   1. In being His Spouse.

   2. In her love of Jesus.

   3. Through the action of her repeated sanctifications.

There are cold, shallow controversies on earth about our Lady's greatness, while at this hour the great St. Michael is gazing on her throne with a rapture of astonishment, a delighted rapture which will grow to all eternity !

VIII.

THE DELIGHT OF GOD IN THE PERFECTIONS OF MARY.*

There has been only one thing from eternity—there is only one thing now—there will never to all eternity be but one thing—the glory of God.

I. The Glory of God.

   1. What it is, and His delight in it.

   2. Its universal empire, and our own concern with it.

   3. The glorious sovereignty of God.

   4. The glorious sweetness of God.

   5. The glorious exclusiveness of God.

II. Mary an immense glory of God ; and God's delight.

   1. In her Predestination.

* Octave of the Immaculate Conception, 1859.

2. In her Office as Mother of God.
3. In her Graces.
4. In her Prerogatives.
5. In the work she does in creation.

III. The reasons of His delight.
  1. Because He sees Himself reflected in her.
  2. Because He is enabled for her sake to love His creation more.
  3. Because through her a greater number of souls are saved.
  4. Because all in her is His own gift.
  5. Because the distance from her to Himself is simply infinite.

This night in heaven: Mary is on her throne, clothed with the sun, twelve stars around her head, sighs of earth coming up to her, and the joys of earth as well. Baptized children, saints, angels, the Sacred Humanity, the Three Persons of the Holy Trinity, are all drinking joy and jubilee out of that one fountain, that dearest of all God's dear glories, the Immaculate Heart of Mary

We too have, we trust, a place kept there, in what part of all that boundless realm of grandeur and ecstasy we cannot know, but it is very beautiful, strangely suited to us, and full of unimaginable delights. Though it is a land of immense distances every one is near to God, every one is near to Mary. Let us think of that dear unseen home, and let us hold on in virtue; let us pray hard; let us love hotly; let us sorrow holily; let us delight in God; and so, dearest children of Mary, shall our whole lives become one long and beautiful Procession of the Immaculate Conception!

U.   ℗

IX.

THE IMMACULATE CONCEPTION.

I.

THE MOTHER AND THE SON.

The history of the Predestination of Jesus and Mary —hence their unity and inseparability. The Immaculate Conception is a mystery belonging to both, and the first mystery of both.

I. The peculiar force and majesty of the mystery of the Immaculate Conception.

1. It is the first dawn of the world's redemption.

2. The fountain of all the other mysteries of Jesus and Mary, and of the seven sacraments, and of the Church.

3. It interprets as nothing else does the character of God, and illuminates His eternal decrees.

4. It illustrates and unriddles the wonderfulness of creation.

5. It beautifies the Church, her doctrines, and her ceremonial, and crowns the desires of holy hearts through many generations.

II. Chiefly, it is the primary revelation of Mary's similitude to Jesus. Points of likeness.

1. She was exempt from original sin, which none ever were before in their conception.

2. The gift of actual sinlessness.

3. She could not be tempted inwardly—the devil had no such power because of her innocence.

4. Her hiddenness and marvellous infancy.

5. A prodigy of suffering, yet not for her own sake.
6. The resurrection of her body.
7. Her Assumption answers to His Ascension.
8. She is treated in the world now as the Blessed Sacrament is, unknown, unrealized, shorn of glory.
9. Her interior—possessing the spirit of Jesus in unknown measure, far beyond her outward resemblance.
10. Her share in the victories the saints have won before and after Christ.
11. In her degree she is the light of the Church— He the Sun, she the Moon.
12. As God communicates Himself through Jesus, so Jesus communicates His gifts through her.
13. Her Queendom, like His Headship, is over angels as well as men.
14. The similarity of her features to His—how wonderful this resemblance must be to the angels, who know God, and gaze on Him Incarnate, a living copy of His creature.

III. It was the grand work of the Most Holy Trinity in power, in wisdom, and in joy; and so love of Mary is, as it were, the signet of the Most Holy Trinity set upon our souls.

1. Love of Mary a power with God, with her, with others, over devils, and over self.
2. Love of Mary a wisdom beyond art and science, literature and philosophy, giving a knowledge of God, grace, sin, creation, Jesus, eternal and invisible things.
3. Love of Mary a joy not temporal, but eternal, and so a shadow of our predestination.

U.   ℞

To know Mary is to love her. How we should bless God for this enchanting knowledge! The ills of life are many, achings of body, pangs of heart, remorse of conscience, peril of salvation, yet it is worth while to have risked all this, and a thousand times more than this, to have gazed on her sweet life, lisped in prayer her most beautiful of names, to have known her, to have loved her, and to be her child; yes, to be as Jesus was, the spotless Mother's Child.

2.

THE MOTHER AND HER MANY SONS.

I. The beauty of Mary is shown by the fact that the Word elected her out of His infinite ideals. She was His mother by choice: she is ours by the appointment of her Son, who shares her with us.

  1. She was no choice of ours, but the merciful ordinance of God; just as He made the privilege of our loving Him into a precept.

  2. We cannot do without her, as the Gospel now stands.

  3. She was given to us from the Cross, to Him at Nazareth: to both of us in the Immaculate Conception.

  2. She has been the ruling power of all the good of our past lives.

  5. That she is our Mother is the great fact of our lives: else we are not of our Brother's family.

U.   ℞

II. The Immaculate Conception as it regards us is a mystery of grace.

1. It is the second greatest mercy human nature could have; the Hypostatic Union being the first.
2. It is the diadem of graces overtopping all that angels and men have ever received.
3. A grace more for the glory of God and the honor of Jesus than any other.
4. A source of perpetual joy in heaven, and boundless confidence on earth.

The five graces involved in the Immaculate Conception. (1) Immunity from all venial sins collectively; (2) Extinction of *fomes;* (3) Ceaseless light of grace; (4) Endless love of God in act.

I know not whether very great saints or very great sinners should most love this mystery: extremes meet: it truly can be no devotion of the commonplace or lukewarm.

III. The exercise of our Lady's Maternal office shadows forth the Holy Trinity.

1. Her immense participation in the power of the Father, the wisdom of the Son, and the love of the Holy Ghost.
2. It is carried on even when we neglect or offend her.
3. Capable of almost numberless degrees, as grace itself is.
4. Desirous of being more and more exactingly called on, just as God loves prayer.
5. On the whole her maternal solicitude is proportioned to our devotion, just as God is gentle with the gentle, liberal with the liberal, and perverse with the perverse.

U.   ℞ .

More confidence! Ask more! Ask greater things! It is no dream: the hour is to come when we shall see her. We shall hear her voice and be delighted by her beauty, and kiss those hands which have sent us so many graces; and then, and not till then, shall we know to the full the abounding joy and exultation with which all heaven and its angels are overflowing because the Queen of paradise, the dear Empress of angels and of men, your Mother and mine, was through the omnipotence of unutterable love, conceived without stain of sin!

3.

THE MOTHER OF THE IMMACULATE QUEEN.

God vouchsafes to make preparations for His great works, as men do, and for our sake: they are full of beauty, wisdom, and winningness. Thus predestination preluded creation.

I. Preparations for the Immaculate Conception.

  1. On earth.

    (1) The yearnings of Eve and of all generations for the Mother of the Deliverer.

    (2) The burden of this desire upon the hearts of the good and holy.

    (3) The weary sighs and tears of the patriarchs and prophets. Elias and Carmel.

    (4) The needs of the sin-desolated world coming to a head.

    (5) The tremulous supernatural expectation diffused over the earth.

  2. In Heaven.

U.   ℬ

(1) Her predestination.

(2) Her not being included in the decree which regarded sin.

(3) The Divine Persons concur in electing her to be the Mother of the Incarnate Word.

(4) The Eternal Son in His wisdom conceives the idea of her glorious soul.

(5) The angels behold the idea of their Queen in Him. Where their sanctity ends, hers begins.

II. The theatre of the actual mystery.

1. Again God chooses, as He chose Mary; His choice must be a great saint, full of the peculiar spirit of Jesus.

2. She must be an image of the suffering and abasement of Jesus and Mary.

3. St. Anne—her life, and that of St. Joachim.

4. The mystery accomplished: announced by angels, hidden like Incarnation, the crown of humility.

5. From that moment St. Anne was the queen of earth; God's gifts to her, retinue of angels, inward holiness and joy.

6. St. Anne begins the devotion to the Immaculate Conception, which the Church now grounds upon an article of faith.

III. The mysteries of St. Anne.

1. To her God's beautiful eternal secret is confided.

2. Her joy in Mary's infancy, and her wonder at her childish actions.

3. Her heroic sacrifice of her in the temple, like Mary's at the Presentation.

4. Her death—she receives from the Soul of Jesus
   the beatific vision—she is with Mary during the
   forty days—ascends with Jesus.

5. Her joy at Mary's Assumption and Coronation.

IV. The prerogatives of St. Anne.

   1. Prerogatives of the saints of the Hypostatic
      Union.

   2. Power with Joseph, as Mary's husband.

   3. Power with Mary, as her mother, like Mary's power
      with Jesus.

   4. Power with Jesus, because of the Immaculate
      Conception.

   5. Power with the angels, as a sort of queen-mother.

   6. Power with the apostles, on the same ground.

   7. Power with the Holy Trinity, as the elect vessel
      and theatre of their greatest grace.

Let all who have a devotion to the Immaculate
Conception put themselves in a special way under
St. Anne. It was St. Anne, who opened in the secret
solemnities of that ever-blessed mystery the everlasting
jubilee of Jesus, and it was within her womb that God
granted the first and the completest plenary indulgence
in the world!

4.

THE IMMACULATE QUEEN.

I. Jesus present in the Blessed Sacrament.

   1. We have to speak of the Mother in the Presence
      of the Son.

   2. He is present as God, with a peculiar presence of
      the Most Holy Trinity.

U.   ℬ

3. As man. (1) Prophet of the world. (2) Priest.
(3) King. (4) Owner of all temporal things.
(5) Judge.

4. To Mary He is in addition—(1) Her God.
(2) Her Creator. (3) Her Redeemer. (4) Her
Son.

5. He is come, we have dared to bring Him to
keep the feast, just as we call her to come
and worship Him for us in the Litany at
Benediction.

II. The three kingdoms of Jesus the King: Mary's
place in them all.

1. Nature.
(1) Below the angels. 1. Joy of this to us.
2. Her gifts greater than theirs. 3. Her
exaltation greater.
(2) The same as that of saints, and sinners.
(3) The same as the nature, by which Jesus is
Blessed Sacrament, prophet, priest, king and
judge.
(4) Both the spiritual and material world were
created because of Jesus and herself.

2. Grace.
(1) All creation, angelic and human, resulted in
a state of grace.
(2) Grace in baptism, of release from original sin.
(3) Preservation from actual mortal sin.
(4) Exemption from venial sin.
(5) Sanctifying in the womb.
(6) Solitary grace of Immaculate Conception.
1. From decree—2. From momentary touch
—3. From root of sin—4. Highest act of
redeeming grace—5. So she needed redemp-

tion most, and Jesus was more truly and highly a glorious Redeemer by this mystery than by the redemption of all the world beside.

3. Glory.

    (1) Baptized infants.

    (2) Multitudes of unplaced saints.

    (3) Angels.

    (4) Hierarchy of the Incarnation.

    (5) Herself.

    (6) The Sacred Humanity, THEN the blaze of the Unspeakable and Incomprehensible glory.

III. Her great *unlikeness* to Jesus was her growth in grace. Hence her growth in the Church. Scripture authority.

1. Growth in heaven.

    (1) Empty throne filled. (2) Accumulated intercession. (3) Love of the angels. (4) Multitude of the daily saved.

2. Growth on earth.

    (1) By doctrines. (2) By feasts. (3) By religious orders. (4) By saints. (5) By councils. (6) By popes. (7.) By devout people.

3. Growth in our hearts.

    (1) Love. (2) Faith. (3) Reverence. (4) Confidence. (5) Thanksgiving to the Most Holy Trinity.

Oh how the spirit of the coming Christmas leaps forward into our hearts to teach us to keep this feast. Angels rejoice and triumph! Oh men, rejoice and bless the abundance of redeeming grace. To-day a Queen is created for you of the House of David, good tidings of great joy that shall be to all the people—a

Mother is given to us, and the government is on her shoulder, and her name shall be called Wonderful, Counsellor, the most high Lady, the Mother of the Lord to come, the Princess of Peace. Her empire shall be multiplied, of her peace there shall be no end. Blessed be the Most High God, above all things blessed for the Immaculate Soul of Mary which He this day so gloriously created, and in the same moment so gloriously redeemed.

Oh Blessed Sacrament, my Lord and my God, my Saviour and my Judge, true Man and Son of Mary, I a sinner have dared to speak of Thy sinless Mother; forgive me and be indulgent to me for every word which has fallen short of her immense dignity and incomparable majesty, and for the sake of her Immaculate Conception grant to every soul here to-night the grace to love Thy Mother according to Thy commandment, and after the measure of Thy Sacred Heart, so that not one among us shall be lost!

X.

PRAYING FOR SINNERS.

The world has a great many wants, and good Christians have a great many wants also; but it so happens that the world's great want is the same as a good Christian's great want—a right appreciation of spiritual things. This want is the source of all mischief.

I. One of the spiritual things in question is the favor of Mary.

1. Intellectually—what is there you would not sacrifice for it.
2. Except the grace and love of God, what *can* come near it?
3. Yet we do not appreciate it as we ought.
4. And this from want of faith in her power, and want of experience of her goodness.
5. This month we are going to offer devotions to her, and likely to secure her favor: and to-day I will speak of praying for those who are in sin.

II. The world of sinners.

1. The dreadfulness of their state in the sight of the angels.
2. Their multitude, and daily increase.
3. Their secrecy—such unlikely persons.
4. The grace they have resisted.
5. Their immense power against God.

Yet on the other side—

1, The good and sweetness there is amongst them.
2. How much also to pity, and often to extenuate.
3. How much struggle also, although inefficacious.
4. What immense capabilities many of them have for glorifying God.
5. How much work one real conversion does, and how many miracles it involves.

III. This is Mary's world.

1. It is given over to her in a special and official manner.
2. She knows how Jesus yearns over it.
3. Hence those have almost a claim upon her mercy, who are so sadly in need of it.
4. How much love of her there is even in that dark multitude.

U

5. Yet in a great measure she has to work through us: just as God vouchsafes to depend on us Himself.

IV. The devotion of praying for sinners.

1. Almost the favorite devotion of the saints.

2. How it cultivates union with Jesus, and fosters love of Mary.

3. Praying for particular sinners, or classes of sinners, or places.

4. Praying, as in the case of the Holy Souls, for those God wills, and leaving all to Him.

Might I speak of the shape of this devotion, which is sweetest to myself? Pool of Bethsaida*—the man who was there for thirty-eight years—so let us pray for the soul which is close to conversion, has been waiting longest, and has none near to put him in. I do not think it would be out of the way to expect to convert one soul a day, and give it to Mary to offer. We should not see our work—it might be by the burning rivers of Africa, or on the icy shores near the Pole, or in the great city, or in the quiet country—it might be one of our own kith and kin, or a stranger and a foreigner—it might be a king or a laborer, a child at school who has just committed his first mortal sin, or an old man in his agony with thousands of them. But these would be among the delightful secrets which we should learn in heaven, and perhaps from Mary's lips.

We should know that we were working for God—we should be sure we were working with success—it would almost be sweeter because it is all in the dark, in that darkness of faith which will one day change so sweetly into light.

* St. John v.

U.   ℞

XI.

THE ASSUMPTION.

To-day is the feast of the beautiful mystery—the first function of the Church triumphant in heaven, the end for which God created the world coming into view; let us see in what light it puts the character of God before us.

  I. Humility. The Assumption is God's coming to crown His own creation.
    1. It is the proper virtue of a creature.
    2. It was so of the angels, and saved them.
    3. It is so of the Church, and is marked in all her worship.
    4. The want of humility in the world is just the evidence of its having fallen from God.
  II. God cannot be humble; yet there is a characteristic of the Divine operations answering to that virtue: we cannot name it; it is shewn—
    1. In the unostentatiousness of creation.
    2. In the renewal and conservation of creation.
    3. In His omnipresence.
    4. In the delay of judgment, and in silence under outrage.
    5. In his quiet hidden way of imparting grace.
  III. God came to practise humility by the Incarnation.
    1. In His choice of poverty and suffering.
    2. In what followed from the Incarnation — the obedience of the Omnipotent, the poverty of the Lord of All, the hiddenness of the Omnipresent, the toil of the Creator.
    3. In the Blessed Sacrament daily.

4. In the humiliations of His dear Spouse the Church.

IV. Mary the humblest of creatures.

1. With the angel. 2. With St. Elizabeth. 3. With St. Joseph. 4. Her purification and obedience to other laws. 5. The silence of the Evangelists.

Thus the Assumption was a consistent manifestation of the Creator's character, a revelation of His taste, a merciful disclosure of His genius.

Oh let us fall in love with sweet humility, let us keep ourselves low, and nestle in the thought of our own unworthiness; let us wonder God should bear with us at all, and so learn sweet manners to bear with the waywardness of others, and this night from the depths of the fallen earth let us look at this grand *action* of our Creator, and worshipping His ways, use our mother's words unto Him: *Magnificat anima mea Dominum, et exultavit spiritus meus in Deo salutari meo:* and why? *Quia respexit humilitatem ancillae suae. Deposuit potentes de sede et exaltavit humiles:* He cast Lucifer from his throne, and set Mary nigh unto Himself.

XII.

THE ASSUMPTION.

World-wearied, sin-stained, earth-bound! What have we to do with this great glory? Yet it has lessons for all, besides the wonder and the beauty and the joy of our mother's glory, and the vision of a mighty work of God.

Vol. I.   U

I. How great nature can be with grace.

   1. She has not outstepped or outstripped her nature.

   2. It would be hard to put a limit to what nature can be.

   3. Yet we are always fancying we have got to our own limit.

II. How little without grace.

   1. For what is Mary's nature in itself?

   2. What has she from nature independent of grace?

   3. Her nature is only visible in the fires of grace as the three children were in the furnace.

III. The abundance of grace.

   1. See what she had in number and in kind.

   2. Yet she has not nearly exhausted the possibilities of grace.

   3. Nay, what abundance have we not had ourselves?

IV. Correspondence to grace is of itself the whole work.

   1. Her correspondence is the nearest interpretation of the mystery of her greatness.

   2. What correspondence is in detail, and how it multiplies grace.

   3. Oh, the room our graces leave us, and our lost opportunities.

Mary is the manifestation of the kingdom of grace, and the type of God's way with all our souls; singular, yet not singular; admirable, yet imitable also; standing alone, yet in the midst of us; moved up to God as His sinless Mother, yet removed from us no further than a mother from her children!

XIII.

ROSARY SUNDAY.

I. The position which the Rosary occupies in the Church.

1. It is not a special devotion, but unites all devotions.
2. It distinguishes no order, but all orders.
3. It is to the laity almost what office is to the clergy.
4. A true Catholic mind can hardly now be formed without it.
5. It is distinguished above all other devotions by the approbations of the Church.

II. The Rosary viewed as an instrument of power in itself.

1. Its peculiar power on earth in forming character. so that it is a Catholic touchstone.
2. Its influence in heaven shewn from its being revealed.
2. Its influence in Purgatory from the immensity of its indulgences.
4. As a profession of faith also.
5. As a shield against many temptations.

III. It is also an instrument of power as a teacher.

1. It illustrates the position of our Lady to our Lord, and is another way of looking at their Mysteries.
2. It teaches also how she is a way to Him.
3. Also it is what she did all her life herself: she rose to great heights by incessant meditation of Jesus.

U.   ℞

4. Therefore it shows us what she wishes us to do; it is her testament, as the Holy Eucharist is the testament of Jesus.

5. Hence it is the truest means of loving her; for love consists, (1) in obedience; and (2) in imitation.

In consequence of all these blessings the devil makes the Rosary a special subject of temptations, weariness, contempt, and the like. Persevere in it, and it will itself be the chain of your own final perseverance.

XIV.

THE LETTER KILLETH, BUT THE SPIRIT GIVETH LIFE.*

People who aim at doing their duty, are divisionable into two classes, (1) they who follow the letter, and (2) they who take the spirit.

I. Our Blessed Lady an exemplification of the spirit, not the letter.

1. She got from the Scriptures a true notion of the Messias and His kingdom.

2. Her conduct to St. Joseph, secrecy, marriage, &c.

3. With our Lord, especially in the marriage at Cana.

4. Her receiving St. John, and us with him.

5. Thus the letter of our Lord's words hurt her not.

II. Conduct of those who take the spirit with regard to—

* Preached to the Enfants de Marie at Roehampton.

1. Genius, and spirit, and movement of the Church, as well as her doctrines.
2. Way of holding doctrines.
3. View of the spiritual life.
4. Promptness of obedience.
5. Intercourse with the world.
6. Supernatural tendency.
7. The Child of Mary ever divining the high and right path.

III. What happens to the mere disciples of the letter. They

1. Often miss real duty, and get gradually entangled in a positively wrong course of conduct.
2. Do no great works for God or the Church.
3. Are less winning and attractive.

The power of high principle and noble purpose and lofty aim, wherein lies the sphere and mission of the Enfants de Marie.

XV.

MEMORIALS OF MARY AND HER SIXTY-THREE YEARS.

1. Her eternal predestination.
2. Her Immaculate Conception.
3. Her first use of reason.
4. Her first act of Divine love.
5. Her pure nativity.
6. Her obedience to SS. Joachim and Anne.
7. Her receiving her beautiful name.

U

8. Her presentation in the temple when three years old.
9. Her holy sojourn and retreat there.
10. Her preservation from all actual sin.
11. Her pure nuptials.
12. The Annunciation.
13. Her humble answer to St. Gabriel.
14. The Incarnation.
15. The perplexity of St. Joseph.
16. The visitation and sanctification of St. John the Baptist.
17. Her innocence declared by the angel and honored by St. Joseph.
18. Her expectation of her delivery.
19. The rebuff from the people of Bethlehem.
20. The entry into the stable.
21. Her ecstatic contemplation of the Incarnation.
22. The birth of her Jesus.
23. The joy of her first services to Him.
24. Her first suckling of Him.
25. The devotion of the shepherds.
26. The adoration of the Kings.
27. The circumcision and naming of Jesus.
28. Her purification, and presentation of Jesus.
29. The joy of Simeon and his prophecies.
30. The flight into Egypt.
31. The return to Nazareth.
32. The loss of Jesus for three days.
33. The finding Him in the temple.
34. Her maternal authority over Him at Nazareth.
35. Her sorrow at the death of St. Joseph and St. Anne.
36. Her joy in following Jesus and hearing His sermons.

37. Her success in obtaining the first miracle at Cana.
38. Her farewell to Jesus when He went to His Passion.
39. Her meeting Him on the road to Calvary.
40. The nailing to the cross and the elevation of it in her presence.
41. Her receiving St. John as her legacy.
42. The death of Jesus.
43. The piercing of His side.
44. The descent from the cross.
45. Her receiving His body on her lap.
46. Her helping to bury Him.
47. Her tears during Saturday's solitude.
48. Her first visit from Jesus risen.
49. Her witnessing the Ascension.
50. Her receiving the Holy Ghost at Pentecost.
51. Her first Communion from the hands of St. John
52. Her solicitude for the infant Church.
53. Her desire for death.
54. Her dying of love.
55. Her burial by the Apostles.
56. The resurrection of her body.
57. Her rising through the air.
58. Her entry into Heaven.
59. Her reception by the Eternal Father.
60. Her Coronation.
61. Her sweet empire over the Angels.
62. Her diligent love of the Souls in Purgatory.
63. Her protection of us poor sinners upon earth.

———

U.

XVI.

THE JOYS OF OUR DEAR LADY.

I. Her seven earthly Joys.
  1. The Annunciation.
  2. The Nativity.
  3. The adoration of the Three Kings.
  4. The Resurrection.
  5. The Ascension.
  6. The coming of the Holy Ghost.
  7. The Assumption.

II. Her Seven heavenly joys, revealed by her to St. Thomas of Canterbury.
  1. Her exaltation above the Angels.
  2. Her seat at the right hand of Jesus.
  3. The obedience of the Blessed to her.
  4. Her being the new Ornament of Paradise.
  5. Her conformity to the Will of God.
  6. Her being the channel of all grace.
  7. The increase of her joys up to the day of Judgment, and their eternity.

Part Third.

OUR BLESSED LADY AND THE SAINTS.

SECTION II.

THE SAINTS.

U.

L

MEDITATIONS ON THE HOLY ANGELS.

I. The silence of God before the creation of the Holy Angels.
1. His infinite happiness without creatures.
2. His independence of all relation to them.
3. The immensity and variety of possible worlds and creatures.

II. The Creation.
1. God's choice of this world out of all possible worlds.
2. The utter dependence of creatures on Him.
3. The eternal silence broken by the beautiful creation of Angels.

III. The existence of the Angels.
1. Spiritual substances possible.
2. Suitable for God's glory and the good of the world.
3. Belief of all ages in the existence of Angels.

IV. The spirituality of the Angels.
1. The substance of the Angels the most subtle in the world.
2. They are more spiritual than the soul of man.
3. Yet gross, and as it were material, compared with God.

V. The great number of the Angels.
1. The ninth choir contains, according to a common opinion, as many guardians as there are, have been, or will be souls of men.
2. Eight choirs remain unnumbered.
3. The great glory of God from the multitude of His courtiers.

VI. The distinction of the Angels.
1. They might have been all of one species.
2. Probably they are of twenty-seven species, three in each choir.
3. Glory of the Creator in this distinction.

VII. The order of the Angels.
1. St. Paul, ravished to the third heaven, classes them in three hierarchies.
2. These subdivided into three choirs.
3. The choirs into three ranks of different species.

VIII. The understanding of the Angels (1).
1. Their substance the most noble after that of God, and so their understanding the most subtle.
2. Their knowledge of the secrets of nature.
3. Their knowledge of theology and the attributes of God.

IX. The understanding of the Angels (2).
1. They receive their ideas and images immediately from God.
2. Their knowledge is intuitive.
3. Their understanding is always in action.

X. The things which the Angels do not know by their natural science.
1. Things future.
2. The secrets of hearts.
3. The Incarnation and its mysteries.

U.

XI. The will of the Angels.
1. The freedom of it.
2. The marvellous power of it as regards God.
3. Their love of each other.
XII. The movement of the Angels.
1. The perfection of it.
2. They move all at once, as being indivisible substances.
3. Their great power in moving other substances, whether spiritual or material.
XIII. The time, place, and end of their creation.
1. The time—when God said, let there be light, or when He created the heavens.
2. The place—in the heavens.
3. The end—to adorn and beautify the heavens for the greater glory of God.
XIV. The supernatural gifts received by the Angels at the moment of their creation.
1. Sanctifying grace, with faith, hope, charity, and other infused virtues.
2. Revelations, as of the Most Holy Trinity, Incarnation, guardianship of men, future events, fires of hell, &c.
3. Actual grace to elicit supernatural acts and merit.
XV. The different orders of Angels.
1. They have received different graces and excellences.
2. They have each distinguishing and special virtues.
3. All other virtues are, however, included in the case of each, in their own special eminence.
XVI. The first hierarchy.
1. The Seraphim, inflamed with love.
2. The Cherubim, glorious for supernatural science.

3. The Thrones, eminent for special submission to the Divine Will.

XVII. The second hierarchy.

1. The Dominations, filled with zeal for the kingdom of God.

2. The Virtues, replete with invincible force in the service of God.

3. The Powers, possessed of marvellous benignity.

XVIII. The third hierarchy.

1. The Principalities, eminent for purity of intention.

2. The Archangels, lovely for their peculiar participation in the virtues both of their superiors and inferiors.

3. The Angels, delightful to God from the humility with which they govern the world.

XIX. The probation of the Angels.

1. The time of their temptation was very short.

2. Two-thirds persevered in their peculiar graces.

3. The battle in heaven.

XX. The sinning Angels.

1. There were some of all the orders.

2. Their sin was pride.

3. Especially, St. Thomas thinks, complacency in their own exceeding beauty.

XXI. The judgment of the Angels.

1. They had a particular judgment, though they will have to appear again at the general judgment.

2. God gave those who had persevered a third beatitude, in addition to their natural and supernatural beauty; it consisted in the Beatific Vision of Himself.

3. The awfulness of His justice upon the evil Angels, though He foresaw all their hatred of Him, and the misery they would cause. ·

XXII. The principal pains of the fallen Angels.

1. The pain of loss.
2. The pain of sense, although they are spirits.
3. The knowledge that it is all irrevocable.

XXIII. The occupations of the fallen Angels against the souls of men.

1. They tempt man, because they envy him and hate God.
2. They cannot hurt man against his will by these temptations.
3. The means of resisting evil angels are prayer, · humility, and the flight of occasions.

XXIV. The possession of men's bodies by the fallen Angels.

1. It is through envy of man, and a blasphemous desire of imitating the Incarnation.
2. This possession is subject to the exorcisms of the Church, though, as it grows more infrequent, it seems more difficult to cure.
3. The misery of possession far less than that of wilful sin.

XXV. The language and light of Angels.

1. They speak to each other by their wills.
2. They ask light of those above them and communicate it to those below them.
3. The words of the superior Angels purify, enlighten, and make perfect those below them.

XXVI. The commissions of the Angels in the world.

1. To move and rule the earth and heavenly bodies.

U.

2. To undertake the protection of kingdoms and
empires.

3. To guard each particular soul.

XXVII. The Guardian Angels; of what order they are.

1. Some say they are from the ninth choir only.

2. St. Thomas thinks that the angels of the first four
choirs never go from the presence of God; and
that the Guardian Angels are from the other
five choirs.

3. Others, taking St. Paul* literally, think that some
of all the choirs are deputed to guard the souls
of men.

XXVIII. The Guardian Angels; at what time they
guard us.

1. They begin as soon as the body is joined by the
soul in the womb.

2. They do so till death, and at the general judgment.

3. The Guardian Angel of Judas did not desert him
so long as breath was in him.

XXIX. The Guardian Angels; how they guard us.

1. With most affectionate condescendance.

2. With inexpressible zeal.

3. With perpetual joy.

XXX. Comparison of men and Angels (1).

1. Men are inferior to the Angels in natural gifts.

2. The Angels are a simpler image of the Divine perfections.

3. Yet the souls of Jesus and Mary surpassed them
in dignity and grace.

XXXI. Comparison of men and Angels (2). They
are equal—

1. In having God for their Creator.

*Heb. i, 14.

U.   ℞

2. In sharing eternal life.

3. In inhabiting the same blessed city.

XXXII. Comparison of men and Angels. (3) Men are superior to Angels—

1. In the Elevation of the Sacred Humanity of Jesus.

2. In that they undergo a ruder probation.

3. In that they rise by repentance when they have fallen.

XXXIII. The worship of the Angels.

1. Because of their eminent sanctity, power, and beauty.

2. By frequent meditation on them, acts of love, prayers, imitations of their perfections, and sweet modesty.

3. Of those Angels particularly of the churches we pass by, of our friends, of our enemies, of our superiors, our own Guardian, the seven that stand before the throne, and especially SS. Michael, Gabriel, and Raphael, whom the Church honors by name with special offices.

XXXIV. The worship of St. Michael.

1. As Guardian Angel of the Sacred Humanity.

2. As Guardian Angel of the Catholic Church.

3. As the slayer of Antichrist.

4. As the sounder of the trumpet at the Resurrection.

5. As the bearer of the cross at the last judgment.

XXXV. The worship of St. Gabriel.

1. As promising the Messias to Daniel.

2. As appearing to Zacharias.

3. As Guardian Angel to our Blessed Lady.

4. As bringing the Hail Mary to earth.

XXXVI. The worship of St. Raphael.
   1. As the physician of the soul.
   2. As restoring sight to the blind.
   3. As knowing the secret powers of nature.
   4. As troubling the waters of Bethsaida.
   5. As binding Satan in the desert.
   6. As guide to man in the pilgrimage of life.
   7. As one of the great and chief seven of the Angels

II.

MOTIVES FOR A PECULIAR AFFECTION TOWARDS OUR OWN DEAR GUARDIAN ANGEL.

I. Because although he is a most noble and pure spirit, and filled with the love of God, the Almighty has deputed him to assist continually a creature so vile and abject as man, and takes pleasure in communicating to us all manner of good through him.

II. Because from the first moment of our life our Angel has taken charge of us with a most tender love, beyond that of brother, father, or mother, and that without any end or advantage of his own; and he employs his entire energies simply for our greater good.

III. Because he never abandons us for so much as a single moment, although we may totally forget him, be ungrateful for his kindnesses, reject his lights and inspirations, and live in habits of sin.

U,　　　　　　　　　　　　R

IV. Because he has taken a most particular care of us when we were children, protecting us and defending us from many dangers to which we were exposed at that age.

V. Because he acts continually as our master, illuminating our understanding with the knowledge of God, and of eternal truths; from him come all good thoughts, inspirations, lights and hints which help us on the way of salvation.

VI. Because he is always endeavoring to incline our will to good works, instilling into our hearts holy affections, kindling heavenly desires in us, and inflaming our love towards God and our neighbor.

VII. Because by his power he is always removing the obstacles which stand in the way of perfection, and dexterously setting aside occasions of sin from before us.

VIII. Because in those occasions of sin, which meet us without any fault of our own, he assists us, gives us interior warnings, or sometimes exterior signs, and animates us to overcome the sin.

IX. Because he bridles the force of the devils, that they may not tempt us beyond our powers, and gives us fortitude in dealing with temptations.

X. Because in troubles of spirit and sufferings of body, he comforts us to suffer patiently, animates our hope, and keeps before us the thought of merit and reward.

XI. Because, when we invoke him in our doubts, he always gives us counsel, and lets us know which are the safest resolutions.

XII. Because he prays continually for us, and offers our prayers to God, and obtains graces for us, and other favors which are not contrary to the Divine Will and to the good of our souls: he also presents all our good works to God, and keeps an affectionately strict remembrance of them himself, against the judgment day.

XIII. Because he advances and promotes our temporal affairs, our fortunes, and the health of our bodies, and is God's secondary cause in all these things.

XIV. Because he is never disturbed, neither does he abandon us when we fall into sin; but he compassionates us with tender love, and stimulates us to penance, and is skilful in devising methods of winning us back to God.

XV. Because when we resist his sweet goads of love, he corrects us, frightens us, punishes us with accidents and sicknesses, persecutions and disappointments.

XVI. Because he sometimes assumes an aerial body and appears in various forms, either for the good of the person he guards, or for the instruction and utility of others.

XVII. Because in our sickness he vouchsafes to humble himself to the most abject ministries for our consolation and repose.

XVIII. Because he assists us at our death with a most diligent solicitude, procures for our souls all external spiritual aids, invisibly defends us from Satan, and comforts us in that tremendous passage.

XIX. Because he does not abandon us in the particular judgment, but conducts the soul to purgatory, consoles it there, and takes solicitous pains to procure our deliverance.

XX. Because when the soul has been cleansed, he introduces it into the glory of heaven, and places it in the place prepared for it among the angelic choirs.

III.

DEVOTIONAL PRACTICES IN HONOR OF OUR GUARDIAN ANGEL.

I. To keep his continual presence in a lively manner before our minds.

II. To preserve careful modesty of external demeanor, so as not to offend the purity of his eye.

III. To get a habit, either in the house or walking out, of spending part of each day in company with our Guardian Angel alone.

IV. To make an act of loving thanksgiving to him morning and evening.

V. To recite nine Paters, Aves, and Glorias in honor of the nine choirs.

VI. To say the little office or chaplet of the Guardian Angel.

VII. To have near our bed, or in our room, a picture of him, and to salute it when we go out or come in.

VIII. On some fixed day in the week to pay him some special tribute of devotion.

IX. To enrol ourselves in some confraternity in honor of the Holy Angels.

X. To propagate devotion to the Guardian Angels among our friends.

XI. To practice custody of the eyes in honor of our Guardian Angel.

XII. To forgive injuries promptly and to restrain the sallies of anger in honor of him.

XIII. To have an especial love of chastity, the virtue most dear to the Holy Angels.

XIV. To practice some particular devotion to the the Queen of Angels in the name of our Guardian Angel.

XV. To select some one of our Guardian Angel's virtues for imitation for a definite time.

XVI. To keep the feast of the Guardian Angels, and also our own birthday, as a feast of our own Angel, who then began his ministry.

XVII. To give alms in honor of the Guardian Angel of the beggar.

XVIII. To salute the Guardian Angels of those whom we meet in the streets, of villages, &c., all which is most acceptable to our own Guardian Angel.

XIX. In entering a church to unite our intention with that of our Guardian Angel to adore the Blessed Sacrament, and then to honor the Angels of the different altars, and the other Angels worshipping there.

XX. To invoke our Guardian Angel at the beginning of all our separate works and duties.

———

Those who from the circumstances of the times and the self-will of the world, or from a strong interior

U   ꟼ

attrait of the Holy Ghost, are drawn to a special devotion to the adorable Will of God, may obtain astonishing graces and favors by showing special reverence and particular love to the third choir of the first hierarchy the Blessed Thrones, on whom the Will of God rests in its might, reposing with inexplicable complacency in the perfectness of their submission.

IV.

ST. JOSEPH.

I. God blessing the world after Creation—how much more was there for Him to love when Mary was born—yet she was a weak damsel whom any one might insult—whom does He choose to protect her? St. Joseph.

II. There was a Babe in the world, and that Babe was the world's God—any one may slay Him, wound Him, trample on Him. God's treasures are now rather on earth than in Heaven—who shall protect them? St. Joseph.

III. There can be no humility in God, but this great mystery was to be in God made Man, obedient to His own creature—who was born to be the lawful superior of God, and to sanctify himself by thus awfully commanding? St. Joseph.

IV. How the Eternal Father seems withdrawn from gaze! the elect are sons of God, and so represent Jesus: the Spirit acts in us;—St. Joseph has imparted to him a shadow, nay a reality, of the Eternal Father's ever-blessed Fatherhood.

V. Brief sketch of his life—suspicion—grief—charity
—Bethlehem—Flight into Egypt—Nazareth—
Three Days' Loss—rules Jesus and Mary—dies
between them.

VI. The love of Jesus and Mary meet in him: he was
spared the Passion: his office is daily represented in mass, procession, and benediction: devotion to him is a short road to the Sacred Hearts
of Jesus and Mary.

VII. His death.—How sweet was the happy solitude
of the House of Nazareth—no secret bower in
the shades of Eden was more sweet than that
sinless house, that heaven upon earth—Would
death dare to come where the Lord of life was
living? It durst not come nigh His Cross until
He bowed His Head in sign that it might come.
Yes! death dared to cross the threshold of the
House of Nazareth. Joseph was now seventy
. years of age, Mary forty-five and Jesus twenty-
nine. He was not ill, but his love of God shook
him in his old age, as it did St. Philip, that
second St. Joseph, after him. The hour came:
he laid himself down to die; and what a death!

VIII. Jesus is on one side of his bed, Mary on the
other: he holds the right hand of Mary in his
left hand in token of his fidelity, and in his
right hand the left hand of Jesus, that with
His right Jesus may give him benediction.
Mary thought of Bethlehem, and of the desert
as they fled to Egypt. She loved him wonderfully: deep thoughts were in her sinless soul
as she watched the coming on of death; she
looked with love on Joseph, and then she

U.   ℞

looked over him at Jesus her obedient Son, and
she remembered how He was the Lord of Life—
He had created and sanctified St. Joseph's
beautiful soul—He it was Who was now bid-
ding death come and fetch it. Oh mystery of
wonder and of love! Joseph need not die, if
Jesus would but will that he should not. Mary
pressed Joseph's hand—she did not pray that
he might live—but looked at Jesus and adored
Him, adored her own Son, who was her God as
well. O death! thou hast travelled the world
over, yet never surely didst thou come on such
a scene as this. God in flesh and blood has
fast hold of the hand of him whom thou hast
come to seek and to strike. Wilt thou dare?
Jesus held the right hand of Joseph—He
whispered in his ear sweet words of thanksgiving for all his care of Him. St. Joseph
looked up into the face of Jesus—his weak
eyes went all over it—the hair, the brow, the
eyes, the moving lips: yes, bold man, thou wilt
see that face once more, Oh how bright and
beautiful! And thou wilt be spared the sight
of it as Mary will see it, covered with blood and
wounds, and mud and filthy spittle. Oh what
a strait to choose in! To die for *us* is to go to
Jesus; for Joseph it was to leave Jesus for
awhile. He looked up into the face of Jesus—
he thought how he had dressed Him, washed
Him, kissed Him as a little one, protected Him,
commanded Him in his poor shop, and he
pressed His Sacred Hand and smiled with love;
and God Almighty, the obedient Son, stooped

down and reverently kissed St. Joseph's hand.
St. Joseph looked to Mary—then to Jesus—
then back to Mary—then to Jesus again. He
looked up into His face;—the smile passed
away—there came a look, most awful, most
heavenly, most wonderful—he saw the Godhead
shine out in the face of Jesus—the most profound and abashed humility passed into his look
—he made an act of fear, because he was a
creature, and an act of love because he was the
foster father—both shook his dying frame.
He adored Jesus his Creator and his Judge—
the dying Saint's guardian angel prostrated
himself adoringly—St. Joseph needed no guardian—God was there. Jesus raised His Right
Hand as Judge and blessed Him; thus He
judged His dying servant even before His death
—that raised Right Hand of Jesus had blessed
St. Joseph—the dying creature whispered softly,
Jesus, Mary, the Creator's ear was close and
caught the words—He stooped and kissed the
lips as they pronounced the name of Mary—in
that kiss of peace the mystery was done—the
soul of Joseph fled away to rest in Abraham's
bosom, to wait till Jesus should have ended four
more years, and be ready to carry it with Him
through the blue skies on Ascension day into
the everlasting joys of heaven.

Oh greatest! Oh dearest of all the saints of God!
may we die the death of the just, and may our last end
be like to thine!

V.

MEDITATIONS ON ST. JOSEPH.

Custos Amabilis, ora pro nobis.

HIS SEVEN DOLORS.

I. His grief in thinking he must put away our Blessed Lady.

1. His horror of impurity, and zeal for the love of God.
2. His refraining from judging her.
3. His discreet and charitable deliberation and delay.

II. His seeing the Infant Jesus in poverty and distress.

1. Seeing Him shiver with cold.
2. Hearing Him cry.
3. The hardness of the manger and poverty of the cave.

III. His seeing His Blood flow at the circumcision.

1. His hatred of sin.
2. He adores the love of Jesus in shedding It.
3. He adores His obedience to the law.

IV. St. Simeon's prophecy.

1. His sympathy with our Blessed Lady.
2. His sorrowful meditation on St. Simeon's words.
3. His continual remembrance of them.

V. The flight into Egypt.

1. The fears, perils, and fatigues of the journey.
2. His watching the sufferings of Jesus.
3. His inability to protect our Blessed Lady.

VI. His hearing that Archelaus was reigning.

1. It dashed the joy of His return from Egypt.

U,

2. His new fears for Jesus and our Lady.

3. His having to live so far from the temple.

VII. His loss of Jesus for three days.

    1. The anxiety of the weary search.

    2. His self-reproach as being the cause.

    3. His misery at seeing our Blessed Lady suffer.

HIS SEVEN JOYS.

I. The angel telling him to take Mary for his wife.

    1. His delight at her innocence.

    2. The honor he pays to her virtue.

    3. Joyous expectations of Jesus.

II. The Ave Maria and Nativity.

    1. His hearing the Ave Maria.

    2. Seeing the adoration of the shepherds.

    3. The homage of the three kings.

III. The holy name of Jesus.

    1. His having to give it to the Child.

    2. His first pronouncing of it.

    3. His pondering with Mary over the mystery of it.

IV. St. Simeon's words about our Lord: that He
    should be—

    1. A light to the Gentiles.

    2. The glory of Israel.

    3. The resurrection of many.

V. The falling down of the idols of Egypt before
    Jesus.

    1. His adoration of the power of the Son of God.

    2. His sympathy with Mary's exceeding joy.

    3. His delight at the glory thus accruing to God.

VI. The command of the angel to return home.

    1. His joy at returning to the land of the true
    Church.

2. To better accommodations for Jesus and Mary.

3. At carrying their Messias to the Jews.

VII. Finding Jesus in the temple.

1. Delight at finding Him.

2. Joy at Mary's joy.

3. Adoration of the wisdom of Jesus.

OTHER CONSIDERATIONS ABOUT HIM.

The ove of God the Father for St. Joseph.

1. In imparting to him His paternal character.

2. In trusting His elect daughter Mary to him.

3. In predestinating him to these two offices.

The ove of God the Son for him.

1. As His father.

2. As the careful and kind protector of Mary.

3. In allowing him to kiss, wash, dress, carry.Him,
&c.

The ove of God the Holy Ghost for him.

1. As a singular vessel of most fragrant continence.

2. As guardian of the Sacred Humanity.

3. As earthly husband of His own Spouse.

The love of our Blessed Lady for Him.

1. As chosen for her by God.

2. As guardian of her purity.

3. As guardian of Jesus.

The love of the angels for him.

1. As so humbly commanding their Lord.

2. As protecting their Queen.

3. In their embassies to him.

St. Joseph model of the Interior Life and Patron of
Mental Prayer.

1. Silence.

U.

2. Recollection.
3. Shunning publicity.

St. Joseph model for priests.

1. In chastity.
2. Devotion to our Blessed Lady.
3. In handling the Blessed Sacrament.

St. Joseph model for the dying.

1. Quiet resignation.
2. On the lap of Jesus.
3. Mary at his side.

St. Joseph model for all the faithful.

1. In ministering to Jesus.
2. In protecting Mary's honor.
3. As a pilgrim with Jesus and Mary in the wilderness.

What our Lady told St. Bridget of him.

1. He was affable, not rude.
2. Defended the absent.
3. Took notice of God's wonderful works.

Also,

1. He constantly prayed for the accomplishment of God's promises.
2. Avoided publicity.
3. Longed for death.

Also,

1. He was very contented in poverty.
2. Very patient.
3. Continued devotion to the will of God.

Devotion to him.

1. Late gift to the Church.
2. Acceptableness of it to Jesus and Mary.
3. Specially extolled by St. Teresa.

Besides these meditations, many more may be made of

U.

the events of St. Joseph's life, especially the eighteen years at Nazareth, when he saw Joseph working, eating, sleeping, praying, &c.; also of the sojourn in Egypt, the two journeys, his accompanying our Blessed Lady at the Visitation, and many more.

VI.

ST. JOHN THE BAPTIST.

I. State of the Jews.
1. Voluptuousness of higher orders.
2. Spirit of disputation and doubt amid the learned.
3. Unsettlement among the people.
II. Appearance of St. John.
1. His wild appearance.
2. His ignorance of human learning.
3. His preaching unfashionable penance.
4. His rude rebuking of the noble.
5. His making no distinction between high and low, simple and learned.
6. His marvellous power and attractiveness.
III. The causes of his power.
1. His truckling to no human respects.
2. His preaching to the heart.
3. His supernatural austerities.
4. His interior union with God.
IV. Similarity between England now, and Judea then. St. John a model for us.
1. In high principles.
2. In cultivating purity of heart.

3. In supernatural faith and perfection, realizing the invisible world.

4. In leading lives of prayer and union with God.

The day of controversy is wellnigh past. The calmness of Catholics in the late troubles excites wonder—now for power with God, and the day is ours; the time will be when men will talk of Protestantism as they do of the old heresies, as a curse which once was and is now no more!

VII.

THE THREE KINGS; OR, ALL GRACES COME OF FAITH.

If the Bible discloses melancholy possibilities of the sinfulness of man, it also discloses magnificences, which perhaps the kingdom of angels can hardly surpass—*e.g.* the Three Kings.

I. The Three Kings.   What immense saints they were —shown

1. From the singularity of their election.
2. From the special graces they received.
3. From the mystery for which they were used—God opening His Church to the Gentiles.
4. From the virtues they practised.
5. From the huge devotion of the Church to them.

II. Their characteristics.

1. They are instances of men who reveal their whole selves in one action: such men are mostly very divine characters; their simplicity is a great power.

U,   ℞

2. Moreover they are saints whose characters are so mastered by their one grace as to lose almost their individuality—yet their offerings bespeak variety of character.

3. They belong to that little class of God's own private saints, the unknown vastness of whose sanctity He irradiates by only one or two gleams, such as St. Joseph, the Baptist, some of the apostles, and SS. Joachim and Anne. These are the Mary-like saints; for this is also her characteristic.

4. Their virtues were—(1) alacrity, (2) courage, especially against human respect, (3) generosity, (4) entireness of heart with God, (5) singular docility, (6) exceeding great joy, as the un-exaggerating Bible calls it.

5. But all these six graces came out of one as out of a fountain, namely, out of faith.

III. Lessons to learn.

1. Faith is God's greatest gift on earth, and is necessary for charity.

2. Of all graces it is the one most capable of increase.

3. It is the most prolific of all graces: and gives us most momentum.

4. It is the source of all spiritual sweetness, and of all joy and consolation in religion.

5. How we can best increase it.
   (1.) By cherishing the thought of God, and culti-vating His fear.
   (2) By a filial and reverential devotion to the Church.

The hidden magnificence of the Babe of Bethlehem compared with the hidden magnificence of the Church.

As we lose ourselves, our own likings and dislikings, our own judgments and criticisms and all the follies of our littleness, in the thought and presence of God, so must we lose them also in the thought and presence of His Church. The grand lesson which He sent the Three Kings to teach the Gentiles was devotion to the Church!

VIII.

ST. THOMAS OF CANTERBURY.*

What a strange providence it is, my dear Brethren in Jesus Christ, that we in this poor faithless land of ours, this poor uncatholic England, should be gathered together quietly this day beneath the shadow of our own blessed and glorious martyr St. Thomas of Canterbury, while the Holy City of Catholics, the home of our affections, the threshold of the apostles, the pilgrimage place of Christendom, is lying waste and desolate and in darkness! How strange, passing strange, it seems that we in this fallen land should be met together to-day to do honor to a name which has been a by-word of scorn and a proverb of reproach in the mouths of generations of our deluded countrymen, while the Holy City is lying waste, because the visible Presence of God passed from it, when His dear and blessed Vicar fled a fugitive along those Pontine Marches through which St. Paul journeyed in his bonds to preach Christ Crucified in the streets of

* Preached in the Church of St. Thomas of Canterbury at Fulham, Dec. 29, 1848.

U.

beautiful Rome! How much is there in this consideration which leads us, almost in spite of ourselves,
to meditate with trembling awe upon the fortunes of
God's Church and her most holy faith, and to watch
with fearful interest the ebb and flow of that empire
of our faith, which, while it loses ground or seems to
lose it in one place, gains it in another, until its wearied
and baffled foes throw down their arms, cease their
calculations, and become stupefied at these repeated
signs of its hopeless and undecayed vitality. But,
my dear Brethren, because things look dark abroad,
because there seems to have come down this night
upon the Church, a night of storm and of eclipse, the
shadow of God's wrath and judgment on the sons of
men, even in the most Holy Place, even where the
bodies of countless saints and nameless martyrs lie,
ought we therefore to lose heart or slacken our endeav-
ors in the cause of God's Church, in other lands or in
our own? God forbid! God forbid that we should
have so little faith in God, or that we should so distrust
the power and heavenly virtue of our blessed faith!
No! we lose not heart, our purposes are not unnerved,
our spirits do not faint or flag, because we know
Whose faith it is, and Whom we have on board while
we are in Peter's bark: and though that bark be now
storm-tossed and in apparent peril, yet when the hour
comes, when our faith has been sufficiently tried and
our sins sufficiently chastised, He will rise from out
His seeming slumber, and with one word will bid the
winds and waves be still.

But while we regard with awe, not unintermingled
with hope, and without one shadow of distrust, the
scenes that are enacting in the Holy Place, how

beautiful, how cheering, how elating is the prospect
around us in this our own dear native land! If the
faith seems faint and feeble and overcast, it is after all
but seemingly so; if it appear to be losing ground, and
to be ebbing from foreign shores, how fast and freely
the tide is flowing in upon our own, and flowing where
it ought to flow, not so much upon the palace steps of
the noble and the rich, upon the change of the busy
trafficker or the hall of the self-wise scholar, as upon
the dense untended multitude of Christ's predestined
poor, upon the friendless, the fallen, the ignorant,
the grief-smitten! How fast is the faith encroaching!
How is it sapping the very citadels of prejudice and
bigotry: how are the hearts of sinners coming into
the fold by scores and hundreds, like the miraculous
draught of old into Peter's net, which at his Master's
word he cast forth into the dark unpromising deep!
Surely we cannot but feel that God has in these days
granted to every one of us, in our own appointed place
and fitting way, without distinction of age or sex, a
kind of universal commission, whereby every English
Catholic is constituted, in his and her place and sphere,
a sort of missionary apostolic to spread the faith; and
the question, the practical question, for all of us to
consider is the manner in which we are to do our work.
It is impossible to look forth on the face of the land,
and not to see that the fields are white for the harvest.
It is impossible to love Almighty God, and not pour
out our souls in secret prayer to the great Master of
the harvest, that He will send forth laborers there-
unto, men of apostolic zeal and apostolic boldness and
apostolic mortification, which alone is the source of
prayer and priestly charity. It is impossible to avoid

seeing that wheresoever the adorable Sacrifice and the rightful priest are to be found in this land of ours, there is the Gospel prophecy fulfilled, that where the body is the eagles will be gathered together.

Yes! the practical question for all of us is how we are to do our work; and surely this feast should be suggestive to every one of us in what way we are to fight the fight :—we are to fight it as St. Thom s did of old. Adverse as the times may seem in outward appearance, there never was an age of the Church when circumstances, both within and without, both at home and abroad, more loudly called upon us to take the blessed St. Thomas of Canterbury for our pattern, our model, nay our living, powerful, and helpful guide, and fight the good fight as he fought it in bygone times, even to the shedding of his blood, or to what men find harder to give than blood, the shedding of their good name by pouring it out to waste upon the earth. Let me then ask you this morning to meditate awhile upon the life of St. Thomas of Canterbury, to put him before yourselves as the great exemplar of those grand characteristics of which he is the special Saint, the special Apostle. He is the Apostle of high principle, the Saint whose every word and work was a condemnation of cowardice, of time-serving, of timidity, of pusillanimity, of all unworthy concession, of all trembling in the face of power, of all bartering of principle for peace or gain, of all circuitous roads to a rightful and a godly end; in a word, of every profane weakness that ever afflicted the Church from within or without, from her children or her foes, he was the unflinching enemy and the pertinacious opponent from first to last. It is on this account that I call upon

U,

you to study his life, and ponder on every word, to
meditate on every action of this most dear and blessed
martyr, whom England gave to the Church of God,
and to put him before us, each of course discreetly, in
his own appointed sphere, and under the obedience of
his spiritual guide, as our model and our patron in the
terrible scandal-breeding strife which seems too probably at hand. If ever there was a time or place
when and where high, obstinate, clear-sighted, and
unflinching principle was the sheet-anchor of the
Church, that time is now, and that place the land in
which it is our lot to live and work.

Let us then look at St. Thomas in three different
states in which his romantic life, so full of wisest
teaching in its minutest details, presents him to us—
St. Thomas in the court, St. Thomas in strife, and St.
Thomas in exile.

First of all, let us look at St. Thomas in the court;
let us look at him after he became archbishop, but, for
his Church's sake, still mingled with the king and the
rude barons and fawning courtiers round him. - What
above all things strikes us in the conduct of this
magnificence-loving man, is the evidence of calm
austerity and of repulsive penance which, amid all the
glory and the brilliance that distinguished the court of
Henry, broke from time to time through that concealment with which Catholic sanctity is wont to shroud
itself. It was said of him, even during his lifetime,
that he degraded and sullied the splendor that was
round him by the dreadful and unsightly austerities
he practised. And is not St. Thomas an example to
us even in this very respect, if at least we desire in
our heart of hearts to see our beloved country brought

back again to God, brought as a modest yet rejoicing
wanderer into the one only fold of the One True
Shepherd? Oh! it is not a work that is nigh at
hand, at least the accomplishment thereof; it is not
a work that is light and easy, neither is it a light or
a little thing to ask of God. But if we do yearn after
this great ennobling end, then must we imitate St.
Thomas in the very matter now before us. Do you
believe that we shall ever convert England, if we are
simply common Catholics, common, good, practical
Catholics, with no aim beyond a state of grace or an
absence of permitted venial sin, moving in the routine
of the far-off feasts and distant indulgences as though
it was a grove out of which our spiritual life would
run to nought and perish? Do you in good faith
believe that this is the material God will use to upraise
a fallen land? Is there here a power of expiation to
thrust aside those tremendous arrears of wrath and
judgment which have accumulated against the land
for three hundred years of augmenting impurity, pro-
faneness, and unbelief? Is this a furnace of love
strong enough to burn away all that needs consuming
among us? Oh how weak and wild would it be to
suppose that we can do great things, that we have the
faith which can remove mountains, and the love which
can cast out fear, and the austerity which can exorcise
the spirits of evil; if we aim not at far higher things
than these. No, my Brethren, it must be something
more than the tameness of a common virtue, something
higher than the level of ordinary attainments, which
will do so great a work for God. We must aim at
perfection; we must strive after the arduous heights
of Christian holiness; we must endeavor to imitate

the saints of God; we must put before ourselves as
possible, aye, and as hopeful aims, their devoted and
heroic deeds.   We must break down all false and
puny standards of virtue which would stunt our
spiritual growth, and abjuring whatever may seem to
have caught by contagion the dominant evil spirit
which surrounds us in this heretic land, we must
throw ourselves heart and soul into the models which
come to us from times which had not lost the faith,
or from lands where amid many hindrances it still
reigns supreme.   Depend upon it there is a host of
sin, a host of God's wrath in arrear, through which
we must press our way before we can come to our
glorious end; and it is not by coldness, by lukewarm-
ness, by indifference, or even by mediocre virtue that
we shall accomplish our purpose, still less by a paltry,
bargaining spirit, that would go to market as it were
with God, and grant him little more than the precepts
of the Church lay upon the conduct and the conscience.
Oh no! it must be a nobler inclination, a more generous
spirit, a spirit that must throw itself fervently and
confidingly into the arms of God Himself, and must
lead us to dedicate ourselves body and soul and spirit
to the trampling the world under our feet as the
canonized saints of God have done, not only in times
of yore, but up to the threshold of these times of ours.
We must be more, ten thousand times more, than common easy-going practical Catholics, if we would convert
for God this deluded and benighted land.

   This surely is the very first thing we must look to,
each one of us to his own practice, each one of us to
his own progress in holiness, and to his own advance-
ment along the road of Christian perfection.   And

U.   ⓓ

why is this? Why is it that I put the austerity of St. Thomas, not only among the examples which that blessed Saint sets us, but the very first and foremost of them all? For these reasons amongst others: because austerity and perfection give us power with God. Oh how useless it is for man or woman to go forth into the world, into the social or domestic circle, and hope to influence their fellow-men for good, if they have not influence first of all in the great court and before the great throne which are on high, if they are not known there as persons of constant prayer, of self-denying lives, of generous sacrifice for the Church and faith of God; and how weak, how powerless, how utterly imbecile will all their most arduous efforts prove to be. Yes! my dear Brethren, we may toil till health of body gives way beneath the burden; but if we have not influence with God, if we are not habitually with Him in the implorings and wrestlings of prayer, in meditation and in secret penance, how powerless, how unprevailing will all our labors be! Our hands will be unnerved, our arms will drop from them, when the hour of victory seems nighest, because we seek to have commanding influence over men, before self-humiliation has earned for us influence with God.

Further, we must strive after these heights of Christian perfection, not only because austerity has power with God, but because it seems on that very account to give a mysterious and disproportionate power to all our actions, even those which are trivial themselves. Common words and common things, when they come from one whose soul is in union with God,—oh! they are like miracles, compared with the selfsame words and the selfsame deeds, when they come

from one who is living an ordinary life. There seems
to be a power in them which emanates from on high,
an abiding presence and unction of the Blessed Spirit
in them. The missionary of hidden austerity may
look outwardly like any other man; he may not
perhaps have human talent, human eloquence, or
human influence; and yet there is something in him,
something that goes from him, which bows the hearts
of men, as the wind bows the reeds when it blows,
and they feel the sovereign influence, acknowledge its
sovereignty, and bend before the words and deeds
which are, as it were, the vessels wherein it is
contained.

There is still another truth to be remarked; austerity,
like other Christian things, is blamed even by those
who are themselves at the moment beneath its influence. While the men of St. Thomas's day found
fault with his want of discretion, and blamed him
because he allowed his rude, uncouth, grotesque
austerities to appear amid the splendors of Henry's
court; yet all the while they were allured and attracted
by it. There is a marvellous power in a holy life;
there is a marvellous influence in austerity, a supernatural power to attract and allure the most alien things
towards itself. Look at the great preacher of penance
in the days of old; look at that unearthly apparition,
that came up from the wilderness after years of in-
human solitude, and the companionship of wild beasts,
and stood before the eyes of men upon the banks of
Jordan. He appeared, in the aspect of his outward
seeming, to have been made only to offend, to disgust,
and to repel. Yet to the Baptist's preaching there
came, wiled as though by an influence they could neither

resist nor divine, the pleasure-loving and sensual officers of the legions from the gay and sinful city; while the cold and sceptic scholars, with their sparkling wit, sarcastic sophistry, and unearnest investigation, were attracted in spite of themselves by this sight of St. John coming up from the wilderness to Jordan's bank, and their eyes were riveted upon him with inquiring awe, although he had no human influence, no show of intellect, nought but the preaching of the most abject penance and undignified humiliation. If there was at that time one object on which their eyes were more anxiously and intensely fixed than another, it was upon this rude forerunner of our Lord, and they stopped to question him, who he was, and what the proofs of his mission were. So will it always be: men will talk to you, criticise you, condemn you, seem to destroy your influence by affixing the slur of indiscretion to your name; but after all, things work round, because there is in an austere life, in one whose soul is in union with God, a secret power of attraction which no other power on earth can give, and which imparts to him who lives that life an empire over the consciences of men beyond the reach of all human calculation.

Let this then, Brethren, be the first lesson that we learn from St. Thomas—the necessity of girding ourselves up to a more holy life, to a more severe penance, and to a closer union with God.

Let us now turn from St. Thomas in the court, with his uncouth austerities, to St. Thomas in his strife. If we look at the accounts given of him even by his own contemporaries, how he was misunderstood, how he was misjudged, how he was described as of a foreign race whose language worldly men could not understand!

No, it requires some hundreds of years to intervene before we are far enough off from the glory of St. Thomas to cast our eyes up to the altitude that was in his noble and sacred character. And what was it, my Brethren, what was it in the manner of his strife, whether with the crowned king upon the throne, or the rude barons, or even, which was harder still, with his courtly brother bishops, what was it that so offended men? It was the seeming hypocrisy, it was the apparent double-facedness of all that he did, it was that holy double spirit which the Church has in her, and wh'ch all the saints of God possessed; that he was humble, with what the world called an affectedly servile humility, to the poor and lonely and fallen and little ones of Jesus; but in the face of the rude king, and in the face of human power and intellect, he seemed proud and arrogant and presumptuous, drawing himself up within himself, and not stooping to make the slightest concession. And here it is that the lesson is for us. We too must be humble—ten thousand times more humble now than St. Thomas was then; our humility must be manly, at the same time that it is meek, to the the little ones of Jesus; but in the face of power, in the face of pride, in the face of unbelieving science, in the face of distasteful and conspiring politics, we must be what St. Thomas was, we must be apparently proud, presumptuous, and arrogant.

It may seem that there is no practical lesson for us in this particular matter; but indeed, if we look closer into it, there is a lesson for us every way. For instance, how many of us, in the private, social, and domestic circle, long with our heart's best affection for conversion to the faith of God of those who are near and dear to

U, ℞

us both by blood and by love. Yes, Brethren, how many of us are there who must entertain such a feeling even in our own hearts, and what a temptation is there here to play false to the faith of God—what a temptation is there here to do the very opposite of what St. Thomas did of old. Beware, in your conversation with others, how you represent the Church of God to those whom you desire to allure within her pale; beware of representing her for one moment as though she were different from what she was in days of old; beware of representing her as abating one jot or tittle of the greatest of those pretensions which seemed most arrogant and most preposterous even in the Middle Ages; beware of representing her as changed one atom in this her temper and her spirit; no, we must adhere strictly and zealously to high principle, disregarding everything that present or temporary advantage may appear to put within our reach. Truth, remember—and this is one great distinction between Catholics and heretics—truth is not ours, but God's. Truth is not ours to bate and pare down. Truth is God's; it has God's majesty inherent within it, and it will convert the souls of men, even when it seems rudest and most repelling; and it will do so for this one reason—because it is God's truth, and because we through the grace of God have boldness and faith to put our trust in it. And again, beware of another evil, that of trying to throw aside or to pare down what seems most faithful and warm in the devotions of foreign lands; do not tell that cruel falsehood, do not tell it to those whom you love, and are longing and yearning to have within the Church, do not tell them that the faith is other here than what it is elsewhere; do not throw aside devotion and sweet-

U.   D

ness, and worship and affection, as though they were not fit for us, as though God's Church were not one; for this is nothing less in reality than to deny the unity of God's Church. Tell them not this. Take not the bread from between their teeth, to bring them within the pale of God's Church, to find that they themselves have been deceived, and that you, while you wished to attract and allure, have only so much the more effectually repelled them, and have taken from them that which, in a moment of faith and love, they would have most generously embraced. This is, indeed, doing a cruel work, and it is in this very respect that St Thomas is to us so bright an example. Believe me, dear Brethren, if there be a land—if there be a people—in which high principle is acceptable from its own intrinsic value, or alluring from the national character of those around us, it is this dear land of ours. Let us have faith, firm, vigorous, unfaltering faith; and, trust me, there is in high principle something which humbles those who hold it. They are never humble who have not high principle. They may be courtly, they may be pusillanimous, but humble they cannot be; for there is in high principles, and high principles alone, that which humbles those who hold them, that which wins those to whom those high principles are put forward; and above all there is in these high principles, and in none other, the plenitude of that heavenly blessing which Jesus has lodged in the bosom of His people.

Let this then be the second lesson that we learn from the life of St. Thomas of Canterbury.

And now let us turn to one more scene in his life; let us turn to the blessed martyr in his exile; let us turn to his bedabbling the floor of his cell at the monastery of Pontigny with his own blood, from the strife of his own chastisement; let us turn to him in his Cistercian Abbey, and let us imitate him in his exile. Yes, Brethren, and let us remember that we are exiles here in the holy faith; that we are pilgrims, exiles and strangers in this very land of ours; and we have a lesson to learn—a lesson of cheerfulness and of hard-working diligence, to learn from St. Thomas in his exile. We have to learn and to lay to heart what we know already:—that weakness is the strength of Christians. Look at the Church of God at this moment. Look how dark, how dismal in many ways the prospect seems; how much evil there seems to be at work, how much conspiring to overthrow her: and then again, look at home, and see what arduous toil is there, and what disadvantages must daily be encountered. Yes, we are weak, but not so weak as some may think we are. They see but the outward seeming and hear but the outward voice, and they think us weaker than we are: but our weakness is our strength; and the weakness which is strength is humility and love; love, suffering love, is the Christian's only victory; Brethren, be not cast down by all that you see and hear around you. Be not troubled by the rumors that come floating across the sea to us, day after day; be not troubled, or cast down, or have your faith fluttered within you. No, but remember that there was a time when Jesus was scorned by His enemies, when He seemed weakest, in the Garden of Gethsemane, when the pale Easter moon was shining down upon the olive-trees, and a band of traitors was round about Him. See how spent He is with His bloody sweat; see how His three hours of agony seem to have exhausted the

very strength of His Divine Nature; and there pale,
pale exceedingly, with these enemies around Him, He
stands as it were betrayed, detected, and surprised.
His disciples have fled from Him, and it seems as
though He did but remain there that they might lay their
rude hands upon their God, and the victory of sin and
evil is complete; and one gentle word from the lips
of Jesus—one sound of those sweet accents, mild, and
gentle, and passionate, and overpowering, caused the
rude Roman, and the ruder Jews, to fall backwards in
wonder and amazement. And wherefore was this,
dear Brethren, but to teach us that in our weakness
is our strength, and that meekness, gentleness, and love
are mightier weapons than all else that the world can
know beside?

But you may ask me what suffering, what trials,
what meekness we shall be called upon to practise or
endure in our warfare in the private or domestic circle?
We shall have to meet with unkindness and cold looks
where we ought to find bright and warm ones; we
shall have to come in contact with cold and freezing
hearts that ought to be beating with the pure fervor
of affection; we shall have to be exiled from the love
of those who are bound most of all to love us. We
shall be misunderstood if we act on high principles,
and scandals must come; remember this is the law of
God's Church; it is the law which distinguished the
life of St. Thomas, and not his life alone, but the whole
history of the Church, from the day when St. Ambrose
humbled Theodosius at his feet, from the day when the
blessed Gregory the Seventh humbled his enemies;
and as in St. Thomas's day, and even now, they who
act from high principle, must not perhaps give scandal,

but be prepared to find that others will take scandal from them: but this must not divert you from the clear path of duty that lies before you. It is the very character of high principles, that the very men who hold them see their way right to the end, they see that their way lies athwart hills and dales, stony places and dreadful deserts, but they turn not either to the right or to the left,—they travel steadfastly throughout. Yes, Brethren, and this is the very thing we must do, even if we be exposed to the condemnation of the good, even if those who are in the bosom of our families, and whom we love and treasure most, think it too arrogant, too enthusiastic, unreal or indiscreet; still we have the good cause entrusted to us, and we cling to it with a holy obedience under the advice and guidance of our spiritual guides. Let us beware how we betray it. What was the characteristic of St. Thomas? It was that he set at nought the judgment of men; it was that God grew upon him in his contemplation; that God grew upon his soul more and more, until God filled his soul, and there was no room for man, no room for human respect, no room for love for the creature. Wherever he turned, there was God in the great and in the small, and therefore he set at nought the judgment of men and exhibited to the world that special characteristic of greatness, that he fought for little things as diligently as he had fought for great ones; and why? Because he was a saint of the Most High; and as in the eye of God there is neither great nor small, so in the eye of God's saints nothing is small that contains one tittle or fraction of high principle; and so it was with St. Thomas. There were little things, there were scruples

that might seem matters of etiquette or indifference.
that might be waived, especially when a king and his
nobles demanded it; but St. Thomas believed that in
these little things there was a portion of the same
mighty principle, and he clung to them with as much
blessed obstinacy, with as much holy pertinacity, as
though the very tiara of the Sovereign Pontiff had
been at stake. It is this very thing that is the special
note of greatness; and in it lies the power which God
has of not dividing things great and small. This must
be our example. If we doubt for a moment, that our
weakness is strength; if we doubt whether or not this
lesson could be read to us in these days,—look not
alone to the picture of St. Thomas in his exile; but
look to another dear and blessed exile now; look to
our Holy Father the Pope, exiled from his sacred city,
driven to the frontiers of another land, or seeking the
refuge of a foreign shelter in a seaport of his own
rightful states. Look at him, and in your heart of
hearts do you not believe that there is strength in our
weakness. Was there ever a time when the throne of
Peter was more firmly rooted in the affections of the
faithful throughout the world? was there ever a time
when thoughtful men, even outside the Church, looked
on the Vicar of God, and trembled with more intelligent awe than they do at the present moment? aye,
when the rebels gathered round him,—even as the
rebels of Nazareth gathered round our blessed Lord,
and pursued Him to the very cliff on which their town
was built,—behold, God's Vicar passed through the
midst of them, and their eyes were holden that they
could not see him. They knew not how or where he
went, because God was with him; and in his exile

U.   ℗

there went with him all his strength, and all his holiness. And at the present moment, who, among the enlightened and intelligent of our holy faith, does not see that the sword of Peter is keener and sharper in the ever-blessed exile's hands than when he reigned within the walls of the vast Vatican at Rome? This is the same lesson that St. Thomas's exile of old gives to us. Wait, Brethren, but a few weeks, or months,— or, if God wills it, it may be years,—and then see how woe will come to them; how bitter and dark their end will be; how shameful and ignominious the life of those, whether of us, or not of us, who dare to raise the whispered voice, or the stealthy hand, against the majesty of Rome in this her hour of eclipse. Wait and see if this comes true. His word is law now more than ever it was before; and the whisper of his exiled voice speaks now more powerfully to every loving and loyal heart, than all the bulls and briefs, and rescripts, that he issued in the days of his glory and his power. And should there, as amid the apostles, be a Judas, who could raise the whispered voice or the stealthy hand, how dark and bitter will be his end,—how dark and ignominious his fate!

No, Brethren, in this way weakness is strength. Be not cast down because ye see many things against us. Look, for instance, at that twin-spirit—that brother-saint of St. Thomas, the sainted Hildebrand. Look at Gregory the Seventh passing down the sunny shore where the Vicar of God, in his exile, has now passed down—visit the city of Salerno where the blue waves beat so gently against the shore, and where all the beauties of nature are gathered together to make a very paradise of peace, a very Eden of delights; and

U.   ℗

go and see that lowly tomb, the tomb of Gregory, who
fell trampled under foot in exile, but whose enemies
died in the very hour of victory, in the flush of triumph,
so broken and discomfited, that the empire of sin and
darkness never rose again.

Yes, my Brethren, so it ever is; weakness is strength.
The strength of Christians is in the cross, and the cross
was a weakness and a shame to Him who hung thereon;
and yet the great apostle of the Gentiles cried, " God
forbid that I should glory, save in the cross of our
Lord Jesus Christ." Oh, it was not when St. Thomas
was in his magnificence—it was not when he was in
his glory and his power—it was not when he rode
through France as the chancellor and ambassador of
England, and astonished men with his unheard-of-
splendor—it was not then that he had power—that
power which lasts to this moment—that power which,
to this very day, is thrilling and trembling through
every nerve and vein of God's universal Church
throughout the world: it was not then that that
power was the mightiest; but rather when he sank
down as his blood flowed on the hallowed pavement
of Canterbury, and when in gentle words he com-
mended his blessed soul to God, our Lady, and St.
Denis.

Yes, my Brethren, all these lessons are for us. We
ought to work hard, and yet not to look for results.
It is not God's way; it is not the fashion of God's
doing. Think how many times the trumpets of God
were sounded round the walls of Jericho ere they fell.
We ought to work as though the conversion of our
native land was at our very doors, and yet as expecting
nothing. It is said that they that sow shall reap; but

U.   ℞

blessed, aye, blessed we, even if we never live to see that day of splendor and majesty in God's Church. The conversion of the people is as the wind blowing where it will; it comes and goes wheresoever it will. In the days of spring, it woos out the green leaves here and there in wanton ways, and seems to have no ruling operation: so is the working of God's Spirit. The two things that we have to lay to heart are gentleness and kindness. Forbearance and forgivingness, gentle and loving words and affectionate treatment, and above all, a secret aiming at perfection in our own lives: these are our missionary weapons, and for conversion we may be content to wait.

If we bear this in mind we shall not lose heart. If to look out upon this empire in its unbelief, its sin, its poor deserted priestless multitude, make the heart sink within us, surely it is not a scene one half so dark as that which the Queen of the apostles saw when she looked from her window over Jerusalem, and over the whole expanse of heathenism that Jesus had given her to convert unto Him. When she and the apostles looked forth on that scene, it was as Noe looked forth from the windows of the ark on the wild and angry waste of waters, and on a tempest-tossed world; on its green things, on its brightness, on its sunshine.

So will it be with us, if we only try, from this day forth, to cultivate a spirit of love and devotion to that blessed Saint whose feast we this day celebrate. It is said, and it is to me a matter of love and interest, that my own blessed father St. Philip Neri, whenever he met in the streets of Rome the English students who were gathered together beneath the shadow of St. Thomas of England, always saluted them in his own playful

U.   ﬔ

way, with the words of the Church's hymn—"*Salvete
flores martyrum.*" And think you that he, whose every
word was pregnant with meaning, did not intend to
commend to them the imitation of that blessed martyr,
under whose shadow they were gathered together?

Yes, Brethren, we must have devotion to St.
Thomas, because he is the apostle of high principle.
Devotion to St. Thomas must be an instinct with us,
even as hatred of Him was an instinct with the wicked
men in the wild and evil days of English apostasy.
Why did they hate the name of St. Thomas? Why
did they tear down his blessed relics? Why did they
erase his name from the calendar? Why did they
trample his sacred memory underfoot, and leave the
other saints of God to go free? Why but because he
was the apostle of high principle? because the devil
inspired them with a hatred of him as with an instinct,
because he knew that the Church was built on a rock,
and that all the power of evil should not prevail
against it. And even as the ashes that Moses threw
upon the banks of the river Nile, brought down the
hateful and degrading plague of blains and boils on
the children of men in the land of Egypt, so have the
ashes of St. Thomas, scattered to the winds far and
wide, brought down God's curse upon the land. They
have brought down the curse of littleness, of pusillanimity,—a curse, the very characteristic of which is
lowering and degrading, even as the curse that came
down on the Egyptians' land. We must cultivate a
special devotion to this mighty saint of God. We
must strive as he strove, in all gentleness, in all love.
We must grasp his principles, and grasp them firmly,
even as the soldier grasps the weapons with which he

U.   ℞

charges in the fight. We must take St. Thomas as
our model and our pattern; and if it be that, in the
intervals of his weariness and strife he beheld visions
of a fair land of peace, beaming with tranquillity and
with all those beauteous and gentle things spoken of in
the pages of the Gospel; if there be a time when
Heaven seems opened, and we behold a land where all
is love and peace—no warfare, no bickering, no chilling
separation—a land where all are crowned kings around
the throne of God, singing sweet songs of everlasting
praise; while we remember that there is such a land of
peace, we must also remember it is not here, that it is
not now. Think you that St. Thomas loved not peace?
Think you that he sighed not for repose as much as
we can do? Think you that, in the recesses of his
sacred cell, he did not many times see Heaven opened,
and behold, more clearly than we can do, bright visions
of this land of peace? But he knew it was not here;
he knew it was not now; and so he fought his way.
Let us fight our way as he fought his. Let us fight
our way, and we shall be one day where he is now.
Oh, it is sweet, it is passing sweet to the spirit to think
of all St. Thomas passed through; it is sweet to think
upon the change that came upon his fortunes; the
change between the great archbishop striving with the
powers of darkness, and the saint at this hour, prostrate
in ineffable transports of contemplation, before the
majesty of the most High, Holy, and Adorable Trinity.
Yes, my Brethren, so it is. His peace-loving spirit is
now at rest. The haughty, imperious, and indignant
word has been subdued into a song of Heaven. The
saint needed it no more; God needed it no more.
Strife has passed away from him, even as a thing that

U.   ℞   •

never was, and he is now canonized throughout the land. Strife has passed away from him like a dream of Calvary, and the scorn of misjudging men like a little shadow of Gethsemane.

IX.

ST. CHARLES.

Men's spirituality depends on the view they take of God. Now the saints seem all of them to have concurred in taking one and the same view of him as the God of the Church. We find this in St. Paul's epistles, and even in the writings of cloistered mystics. There were others whose life was part of the life of the Church.

I. So St. Charles.

  1. He was part of the life of the Church.

    (1) He was a saint of fewer peculiarities than most saints.

    (2) His personality was almost merged in the Church: he had nothing new to teach, no peculiar spirit to communicate.

    (3) He left fewer things said than most saints of whom so much is known.

  2. He was a reformer: one of God's reformers, and so his example is full of lessons to all men in different times.

II. In these two things we find his fitness for our times and for our present troubles.

  1. The state of the Church makes it needful for

the lives of all of us to be in their measure part of the Church's life. The state of the Church must give us the character of our piety: it must be in us the cause of most that is spiritual about us. It is not a question of politics, of historical sympathies, or of interesting opinion. It is part of our relation towards God, of our duties to Him, and of our worship of Him.

2. When God punishes us, He is calling upon us to reform.

3. Now let St. Charles teach us what manner of reform we must aim at.

   (1) It must be one of personal holiness, and St. Charles would have it turn especially upon our ordinary actions.

   (2) It must be a growth in profound, universal humility, a constant wonder that God should bear with us—for what good have we done, and what good have we not spoiled? Our own want of inward purity and of generous holiness—how may it not explain many of the misfortunes of the Church?

   (3) It must be a special cultivation of *simplicity*, the only gift which God seems to be blessing now, from the Sovereign Pontiff downwards. This simplicity will lead to childlike obedience of the intellect, for that alone is the possible or practical obedience of most men—and to self-denial, and so will set us against expensiveness and enable us to give more alms to the poor—which is a

special thing to do in dark and difficult times.

III. The spirit of St. Charles should be our spirit.

1. Eminently a spirit of faith, believing nothing impossible, with hatred of heresy, and with kindness to heretics, which is mostly in proportion to a man's hatred of heresy.

2. From this spirit of faith came his two characteristic graces, fortitude and calmness. His fortitude seemed to go beyond prudence, yet was the real prudence of the Gospel, because of his faith.

3. Calmness—a wonderful feature of this was that he seemed hardly even to deliberate. He was so master of his principles, that all the excitement of plans was gone from him: how like in this to our Lord in the Gospels, how like to God in the adorable simplicity of His action.

What is the end of it all? intense filial love of the Church, and more and more hungry pining after God, and yet a most patient cheerfulness, a most serene confidence, nay, even a modest elation of heart and soul, as if Jesus was for ever saying in our ears, with the piteous sweetness His Blessed Voice must have had that last Thursday night—*In mundo pressuram habebitis: sed confidite, ego vici mundum.*—In the world you shall have distress; but be confident, I have overcome the world. (St. John xvi. 33.)

X.

NOVENA OF ST. PHILIP.

1.

SKETCH OF THE SAINT'S LIFE.

All lives of men are beautiful in their changes and vicissitudes, all full of romance and poetry: or like various music, a quiet pastoral, a stirring march, a pathetic drama, a touching elegy, or strains of mutable, fitful sweetness. Such is man's life as outward Providence ordains it: sin mars it. We are concerned now with a life lived in the sixteenth century in the great city of Rome, which with manifold vibrations is working still on earth.

I. St. Philip's Picture.

  1. The aged priest for the most part ashy pale, not foreign-looking to us.

  2. With a soft mellow sweetness as of one to be familiar with, yet with a sternness underneath as of one not to take liberties with.

  3. Very simple and childlike, yet with a depth as of one who knew secrets and had seen visions. We do not exactly know why, but as we look on him we think of St. Joseph.

II. The Boyhood.

  1. He was born in beautiful Florence on the eve of St. Mary Magdalen. The gravity and sweetness of his childhood, which yet was not without traits of humor and fun and geniality.

  2. Gaeta—the cleft mountain—the inheritance renounced.

III. The beginnings at Rome.
 1. He was drawn there by instinct, and lived there
     at first as a tutor in poverty and silence.
 2. In catacombs, and studying in moonlit porticoes.
 3. Receiving pilgrims and visiting hospitals.
 4. Priesthood—St. Girolamo—the Seven Churches—
     beginnings of the Oratory—his penitents.
 5. The Vallicella—and the Congregation founded.
IV. The sort of life.
 1. Absence of all singularity.
 2. Miracles daily, and ecstasies almost continually.
 3. Apostolate of conversation and supernatural out-
     breaks of devotion.
 4. He silently took possession of all Rome as a per-
     fume fills a room.
 5. After eighty years he dies. And this life so
     beautiful on earth was quietly translated to
     heaven, to be continued still more beautifully
     —and on earth houses rose up all over the
     world to catch the image of that life, and to
     try to live it over again, and everywhere loving
     hearts gather round these houses and feel instinct-
     ively a joy and a security in belonging to St.
     Philip.

2.

THE LOOK OF COMMONPLACENESS WITH SUCH A SUPERNATURAL LIFE.

Let us go as foreigners to Rome in the sixteenth
century ; it is full enough of associations, and of relics,
and of shrines, and of the Sovereign Pontiff, to hide in
the beauty of its spiritual brightness a thousand living

saints as completely as if they were shrouded in the earthly gloom of the catacombs. We hear talk of Father Philip, and listen, and go to see him. We write home what we have seen and heard. We see him in his room—the vineyard—the street.

I. The look of his life.

    1. A kindhearted priest with much zeal, yet somewhat irregular and eccentric in his zeal—otherwise commonplace enough.

    2. He has joined no religious order, and seems to have formed no extensive plans.

    3. He is shy and has rather to be sought than comes forward.

    4. There is no look of austerity about him—he is rather free and easy and jocund.

    5. Surely it is an exaggeration to speak of him as a saint; for there are no secrets about him; we see the whole of him, perhaps a man to love rather than revere. Yet we left him with our hearts softened and heated and gently filled with God—undoubtedly a good man, a very good man.

II. The reality of his life.

    1. His heart miraculously filled with the Holy Ghost: his ribs broken.

    2. His Mass of five hours daily.

    3. His constant reading of the secrets of hearts.

    4. Surrounded with light, and distilling strange perfumes of some aromatic heaven.

    5. Miracles going out from him almost like ordinary actions, and his living without food.

III. This contrast is the type of his holiness: the there hidden lives of Jesus, divine eclipsed by

human, glorious by passible, holy by unaffected-
ness—such was St. Joseph's holiness, and such
St. Philip's

1. St. Philip's studious pursuit of secrecy—he risked
   scandal rather than be found out.

2. His looking only to ends and not to means, to
   God, not to devotions, &c.

3. His finding God equally or even preferably in
   very little things.

4. His meekness, though he knew he was going to
   be canonized.

5. Yet it was the very wonderfulness of his sanctity
   which caused him to look so commonplace.

Should we know a saint if we met one? I doubt
it. This is sad to think, but very profitable. How
we might have left St. Philip, and turned down
the Banchi toward St. Peter's, and thought how
commonplace he was, how he talked on ordinary
subjects, how careless about giving edification, what
light odd things he said for a grave old priest, and
what a sly look of mischief there was in his eye when
we parted. And while we walked and thus criticised,
behold! he in the secret of his room is floating in the
air, waving to and fro like a branch in the summer
wind, girdled with a golden light, hearing unutterable
words and seeing unutterable things down deep in
God!

3.

HIS SPIRIT OF LIBERTY AND ABSENCE OF METHOD.

I. All saints seem to have given scandal in their day,
St. Philip is no exception.

U

1. This taking scandal at saints is an evidence of corruption.
2. It was the same with our Blessed Lord. And the world never learns; it would take the same amount of scandal, both in amount and kind, if He came again.
3. That in which each saint gives scandal, is his characteristic peculiarity; and in that will be found to consist the eminence of his holiness and sanctity in its earlier stages, not very easily distinguishable from eccentricity.

II. What people took and take exception to in St. Philip is his liberty of spirit and absence of method.

1. As a saint in his own life.
   (1) He was long years in Rome and yet joined no religious order.
   (2) He took all his steps as direction and obedience suggested, but even then formed no great or definite plans.
   (3) He was ready to give up his works at any moment.
   (4) His own spirituality was singularly free, and left to God's action on him day by day.
2. As a founder and superior.
   (1) The way his Congregation grew up piecemeal.
   (2) He would not let his subjects have their time to themselves.
   (3) He would not have vows in it.
   (4) He made the separation of each house essential, that they might not band together for any common end, or to forward any definite views.

U.

　(5) His dislike of attachment to their work in his subjects.

　3. As a master of the spiritual life.

　　(1) Absence of set rules and methods; each day was to supply its own materials.

　　(2) His penitents were to keep in their own spheres and at their social duties.

　　(3) His little interference with their external things.

　　(4) His spirit of prayer so full of liberty as to method.

　　(5) His variety of direction without any recognizable technical peculiarity of his own.

III. Two schools of holiness in the Church, the school of captivity and the school of liberty. St. Philip, like St. Francis of Sales, singularly of the latter.

　1. It came from his immense devotion to the Person of the Holy Ghost. Docility to inspirations was to him instead of rule.

　2. This made him immensely interior. God was his one demand in himself and in others.

　3. His horror of mere formality and habit, or *woodenness*, or anything cut and dry. This made him negligent, sometimes startlingly so, of externals.

Both systems are holy; I do not say that one is in itself better than the other; both are from God. But I bless God that He has given to His Church the system of liberty as well as that of holy captivity; because I feel for myself that I never could be spiritual on the captivity system, whereas I hope that I may some day or other attain to spirituality on the other system.

U.　　　　　　　　　　　　　　　　　ᴆ

IV. Living with St. Philip daily.

1. Meeting his clear quiet eye every morning, feeling that we were seen through, that nothing was unnoticed, nothing unremembered.
2. Feeling how easily and also how deeply pained he could be, how he revolted from all insincerity and pretences.
3. Made uncomfortable by feeling that we had weaknesses, he had not.
4. In good times we should enjoy it, in bad chafe under it.
5. His sternness would grow on our notice—and yet his sweetness be ever gaining more empire.
6. Why should such a man attract? Because we have all a distrust of self at bottom—we do not like standing alone—life is a grave thing—we like to lean on some one of whom we are sure— and in sorrow and such like times he was all sweetness and support.

4.

HIS REALITY.

I do not think that any devout person can look long on St. Philip's picture without growing somewhat afraid of him. He is the apostle of liberty, and yet somehow not a man to take liberties with.

I. We meet with men in the world

1. Whom we admire and love—yet are not at ease with—feel untruthful with. We have an instinctive fear of their influence, and are restless when we have to do with them.

U.   ℞

2. There is something in them which we wish away: and yet if it was away they would not be the same men, nor should we ourselves love and admire them so much.

3. It is their reality—their genuineness—their truth —not so much their truthfulness as their truth.

II. Reality.

1. A real man is a man without secrets or diplomacy.

2. His extreme simplicity, and his singleness of purpose, invest him with a kind of sternness, so that we feel rebuked in his presence.

3. Yet his heart is always full of gushing sympathies and kindness.

4. He has a sort of impatience with foolishness, insincerity, and circuitousness.

5. He sometimes tries us by the way he keeps to the one point, and slips off disguises, and walks on such a very straight road.

III. To live with such a man is an education in itself, and this is just what St. Philip was. I dare say sometimes men thought him even *wooden*, because he was so pertinaciously real, never unbending from his simplicity, never giving his genuineness a holiday.

1. His common sense in plans, in government, in direction : his dislike of changes, and of non-sense talked in the confessional.

2. His sternness which flashed out when any insincerity came in his way, or any making of difficulties.

3. The stress he laid on perseverance, by which he prevented liberty of spirit from degenerating into off-handness and free-and-easiness.

U.

4 His crusade against human respect—the queer things he did himself and made his people do. All meant nothing more or less than this.

5. His mortification of the judgment also made men real, while it hindered liberty from becoming license.

Of all the things which I admire in our Holy Father I admire none so much as his reality. It is the great want of the times. It is the grace of all graces which we every one of us stand most in need of.

5.

ST. PHILIP'S SPHERE.

While all saints do all the good they can find to do, each has a sphere peculiarly his own, a work which peculiarly belongs to him, and by which more especially all after ages will know him in the Church. Now what was St. Philip's sphere?

I. The spheres of saints.

1. There are aggressive saints like St. Ignatius: there are also inventive saints.

2. There are revolutionary saints like St. Francis.

3. Historical saints like St. Athanasius—raised up to save an epoch.

4. There are reforming saints like St. Charles.

5. There are saints who perfume the Church like sufferers and contemplatives.

6. How St. Philip had an element of all these saints in him.

II. His choice of a sphere.

1. He was not allowed a foreign missionary field.

2. He sent many into religion, but did not enter it himself.

3. His associations and instincts were all for primitive times; not for mediæval saints, who would hardly allow salvation out of the cloister; nor for modern ideas, which refused perfection out of convents.

4. St. Philip took *the world;* took pity on it, and taught that men and women might live in the world, and be as perfect as the highest saints.

III. How he exemplified this.

1. In his dislike of change—home is not the world, as convent people say it is.

2. In his stress laid on the *heart*—so like a thorough Scriptural saint!

3. In founding his Congregation for the help of those in the world.

4. In his wideness of spirit admitting all varieties and even *opposites* of goodness.

5. In his choice of great cities for his sons to work in.

IV. His peculiar attraction.

I observe that those who have a devotion to him mostly have an enthusiastic devotion. Yet they can hardly say on what it rests: it is rather some nameless attraction than any specific grace or sweetness. Also it is not to his work, or to his grace, but to himself—it is not to anything of St. Philip's but to St. Philip. This nameless attraction is fitted for a sphere consisting of such diversified materials. It is justly called an attraction, an instinct, a spell:—it draws us to him, quietly moulds us—quietly heats us—quietly changes us—quietly makes us all for God. I have often wondered what precisely it is, this nameless charm, but I do not know. We feel it—and are silent, and our hearts fill with it, and we are happy in being his children and at his feet:—and somehow all he does for us, and all he does in us, and all he makes us do, and all the liberty he gives us, and his loving of us, and his frightening of us—all somehow brings us round to God!

XI.

FIRST VESPERS OF ST. PHILIP.

All God's works come to an end, and for the most part their end is more beautiful than their beginning; and the end is often the beginning of a more heavenly and eternal beauty How true this is of the deaths of the saints.

The feeling in the morning all through the house, and then all through Rome, when St. Philip's death was known. What it must have been to have lived with a saint!

I. As if the end of the world was come; what next? there is no *next!* He had grown into the habits of men's lives; and yet, though warned in every way, they found themselves unprepared.

II. His ways, his words, his looks, his haunts, all grow vivid and into a unity to them; they begin to understand him.

III. Hence they want him most, now that he is gone; to whom are they to go to confession? How are they to do without his room, now become like a sacrament to them? He has been so quietly necessary to them, that it is incredible he should be gone. They feel as if they also should have died with him, for how can they go on?

IV. Yet, strange to say, a growing joy makes itself felt in their hearts. The joy comes from within, and without any apparent natural cause.

V. They see him on his bier in church, and as he gave light and perfume in his life, so he gives light and sheds sweet odors down on the souls of those who kneel there. It is the light of God, the sweet odor of Jesus Christ.

VI. Spiritually he will continue to give this light and to shed this perfume in our souls in an especial manner on his feast-day year by year until Jesus comes to Judge the world.

He has many places to look to this evening, many Oratories to bless with his paternal benediction; many hearts to touch with his love, many benefactors of his Congregations to enrich with especial graces; many souls to fill with his light and perfume: but the Blessed can do all these things quietly in God. I feel that his light and perfume are coming to us here. By the light we see God and the shores of the Eternal Land more plainly. By the perfume we lose more and more of our relish for earthly things and are secretly drawn to Jesus. O St. Philip, St. Philip! my Father and my Master! how fair is that light, and how peculiar is the fragrance of that perfume! Sweet light of St. Philip! oh that we may always walk by it! Sweet perfume of St. Philip! oh that it may always cling about our souls like a sensible presence of our

Blessed Lord! Father, be not afraid, do not doubt we will come to thee in Paradise!

XII.

ST. PHILIP'S DAY.

I. For two hundred and sixty-six years St. Philip has been looking upon the Face of God: he has never wearied. It is ever new; the years have sped silently away; they have not been like years; no springs or autumns, no winters or summers; there has been the calmness of eternity.

1. How much the world has gone through since, and his own favorite Rome.

2. His own work, how it has lasted and spread—and to how many souls it has gone!

3. Does not the thought of him, and of his calm looking upon the Face of the Most Holy Trinity this day, make us long for heaven. The times are evil—that makes us long for heaven. We are evil ourselves, we are wearied of our own foolishness—oh how we long for the security, the peace, the truth, the charity of heaven! Oh yes! most of all for the *charity* of heaven.

II. But there are lives on earth which have a look, a feeling, a fragrance of eternity about them. This was quite a distinguishable characteristic of St. Philip's life.

1. How his years were like eternal years—so still, so swift, so calm, so like each other.

2. Full of crosses, yet no ripples, no rufflings, no sounds at all—it was too deep.

3. He was called an apostle—think of Roman roads and hurrying toil—he in his room for the most part, or in quiet churches, or leisurely pacing the streets of Rome: *he* stationary, and Rome flowed by him, touched at him as at a harbor, and went on all controlled by him.

4. Yet he was like an apostle in his love of the primitive times, and early Christian life; hence his simplicity, his unity—he kept aloof from the world, yet exercised an almost ubiquitous influence, through his simplicity and his love. People told him he might influence it more by leading a more public life. No! he knew his place; he had ascertained his calling: he was stationary, like eternity.

5. His unity was like eternity. He had only one thought, only one secret, only one way, only one work: to make God dearer to men, and that in direct ways, not in indirect, however excellent. Hence his success, hence that remarkable, and it would have seemed so unlikely, oracle of the Church, which authoritatively conferred upon him the title of Apostle of Rome. Is it not strange? An apostle shy and hidden, keeping out of people's way, shunning every kind and shape of notoriety; a light whose power was in its being wellnigh invisible.

III. How did he work upon his times? What did he tell people to do? His times were bad, as ours are. and he was raised up, remember, to

be the apostle of his times in the centre and
capital of all Christendom.

1. The things he did *not* do; yet other saints *had*
done them. -

   (1) He never went the world's way, nor bor-
rowed its methods, however good or promising or lawful they might be.

   (2) He preached no reforms, but the secret reforms of single souls.

   (3) He founded no intellectual school of philosophy or theology.

   (4) He stood aloof from all political movements,
or views, as things not to his purpose. Indeed I cannot fancy St. Philip having any
views; his whole soul was in the Church;
his views were not views, they were faiths,
principles, obediences.

   (5) He attacked nothing, unless indeed it were
sin, frivolity, worldliness, and the reluctance
of rich people to give large alms; not even
did he attack dress or expensiveness, intensely as he hated both the one and the
other.

2. What did he tell people to do? Oh strange
foolish wisdom of the Gospel!

   (1) To keep in their own places, and attend to
their ordinary actions, avoiding change,
avoiding excitement.

   (2) To be exceedingly simple, and not to mind
criticisms and talk. If you are devout to
St. Philip, he will give you the grace not to
care what people say of you—and is not
that perfect happiness?

U.

(3) To be always reading the lives of the saints, because that makes an atmosphere, and excludes worldliness without trouble.

(4) To pray, frequent the sacraments, and hear a great many sermons.

(5) To love everybody, to praise everybody, and to find good in everybody. And all this because of the one mastering thought and sovereign love of God.

What was there wonderful in all this? Was it not strangely commonplace, for a saint in whose broken heart the Holy Ghost dwelt supernaturally, and who was the recognized Apostle of great Rome? Yes! *this* was wonderful,—that he kept to it, that he mixed nothing else with it, that he added nothing else to it, that he persevered in this bare singleness of purpose. This is in my eyes a greater miracle than we read in any of the lives of the saints.

See then, brethren, to what a conclusion we have come! The saint, who had the Holy Ghost in his miraculously dilated heart, is the most commonplace of saints; yet he is also the most peculiar and individual of saints, because of the persevering simplicity of his commonplaceness. Oh how much there is to learn, how much to learn of God and Jesus Christ in this one fact that St. Philip became the Apostle of Rome, a second Peter and a second Paul in his one self, through the mere perseverance of his enthusiastic, unadventurous simplicity!

———

XIII.

ST. FRANCIS XAVIER.*

Work your work before the time, and He will give your reward in His time. (Ecclus. li. 38.)

No scene in history is more significant than the few apostles with the world before them.

I. Character of our own age.

    1. It is an age of enthusiasms; partly material, and partly intellectual: concerning science, commerce, discovery.

    2. The impossible seems almost fading out of view; what a lesson the world is reading to us.

    3. Why not an enthusiasm all for God? a sober, steady, business-like enthusiasm, like the material one we see around us.

II. Lesson of St. Francis Xavier's life.

    1. What one man can do, who is all for God,

    2. Who has begun with sanctifying himself,

    3. And who then keeps within his own appointed sphere.

    4. The sobriety of his enthusiasm kindling, not stifling, his fervor is the wonder.

    5. It is a characteristic of true enthusiasm to neglect no means of grace.

    6. Now living in an unbelieving country is a means of grace both to ourselves and others.

III. We are all missioners, and England is our Japan. Let us convert it.

    1. By example.

* Preached at the Church of the Immaculate Conception, Farm Street.

U.

2. By sweetness, yet by gravity in our sweetness.
3. By incessant prayer.
4. By works of mercy to others.
5. By union and absence of jealousy among ourselves; for what the world envies is our
   union.
6. By holiness, which is a power and an attraction
   beyond all others.

When we look at the map of the world, and see the countries which St. Francis overran, when we think of the thousands and hundreds of thousands of those whom he baptized, when we weigh up his difficulties, count up his failures, follow him in his toils and learn sympathetically to estimate his disappointments, we are amazed, and humbled and gladdened also while we are amazed, to think how much one man can do, to whom nature gives an enthusiastic loving heart, and grace the magnificent gift of being simply, always, and only —All for God!

XIV.

THE FEAR OF THE SAINTS.

Meddle not with the names of saints. (Ecclus. xxiii. 10.)

The reason of unanswered prayer and of inefficacious devotions is the want of more fear. This applies very much to our devotion to the saints.

Our view too often is that they lived holy lives, worked miracles, have gone to God, are crowned kings in heaven, and are now conveniences to us as additional means of grace, and doubtless are fresh ornaments of heaven. We do not *fear* them.

But there are motives for other devotion than this.

I. How majestic a saint is in himself. Great holiness is a thing to fear.

II. The greatness of his power and glory in heaven.

III. The honor of God, which is deeply implicated in the worship paid to the saint.

IV. In some sense He is more jealous of it than of His own; less patient of levity with them than with Himself, and frequently punishes persons for this.

V. The saints themselves have also entered into the dispositions of God, and, with a sort of vindictive holiness, hard for us in our present state to understand, resent familiarities and impertinences. We regard them too much as on our side, to get things from God for us. Some saints have shown this vindictiveness more than others.

VI. Faith is the chief ingredient in a true devotion to the saints; faith in the reality of their power, and of their relationship towards us. It is a great sign of a man being supernatural when he fears to offend a saint.

VII. The favors of the saints form a great department of the Divine mercies, and play an important part in the sanctification of holy men. Often the punishments of the saints do this last also; and this is especially the case with founders of orders, both to their children and to the enemies of their orders.

VIII. Weakness of prayer is one of the feeblenesses
   of our times, through want of faith and fear:
   this is one way to set them right. We always
   fear those in whom we have confidence. We
   cannot ever put confidence in those whom we
   do not in some way fear.

The Church expresses the old-fashioned devotion to
the saints by threatening disobedience to Bulls, &c , with
the anger of the holy Apostles SS. Peter and Paul.

U.   ℞

INDEX.

383

U.   R

U.   ℞

U.